RECALLING THE CALIPHATE

S. SAYYID

Recalling the Caliphate

Decolonisation and World Order

HURST & COMPANY, LONDON

First published in the United Kingdom in 2014 by
C. Hurst & Co. (Publishers) Ltd.,
41 Great Russell Street, London, WC1B 3PL
© S. Sayyid, 2014
All rights reserved.
Printed in the United Kingdom

Distributed in the United States, Canada and Latin America by
Oxford University Press, 198 Madison Avenue, New York, NY 10016,
United States of America.

A Cataloguing-in-Publication data record for this book
is available from the British Library.

ISBNs: 978-1-84904-0020 (hardback)
       978-1-84904-0037 (paperback)

www.hurstpublishers.com

This book is printed using paper from registered sustainable
and managed sources.

In memory of Kishver Nasreen Shah

CONTENTS

ACKNOWLEDGMENTS

It is inevitable that an enterprise stretching over many years and several continents would incur debts from friends, colleagues and fellow travellers. To paraphrase an African proverb (apparently) it takes a village to put together a book. As I lack the means to repay my debtors, I am more than happy to confess the unstinting assistance of my fellow virtual villagers that helped make this book possible. I would like to thank AbdoolKarim Vakil and Barnor Hesse for generously donating so much of their hard-pressed time to comment on various drafts of various chapters. Ramon Grosfoguel and Brian Klug have over the years become conversational sparring partners and I have learnt as much from our differences as from our agreements.

Riding around the streets of Ankara in a crammed white Renault after dark is not a bad way to meet kindred spirits, and since that spiritual car journey Yasin Aktay, Cemal Haşimi and Nur Yilmaz have done much to show that decolonisation is not only theoretical speculation but a lived practice.

I was fortunate while writing this book to be engaged with a critical race theory research team arranged around the TOLERACE project. This provided a convivial space to discuss and debate ideas, some of which have come to animate this book. In particular I want to recognise the contributions of Marta Araujo, Silvia Rodriguez Maseo, Katypal Sian and of course Ian Law, with whom I shared many conversations—none more cinematic than during a frantic drive across Europe when volcanic ash from Iceland had left us stranded in Lisbon.

ACKNOWLEDGMENTS

My Antipodean sojourn would have been arduous if it had not been for the generosity, good humour and diligence of a number of people I was lucky enough to meet. I would especially like to mention: Minerva Nasser-Eddine, Lyn Browning, Sanam Saitov and her family, and Mary Jolly. Shvetal Vyas-Parae whose effervescent intelligence and boundless enthusiasm made her an excellent research assistant and whose efforts (ably supported by the stoicism of Vipal Vyas) were invaluable in bringing this book to its conclusion. Of course, this book would have been the much the poorer without the interventions and interruptions provided by Amir, Yamina, Lilian and Imran.

The ideas contained in this volume were aired in a number of venues, and I am grateful for the various institutions and groupings whose invitations provided a platform for me to sharpen my arguments. I would like to single out South Australia State Library Study Circle and in particular the participation of Uzma Jamil, Muhammad Kotan and Lejla Voloder; they gathered weekly to discuss hegemony and the relationship between the ethical and the political, often in the most exacting circumstances.

Finally I would like to thank a number of people including Warren Chin, Tariq Modood, Amr Sabet, Paul Taylor, Hatem Baizan, Houria Bouteldja, Veena Ahmed, Junaid Ahmad, Farid Esack, Itrath Syed and M. G Khan, as well as the Brighton Beach Reading Club for their *en passant* promptings and impassioned positionings.

Earlier versions of some of the chapters in this book have previously been published in various forms and are included here with the permission of the publishers or editors of the journals and collections listed below.

Chapter 2, Liberalism, is a slightly modified version of an article published as 'After Babel: Dialogue, Difference and Demons' in *Social Identities: Journal for the Study of Race, Nation and Culture*, Volume 12, Issue 1 (2006): pp. 5–15.

Chapter 3, Secularism, is a revised version of a chapter that appeared as 'Contemporary Politics of Racism' in Levey, G. & T. Modood (eds), *Secularism, Religion and Multicultural Citizenship*, Cambridge: Cambridge University Press, 2009.

Chapter 4, Relativism, is substantially re-written, elements of it appeared as 'Bad Faith: Anti-Essentialism and Universalism' in Brah, Avtar and Annie. E. Coombes (eds), *Hybridity and its Discontents*, London: Routledge, 2000.

ACKNOWLEDGMENTS

Chapter 5, Democracy, is re-written version of an article that first appeared as 'Mirror, Mirror, Western Democrats, Oriental Despots?' *Ethnicities*, Vol. 5, Number 1, March 2005, pp. 30–50.

Chapter 6, Futorology, is a re-drafted English translation of a chapter that first appeared in Spanish as 'Dune, Decolonizar el futuro' in Vzw, C., (ed.), *Suturas y Fragmentos: Cuerpos y Territorios en la Ciencia Ficcion*, Barcelona: Fundacio Antoni Tapies, 2006.

Chapter 7, Diaspora, is a modified and updated version of a chapter that appeared as 'Beyond Westphalia: Nations And Diasporas', in Hesse, B. (ed.), *Unsettling Multiculturalism*, London: Zed Books, 2000.

Chapter 10, Hermeneutics, is a largely re-written version of an article published as 'Rituals, Ideals and Reading the Qur'an', *American Journal of Islamic Social Sciences*, Vol. 23, No. 1. Winter 2006, pp. 52–65.

1

NAMES

The vanquished always want to imitate the victor in his distinctive characteristics, his dress, his occupation, and all his other conditions and customs. The reason for this is that the soul always sees perfection in the person who is superior to it and to whom it is subservient. It considers him perfect, either because it is impressed by the respect it has for him, or because it erroneously assumes that its own subservience to him is not due to the nature of defeat but to the perfection of the victor.

Ibn Khaldun (1978: 116)

I

Islam is the name that gives Muslims a name. For Muslims it is perhaps the most proper of names, a name that loses its singularity when transcribed outside Muslim contexts. After all, what is Islam in a world dominated by the Western enterprise but a scandal? The contemporary struggle around the name of Islam takes place against the background of a kind of defeat that on so many levels seems proximate to that described by Ibn Khaldun in the quotation that is the epigraph for this volume. Ibn Khaldun seems to suggest that the defeated see the judgement of defeat in terms of the qualities of the victor, for this defeat is not purely military but can have profound cultural impacts. Does this description not capture with great acuity the condition of the *ummah*?

The analysis of the cultural effects of military and political defeats experienced on a grand scale over a *longue durée* could be said to resonate in the contemporary world under the broad heading of postcolonial thought.[1] The conflict that haunts postcolonial writing was inaugurated by Christendom's appropriation of the Western hemisphere and the subsequent expansion of Europe through the process of conquest, and the establishment of a planetary colonial political economy (Venn, 2006: 47–58). In this defeat the line between the West and the non-West became the axis of the world. In this world the superiority and normality of the West was institutionalised and constantly contrasted with the inferiority and abnormality of the non-West.

The reconfiguring of the world along the lines of a violent hierarchy between West and non-West came to consume the *ummah* as part of the subjugated non-West. In the *ummah*, efforts to come to terms with the cultural challenges of Western colonial military victories have often meant trying to hold on to Islam as a proper name. It is in the name of Islam that many have taken up arms, taken to the streets and, most of all, taken to calling themselves Muslims, even in circumstances when such declarations can invite suspicion, surveillance and subjugation. A name is not only a shorthand expression of something that already exists but, more profoundly, it is through the process of naming that the thing being referred to enters our consciousness.[2] A name is not just a label that can simply be attached to something that is already there: it is the means by which heterogeneous elements are marshalled together to become the intrinsic features of the named entity. What these features have in common is nothing but the name itself. There is no ultimate necessity to the features denoted by a name. The act of naming is also the act of becoming. The act of naming is an exercise in history making: only those with names can write their own history; only those with names can give themselves a destiny. Thus, the division of the world between the named West and nameless non-West becomes a division between people who have their own history and those who do not. The name of Islam has brought Muslims into history and, in circumstances when the name cannot be evoked, Muslims become a 'people without history', thus ceasing even to be a people.[3] People become without history not because they lack a past but because, paradoxically, they cannot narrate themselves into the future. People without history are either nameless (and thus not really a people) or they are named by others.[4]

The great defeats deny destiny and if the defeat is profound enough it can erase a name.[5] During the nearly 1400-year period of Islam's existence, the intensity of its utterance, range and meaning has not been static. There have been moments when it has seemed close to erasure; for example, perhaps if the Mongols had not been defeated at Ain Jalat (658/1260),[6] or perhaps following the reforms inspired by the example of Mustafa Kemal when Islamicate public space virtually vanished from the world.[7] In the various shifts one cannot discern (outside teleological and determinist historiographies) a distinct pattern of brilliant beginnings and long drawn-out decline.

At certain points Islam has meant a whole way of life; on other occasions it was thought to be no more than just one name among many. Mapping out the fluctuations in the significance of Islam would tell us a great deal about the place of Muslims in the world. For Islam is the knot that stitches together the many strands that make up the *ummah* in all its diverse, textured richness. The name of Islam not only ties up Muslims and binds them to each other; its meaning also determines who Muslims were, who Muslims are and who Muslims ought to be. Without Islam, there would not be any more Muslims. This does not mean that those who are Muslim beings would vanish from the earth but, simply, being Muslim would no longer be possible.

The fate of Muslim beings and being Muslim hangs upon the name of Islam. Thus, the interrogation of Islam has become one of the most pressing questions of our time. The Muslim question (with its echoes of the Jewish question and the Eastern question before it) refers to a series of interrogations and speculations in which Islam and/or Muslims exist as a difficulty that needs to be addressed. Thus the Muslim question is a mode of enquiry that opens a space for interventions: cultural, governmental and epistemological. How a fifth of this planet's population comports itself in the world depends on its answers. The Muslim question encompasses the difficulties associated with the emergence of a distinct political identity that appears to be transgressive of the norms, conventions and structures that underpin the contemporary world. Reflecting on what he observed while filming in a US prison in Arizona, the vernacular intellectual Richard Pryor (1982) remarked:[8]

[I]n the penitentiary man they got all them racist groups. They got the white groups. They act like they're in New York. They got the Nazi party and the— what do they call it? The Ku Klux Klan. The Mexicans got them gangs you can't pronounce the names. And they don't wear no shirts. Black people got the Mau Mau, Muslims, Double Muslims. Them's the ones you don't f**k with—them Double Muslims. 'Cause them motherf****** can't wait to get to Allah and want to take eight or nine motherf****** with them.

The on-going 'War on Terror' seems to be predicated on both a rejection of Pryor's advice, but also, an acknowledgement of its basic premise that the transcendental motivations of 'extremist' Muslims is such that exceptional levels of violence are necessary to contain them. It is this assumption that has produced one of the most iconic images of the War on Terror: men clad in orange jump suits, sensory deprivation, goggles and headphones, bound and silenced—their 'Double Muslimness' justifying their living mummification. In contrast to the 'Double Muslim', who needs to be bound because he may attack, the Muselmann would not even try and defend himself when attacked (Žižek, 2001: 76). This representation of the incarcerated 'Muslim' arose from the argot of the concentration camp. A Muselmann was an inmate who had recoiled from the horrors of the internment and become 'absolutely apathetic', able to endure everything not because of courage but as living death (Agamben, 1998: 185). The Muselmann is defined by non-thinking (Žižek, 2003: 157–9; Goldberg, 2006: 336). What is interesting is unlike Pryor's Double Muslims, the Muselmann does not have to be an actual Muslim.[9] Rather it is the idea of a Muslim as a fatalist that is at play and in passing demonstrating the deep-rootedness of Orientalism in European society. The Double Muslim is a fanatic par excellence and the Muselmann the fatalist, the range from fatalism to fanaticism sums up the spectrum of subject positions available to Muslims within the Western imaginary. This distinction between Muslimanner and Double Muslims is played out in a variety of registers: moderate and extremist Muslims, liberal Muslims and radical Muslims, good Muslims and bad Muslims. The War on Terror and its attendant torture and incarceration system can be read as a sustained effort to discipline the Double Muslim into becoming a Muselmann. One could ask what motivates the attempted zombification of those whom the American government has identified as 'enemy combatants', why the visceral humiliation and violence is necessary, why the normative claims made for the humanness of Western plutocracies are suspended with such disdain (Asad, 2007).[10] The radical richness of Pryor's observations presents the possibility of a decolonialising inversion of Orientalist tropes, unlike the figure of the

Muselmann who conforms to the assumption that Muslims lack agency. In Pryor's figure of the Double Muslim one can see the transformation of the fanatical zeal associated with Orientalist caricatures into a strangely liberating assertion of autonomy within the context of the American penal system.[11] Pryor's passing reflections contain three themes which can be useful in illustrating the position of Muslims in the contemporary world.

First, there is the setting of an American prison, in which various marginalised groups are to be found: poor whites, Latinos, Blacks and Muslims, which seems an apt metaphor for a hierarchical world in which American power contains violent contending tribes of the dispossessed. Second, there is a distinction between ordinary Muslims and more dangerous Double Muslims. A version of this can be found in various accounts which seek to distinguish between moderate Muslims and radical Muslims, progressive Muslims and traditionalist Muslims—which can be described as the dialectic of good Muslim and bad Muslim.[12] Third, implicit is the idea that the Double Muslims are beyond rational calculation and their ability to carry out violent acts is transcendentally motivated and cannot be rationally contained. The consequences of such a view can be seen in the treatment of suspected Muslim terrorists—from the orange-clad forgotten inmates of Guantanamo, to the disappeared of secret prison complexes and virtual entombment in supermax prisons—which all point to the practical problems of suspected Double Muslims. The problem of the Double Muslims and their difference from other Muslims is one of the key tropes in the Muslim question.

II

The question of what Islam is commonly elicits replies along the lines of: Islam is a militant faith; or it is a religion of peace; or it is another form of totalitarianism. Answering the Muslim question requires an understanding of the meaning of Islam. What we believe Islam to be is one of the means by which we seek to apprehend the way the world is. Most Muslims would agree that Islam is formed by belief in the oneness of God, in the Prophethood of Muhammad (pbuh), the divine nature of the Qur'an and so forth. Many Muslims would add that certain key rituals and practices are also associated with Islam in a manner that is, for all intents and purposes, fixed and Muslims in Indonesia or Surinam or Arabia would certainly know how to pray, which direction to pray in and what to do during Ramadan. Even if the conduct of individuals or communities is at variance from what is considered to be proper they would act in that knowledge. Thus Muslims who do not fast during Ramadan give reasons that range from fasting not being central, their own spiritual weakness, or their belief that it is an unhealthy practice. Similarly, those who do not pray five times a day provide all kinds of justifications, from arguing that prayers are excessive, that their work is their prayer, an admission of their failings or a denial that praying is that crucial. These rationalisations take place in relation to conversations and admonishments (projected or experienced) that fasting is central or prayer is crucial. These responses to describing Islam are elaborated by references to its features, such as the 'five pillars', references to customs and practices associated with the Prophet (pbuh) and his companions, and ultimately to the Qur'an: the word of God.

At every point in these conversations and debates about the proper behaviour for a proper Muslim, the limits of language get in the way. At every point there is a battle of interpretation, from what the Qur'an means, to debates about whether there are indeed five pillars and not six, or if the pillars each have equal weight, or to what degree the kernel of Islam can be reduced to the architecture of its pillars. These interpretations—sometimes debated between family members and friends, at other times between members of a community, and sometimes between those who hold public office or those who have institutional authority—take place over an uneven terrain. Not only are interpretations widely disputed; not all counter-interpretations enjoy equal support. The meaning of Islam is struggled over in the context of wider conversations about Muslims, including the ethnography of actual Muslims, or the history or what Muslims actually do when they 'do' Islam. These kinds of responses are commonplace and are the currency by which Islam is debated. All these takes on Islam emphasise the ontic: Islam is something that can be apprehended by positive apparatuses of knowledge formation. This understanding of Islam grounds and guides investigations into its nature; it determines what things can be said about it and be considered as serious and significant.[13] This way of approaching Islam does not take into account the background practices and assumptions that allow it to be disclosed as such. The background practices and assumptions of a particular context ground the field of its intelligibility.[14] These parameters of intelligibility are not permanent, nor are they merely random or free-floating, but rather they are grounded in specific historical transformations. This context is not based on an invariant and immutable core that determines its contours, nor is the context a random amalgamation of elements. Rather the context is the crystallisation of particular philosophical and political struggles.

Islam names a distinct historical mode of comporting oneself in the world. It is not that Islam in today's world has been reinvented, but rather that it is always being reinterpreted. What Islam has meant in the past, what it means in the present and what it could mean in the future do not signal a series of reinventions but rather interpretations of interpretations. The ontically inclined answers to the Muslim question often take the form of an enumeration of the various kinds of subject positions: moderate Muslim, liberal Muslim, the oxymoronically self-styled ex-Muslim and of course the dangerous Double Muslim. The variety of forms of Muslim is used to indicate that Islam is not monolithic. Muslims are varied, various and often at war with each other. The fissiparity of Muslims it is argued is manifested in cleavages along the lines of ethnicity, nationality, class, gender—in other words, a Muslim is someone who is really someone else, someone whose Muslimness is a cover for who they really are—a woman, an Uyghur, bourgeois, Canadian…

Many Muslims, it is suggested, are nominally observant of religious practices, and as such any attempt to articulate a Muslim subjectivity is illegitimate and shows the work of the politically motivated, based on instrumental rationality rather than sincere faith. It is assumed that religious forms of identification are less legitimate than other forms and that Islam is a religion. It therefore follows that Muslims are imposters or ghosts (Sayyid, 2003; Tyrer and Sayyid, 2012). To argue that a Muslim subject position is not inauthentic does not mean that I think it is authentic, or to put it another way, the authenticity or inauthencity of being Muslim is no more or no less than the other forms of collective identifications. It certainly does not mean that I believe that Muslims do not form an 'imagined community', do not have 'invented tradition' or are exempt from the ideas and academic practices that emphasise the social construction of knowledge.[15] Muslims are as imagined, invented and socially constructed as Chinese, as Americans, as socialists, as Buddhists, or any other form of collective identification. No doubt there are accounts of collective identities which see an essence in being British

7

or being gay or being Japanese—similarly there are essentialist accounts of being Muslim. There is also little doubt that popular conversations often betray an essentialist understanding of collective subjectivities. The problem with Muslims is not that many use essentialist tropes to describe themselves, but rather that the assertion of a Muslim identity occurs in a world in which there is no epistemological or political space for it. The question of the relevance of Muslim identity turns on a theory of collective subjectivities. A collective identity is not something that is a product of economic processes or ethnic consciousness or common language, or religious affiliation or shared cultural practices. It is not something that is found but rather something that is made. It is not the case that being Muslim is less authentic than being a Bengali, which is less authentic than being a Sylheti.[16] Or that a moderate Muslim is more authentic than an 'extremist' Muslim, and nor is it the case that an extremist Muslim is more authentic than the 'moderate'. No doubt Muslims in Germany, in Paris or in Bradford have particularities that they may not share with Muslims living in Thailand, in Bamako or in Utrecht. These local inflections however do not constitute distinct multiple 'little Islams'. The attempt to argue for a world of multiple Islams is a rather hurried response to the threat of essentialising Islam. Multiple Islams would only make sense if they could be said to exist in splendid isolation from each other, hermetically sealed and unaffected and fully self-contained in whatever locale (it is not clear what proper zones of demarcation of these multiple Islams would be; would there be a British Islam or an Islam for London or Manchester?). One does not need to posit an essence to Islam to argue that Islam is not reducible to its ontic manifestations. All the particular expressions of Islam exist as a part of a singular Islam: at the most we have rival projects to interpret a singular Islam.[17] Indeed, it is precisely the existence of a singular Islam that allows the constitution of an Islamicate politics, in which Muslims (and also non-Muslims) wage wars of interpretation to attach Islam to various specific projects. The knowledge that Islam may be used as the means of articulating a multiplicity of positions is not grounds to assume that we are dealing with distinct multiple Islams.

At stake is a struggle as to what we understand Islam to be, for its ontological characterisation determines its ontic manifestations. The answer to this question of what Islam is establishes the most fundamental parameters of intelligibility. The broader context for all these interpretations of what Islam is and what Muslims are or should be (or even perhaps what books like this could be) can be described in a number of related ways: the epoch of technology, the age of Pax Americana, the modern age, late capitalism and so on. My preference is to see the contemporary emergence of Islam taking place in a world marked by the logic of postcoloniality. That is, in a world in which the cultural underpinnings of the West find it difficult to translate Western military and political power into a planetary hegemony. This inability, however, occurs in a world order that is largely a creation of the interaction between the West and the non-West. The designation of the West (here and in the rest of the book) is neither geographical nor is it essentialist or overarching. Arguments that point to the diversity of the West often neglect the way in which construction of all identities involves an erasure of differences. (Nor are these differences monadic elements; they are in themselves identities that erase other differences, which are also identities that erase further differences. The point is that there is no ground, no final identity, beyond which there is nothing.)

One of the most significant attempts at understanding the meaning of Islam can be described as Islamism. If Islam can be understood as the name by which a set of narratives and practices, heritages and futures are marshalled, then Islamism is an attempt to give the name of Islam a political charge. Or, put more prosaically, Islamism seeks to establish a political order centred on the name of Islam. The relationship between Islam and Islamism, then, is intimate even if it is not intrinsic. The relationship between Islam and Islamism, however, is not one of derivation or distortion or ideologisation. Islamism is neither derived from Islam, nor is it a transformation of Islam from religion to ideology. Islamism is not a replacement of Islam akin to the way it could be argued that communism and fascism are secularised substitutes for Christianity. Nor is it very useful to argue that Islamism is a falsification of Islam; rather, as I have argued elsewhere, Islamism is a constellation of political projects that seek to position Islam in the centre of any social order (Sayyid, 2003: 17).

Throughout the *ummah* attempts are being made, although hesitant and difficult, to forge another way of speaking, through Islam. Thus, Muslims often find themselves in a situation in which the dominant descriptions of the world conducted in 'Westernese' are no longer adequate and the project of speaking through Islam is, as yet, not fully

developed.[18] Thus, Muslims have to muddle through, bilingually starting in one language but trying to develop another language, as yet
unrecognised, a language considered at best a dialect. The effect of this
is to maintain Islam and Muslims within a colonial framework from
which it is impossible to generate enduring solutions to the many problems and difficulties that confront the *ummah*. Ways forward require the
decolonisation of the *ummah*, not only in terms of its cultural, economic
and political subordination but also in terms of the states of knowledge
that enable such subordination. This is the project of Islamism. This
project articulates a globalised Muslim subjectivity, which increasingly
transcends the Westphalian template and finds Westernese less and less
credible. Islamists have successfully and ostentatiously inserted a Muslim
subjectivity into the contemporary world. From the perspective of the
division of the world between West and non-West, the ability of Muslims to insert the name of Islam destabilises the order of coloniality.
Islam appears to announce a third position that can be called by its own
name. In other words, we must forge new conceptual and analytical
tools and new discursive approaches that go beyond the rejection of
Orientalist framings and move beyond traditional Islamic approaches.
This calls for an approach to Muslim politics with all its complexities
and diversities as a field of contestation between those who interpret
Islam and Islamicate history as necessitating the institution of a political
and social order, and those that reject such an interpretation.

III

The books we write are products of the conversations we have had and
the books we have read. This book is a tracing of many conversations
across several continents over many years. No doubt if I had read different books or had different conversations then this book, if it had existed,
would be very different. This is a truism that is often forgotten when
demands are made by dissatisfied readers for a different kind of book: a
book with more ethnography, a more empirical book, a more autobio-
graphical book.

The current volume is organised around two broad sets of conversations: those that deal with the various attempts to block Muslims from
becoming the authors of their own history, and those that try to imagine
what kind of history Muslims could write. The ability to articulate Mus-

lim autonomy with consistency and hope, which demands that Muslims engage in the difficult but necessary task of writing their own history as Muslims, requires as the first step a clearing of the ground, a clearing of the objections that are constantly made and endlessly recycled. It is sometimes difficult to get to a more constructive discussion, since the voices that wish to drown out the possibility of a Muslim subjectivity appear so numerous and so insistent that those who advocate Muslim autonomy must repeatedly ward off accusations and counter-arguments that problematise the very idea of Muslim identity.

As late as the last quarter of the twentieth century there was a confident expectation that Islam would dissipate as the global advance of Westernisation brought secularisation and modernisation in its wake. Not only has Islam failed to follow the trajectory pursued by variants of Christianity—namely confinement to the private sphere and depoliticisation—but it has, in contrast, forcefully reasserted its public presence in the world. Mobilisations in the name of Islam have presented a series of challenges to the current world order that have taken the form of geopolitical, cultural and philosophical contestations. The quest for Muslim autonomy has become one of the main fault lines around which a variety of positions—local and global, extremist and moderate, conservative and revisionist—are arranged. In the light of these developments the recycling of conventional narratives about Islam seems redundant and increasingly problematic. Consequently, there is an urgent need to work out how the West and Islam fit into the world. *Recalling the Caliphate* is a contribution to this working out process. In a series of overlapping arguments I interrogate the interactions between Islam and the political, in the context of a postcolonial world order that seems to promise and yet at the same time defers any deep decolonisation.

IV

What follows is a series of interventions that aim to clear the ground for sustained reflection on the relationship between Islam, Muslims and the postcolonial context in which they are currently disclosed. These interventions are not point-by-point refutations of positions taken against the possibility of Muslim identity, since an exchange would already concede too much to the philosophical ground that is at stake in these interrogations. They can be grouped together under the rubric of Critical Muslim Studies. By Critical Muslim Studies I refer to a field of investigations into matters associated with Muslims which are framed by three related epistemological stances. It is characterised by systematic enquiries that are post-positivist, post-Orientalist and decolonial. By post-positivist I mean that it rejects the dream that has haunted social sciences from their inception—the aspiration to be a natural science. In this rejection, there is also an abandonment of a desire to come to some substantive understanding of what Islam really is or what Muslims ultimately are. Critical Muslim Studies shift the focus of research into matters Islamicate from ontic to ontological enquires. Post-positivists are keen to see the difference between natural and social sciences, not in terms of underdevelopment but in hermeneutical contestation. In other words, natural sciences are located in a paradigm that is hegemonic and which sees interpretive activity as being external to the actual constitution of its object of study. Post-positivism is simply a broad label for developments within the social sciences that have taken the critique of essentialism to heart.

By post-Orientalist I do not mean that it is informed by an attempt to 'reverse' the assumptions of the critique of Orientalism made by Edward Said and others, in which the category of Islam and its cognates is dissolved as a reaction to the essentialist fixation on Islam by mainstream Orientalism. Rather, it provides an analysis of the use of the signifier of Islam. Post-Orientalism is consistent with the 'strong' critique of Orientalism that can be found in Said's work alongside the 'weak' critique, which sees Orientalism through the prism of a sociology of knowledge. 'Strong' Orientalism is based on a set of arguments that the Orient is a construction of Orientalism; that is, Orientalism is not a distortion of an actual existing Orient that can be corrected by better informed, less biased writing and so on, but rather that the Orient is a product of the Orientalist imagination. Orientalists construct what are considered to be non-Western societies and histories as a residual category of the West. Orientalism tells a story about the West through the Orient.[19]

By decolonial I mean that Critical Muslim Studies is aligned with a wider project of 'epistemic disobedience' (Mignolo, 2007). Decolonial thinking takes the problem of Eurocentrism within the production of knowledge seriously and profoundly. The decolonial project developed a rich literature that is primarily focused on Latin America and on the articulation of a global South. These pioneers have begun the difficult task of rewriting an account of the emergence of Western modernity and thus of Western global hegemony. Decolonial thinkers seek to demonstrate the deep imbrications between coloniality and modernity as a prelude to unravelling the 'modern/capitalist/colonial/patriarchal world system' (Grosfoguel, 2006).[20] At first glance, decolonial thinking would seem to be related to the various projects on the Islamisation of knowledge initiated by scholars such as Syed Muhammad Naquib al-Attas and Ismail al-Faruqi. The aim of the Islamisation of knowledge projects has been to rein in modernity through the application of Islamic morality as a system of brakes.[21] In other words, Islamic prohibitions would corral modernity's will to power. For example, it is argued that scientific progress would be curtailed by following Islamic moral precepts, or that the economy would be more just if the Islamic moral prohibition on usury was followed (see Chapter 10). Clearly there are some overlaps between decolonial concerns and the Islamisation of knowledge, and one could see the works of al-Attas and al-Faruqi as part of the global South. There are, however, important differences. In particular, I remain somewhat sceptical of normative attempts to restrict modernity's will to power that are not embodied within hegemonic cultural practices. Such normative interventions are external and prohibitive. This is not to argue that the normative is not present in modernity. Nor is it to accept that modernity is an objective and neutral process without any particularities, or that no norms are involved in the construction of positive sciences, but rather to argue that such norms enter at the moment of the constitution of a system of structured enquiries, and are thus intrinsic and constitutive.

The decolonial nature of the enterprise of Critical Muslim Studies cannot be simply related to a different and distinct point of enunciation, since it is not clear that such points of enunciation can exist outside the framing of coloniality. The decoloniality of Critical Muslim Studies arises from an experiment with the provincialisation of the Western episteme. The decolonial refers neither to an erasure of all power relations (whatever that may mean), nor is it an attempt to found a utopia beyond all possible camps, but rather has the more limited aim of rejecting the continuity of the founding axiom of coloniality/modernity: the violent hierarchy between the West and non-West.

Decolonial projects, post-positivism and post-Orientalism are related through the way in which they are a response to the possibility of decentring the sign of the West. Science has a name; modernity has a name;

coloniality has a name. It is a name that has prevented the possibility of other names. Of course, all three positions contain within them a host of heterogeneous outlooks and proclivities. What unifies these positions is not any particular essence, but rather the possibility of being in fruitful conversation with the project of Critical Muslim Studies. The epistemology and methodology of this volume is informed by my articulation of these three positions.[22]

V

This book is an exercise in Critical Muslim Studies. It is self-consciously distinct from conventional paradigms for addressing Islamicate phenomena whether they be in the field of anthropology, Islamic studies or area studies. In the first section of this book I offer a critical engagement with the ways in which Muslim mobilisations are inflected by various themes such as democracy, relativism and secularism. I demonstrate the nexus between cultural, philosophical and governmental interventions that shape the interactions between demands for Muslim autonomy, and domestic and global structures of the world order. The backdrop to these engagements is provided by the still simmering War on Terror, that is, a 'dirty war' waged on a global scale.[23] This is not only a military enterprise but also a cultural project (Bhattacharyya, 2008: 4). The logic of the War on Terror has helped to fuse many disparate conflicts into regional fronts of a global conflagration, uniting both domestic and external zones of state activities. The eradication of extreme Islamism has both what military theoreticians call a kinetic dimension (drone assassinations, rendition, torture, assassination, war and threat of war), and a campaign to win the hearts and minds of the Muslim masses. The central component of this campaign is dismantling the narrative of Islamism and thus Islamism itself, and in doing so re-asserting the hierarchy between the West and non-West. In this section of the book each of the chapters analyse the displacements and evasions by which the decolonisation of the *ummah* continues to be disavowed and deflected by attempts to defer and disarm Muslim capacity to project themselves into the future. Thus, interventions dispersed in theme and time have a coherence arising out of their decolonial trajectory. In the process of decolonising the Muslim question, these interventions can be seen as building on the work of those who challenged the epistemological grounding that has dominated (and for the most part continues to dominate) the representations of Islam and Muslims, be it academic, popular or merely 'middle-brow'.

The second part of this book is a series of reflections on what an alternative to the current way of dealing with Muslims and Islam might look like. In this section of the book I draw attention to the configurations of various attempts to decolonise the *ummah*. I sketch out the consequences and parameters of a global institutionalisation of Muslim autonomy. These reflections are not blueprints for a future that is around the corner, nor are they specific plans ready to be implemented, but rather sketches of some possibilities akin to speculative fictions. The reflections are related to each other as they form a strand in broader arguments about projects for Muslim autonomy. These reflections meditate upon the dangerous impossibility of the very idea of the caliphate. It is dangerous because it threatens to overturn the current ordering of the world. It is impossible because it seems it cannot be realised. The caliphate is a metaphor for the struggles between Muslim aspirations to reorder the postcolonial world and the investments in the continuation of the violent hierarchies of coloniality. At the heart of this section is the tension between Islam and the Islamicate. That is, what is Islam and what is inspired by the venture of Islam? The division between clearing and dreaming cannot be absolute nor is it in the case of this volume, rather it ranges along a spectrum on which one end is dominated by critique and alternative language games are put forward at the other. *Recalling the Caliphate* then is not about remembrance or restoration but rather about reconceptualisation—a reconceptualisation that opens a decolonial horizon.

2

LIBERALISM

I

I do not know much about devils, but I know that Ayatollah Khomeini considered the United States to be the 'Great Satan'. This vision of a world polarised into contending 'civilisations' is one of the most popular ways of understanding the post-Cold War world. It can also be seen against a larger context as an attempt to deal with the problem of the decentring of the West and the associated undermining of a universal language based on the idea of the West as universal culture. In 1999, Ayatollah Khatami, the then newly elected president of Iran, suggested the possibility of an alternative to this vision of intercivilisational conflict.[1] His proposal was for a dialogue of civilisations, a proposal that was taken up by the United Nations. Khatami seemed to hope that the polarisation based on geopolitical differences and represented through the clash of civilisations could be overcome by better communication. In other words, dialogue would overcome difference. As the news of the attacks on New York and Washington in September 2001 spread across the world, a number of Iranians from north Tehran took to the streets and held vigils in support of the people who had died as a result of the attacks. It seemed this act showed the common human nature that lay beneath our cultural skins; underneath all our differences we were basically the same. Thus, a universal language could be an expression of our common humanity. The idea of a common humanity carries with it the connotations of an end to trouble and strife. Various individuals and groups argue that if we were to recognise that we are the same, the world would be a better, more peaceful and more just place.

II

When the towers of the World Trade Center were built they were supposed to be the tallest buildings in the world; proud towers that demonstrated the power and achievements of the American enterprise. But, perhaps one of the most ancient, or at least one of the most famous stories of a proud tower, is the story first recorded in one of the lands until recently under direct US occupation. The story goes that after the Great Flood, the Black-Headed people wanted to build a city with a great tower. The tower of Babel was built—perhaps, as is suggested by its possible etymology—as a Gate to God, as a demonstration of the capacity of humans to transcend their humble beginnings, and to recreate divine order on earth. Before the tower of Babel was brought down, the story goes, 'the whole earth was of one language, and one speech' (Genesis 11). The whole world was united and humanity was just one happy family (give or take a little fratricide). There were no collective entities in struggles with each other. There was no state, no nation. It is a vision of humanity that is resolutely prepolitical. This prepolitical world is often what people have in mind when they appeal to common-sense ideas of all humans being the same and conflict arising out of misunderstandings or manipulation by a few evil men. When the tower of Babel was struck down, the happy human family was torn asunder into distinct nations or tribes, and distinct language groups. The loss of common language opened up the world for conflict: apparently, it made diversity possible and community impossible. For the break-up of language not only meant the introduction of linguistic differences, but also the loss of our ability to communicate with each other and antagonisms emerged in the absence of such communication. It is the desire to control the production of antagonism and overcome differences that suggests the necessity of a universal language.

The destruction of the tower of Babel can serve as a metaphor for the transformation of the organic to the social. Or, to be more precise, it marks the emergence of the political itself. That is, society has to be established by managing differences. Organicist notions of identity give way to forms of subjectivity based on the identification of enemies and friends. In other words, the political is a means of mastering difference, but at the same time its condition of possibility is difference itself. However, we now live after the fall of the tower of Babel, and thus we are condemned to babble incomprehensibly with each other. In our inability to communicate, suspicion takes hold and violence becomes endemic. Dialogue, then, is a means of recovering that unity and, by mastering communication, of overcoming incomprehension and ignorance, and developing/articulating a language that would allow humans after the fall of the tower of Babel to overcome strife and conflict. Such a language was provided by the Western enterprise.

In its 500-year history, the Western project sought to establish a language that would enable the world to be comprehended in its totality. The name of this system of significations varied with context: sometimes it was called Reason, sometimes History, sometimes Science—but I prefer to call it Westernese. For this language game arose from extrapolating a very specific reading of the West and projecting it into the future as the destiny of the planet. During the short twentieth century the proud towers of Western enterprise crumbled, and with them the dream of Westernese replacing the chaos ushered in by the fall of the tower of Babel. It is this vortex created by the abandonment of Westernese that has introduced a series of crises ranging from the so-called 'culture wars' in US campuses to the emergence of Islamism throughout 'Muslimistan' and beyond.[2] The discourse of the clash of civilisations represents an attempt to come to terms with the dislocatory effects of the unravelling of Westernese. With the abandonment of Westernese as a universal language, we are confronted with a dangerous world of difference.

It is in order to find a way around the clash of civilisations and the binary opposition between Islam and West that Hamid Dabashi offers a 'hermeneutics of alterity' that rejects the 'metaphysics of identity' (2013: 159). It is in this light that we see the attempt to articulate a global public joined in an ecumenical embrace that disarms warring factions and refuses the choice between imperialism and terrorism (Buck, Morss, 2003). The idea that the clash of civilisations can be replaced by a conversation between civilisations seems to have instinctive appeal. This appeal, however, is also a reflection of the hegemony of liberalism. This is the version of liberal philosophy which is based around the primacy of the rational individual and sees conflicts as being the result of the failure to find apodic solutions, a failure that is temporary and that can be defeated by the exercise of goodwill and reason. According to this view, the existence of difference in the world reflects an empirical rather than an ontological limit.[3] In the rest of this chapter I want to focus on the attempt by Ayatollah Khatami to cross the frontier between Islam and the West.

III

In an interview with CNN correspondent Christiane Amanpour (1998), Khatami explained that the aim of his idea of a dialogue of civilisations and cultures is 'a world in which misunderstandings can be overcome, nations can understand one another and mutual respect and logic can govern relations among states'.[4] Clearly, he sees dialogue as a means of overcoming difference, and difference as contributing to the existence of antagonisms. The liberalism of Khatami's approach becomes even more explicit when Khatami recommends that the United States abandon its 'instrumental rationality' and embrace a foreign policy approach based on communicative rationality. To make this transformation possible, Khatami's next move is to demonstrate to his American audience that 'communicative rationality' is not alien to American culture but completely compatible with it. He then proceeds to show how the foundation of the United States was based on 'the vision, thinking, and manners of the Puritans'. For Khatami, the Puritans are a religious sect who combine a strong belief in God with a strong commitment to 'republicanism, democracy, and freedom'. In the Puritan colonisation of the Americas, Khatami sees one of 'the biggest tragedies in human history', that is, the belief that religion and freedom have an antagonistic relationship. By escaping religious persecution in England, the Puritans elaborate a way of life which sees liberty as only possible without religion, and that an official religion has no room for freedom. At this point in his analysis Khatami introduces Alexis de Tocqueville's *Democracy in America*, which he touchingly assumes most Americans to have read. According to Khatami's reading of Tocqueville, the importance of American civilisation was that religion and liberty became mutually supportive of each other. Khatami deploys Tocqueville to undermine one of the most cherished American visions of America: that in the

United States there is a strict separation of church and state and it is this separation that is the foundation of freedom in the country. In contradiction to this belief, Khatami argues that American experience demonstrates that 'religion and liberty are consistent and compatible' and that 'even today Americans are a religious people'.

Regarding the Iranian revolution, Khatami then draws analogies with the American War of Independence: 'With our revolution, we are experiencing a new phase of reconstruction of civilisation. We feel that what we seek is what the founders of the American civilisation were also pursuing four centuries ago. This is why we sense an intellectual affinity with the essence of the American civilisation'. Throughout this exchange Khatami is keen to try to establish commonalities between the formative period of US history and the foundation of the Islamic republic, in the hope that by highlighting these similarities he would be able to transcend the differences and suspicions that have arisen between Iran and the United States. Khatami is keen to argue that Tocqueville's privileging of freedom took place in the context of religion and that, as such, the religious milieu of the Islamic Republic of Iran points to a similarity between the American and Iranian revolutions, a similarity that US foreign policy fails to acknowledge.[5]

Khatami hoped that the text of *Democracy in America* would provide the common language that would enable dialogue between Islamist Iran and capitalist America. To do this, Khatami had to present, as Donald Pease puts it, '*Democracy in America* as an intercultural artefact that permitted the construction of homologies between Islam and US culture' (Pease, 1999: 82). This change in the status of *Democracy in America* from a clearly Western text to an 'intercultural artefact' available to be deployed by a scholar steeped in Islamicate education presents a series of challenges to the nature of US/Western identity. Pease offers a critical (deconstructive?) reading of one part of an editorial in the journal *New Republic* (tellingly entitled 'Tocqueville and the Mullah') that sought to intervene in the debate ushered in by Khatami's interview.[6] Pease exposes the way in which the Western supremacist discourse insists not only on its universal nature but also on the impossibility of reaching the universal through any other reading except the one steeped in Westernese. For the editors of *New Republic*, the Khatami interview poses a threat to the US policy of isolating Iran as a 'rogue state', but more generally poses a threat to the very constitution of a world order that is constructed by the 'externalisation of Islam as its historical and cultural Other' (Pease, 1999). This articulation is built on the myriad Orientalist representations of Islam found circulating within Western culture at popular, academic and public policy levels. The neo-conservative spin on these representations defined Islam as 'a transhistorical cultural essence whose irreducible disparity from universalist notions of civilisation rendered it similar to communism in its radical otherness' (Pease, 1999: 82). As a result, the editors of *New Republic* neither tried to debate with Khatami, nor did they discuss whether they disagreed with the specific reading Khatami offered—instead they attempted to rule Khatami out of order, to excommunicate him. As Pease puts it, the editors did not use the text of *Democracy in America* as an 'interpretive authority for their argument' with Khatami, rather they used it as a juridical device to invalidate his reading by denying him the right to be part of the international community in which dialogue can be conducted, by insisting on the exteriority of Islam from the world order. This expulsion of Khatami could only be achieved through the exercise of a 'symbolic violence' that the editors of *New Republic* had articulated as being characteristic of Islamist terrorism (Pease, 1999: 92).

Khatami's interview can be seen as an attempt to break the 'Plato to NATO' sequence of historical narrative grounded in Westernese, by grafting onto it another reading that interrupts its teleology. So the canonical sequence of the metaphors of Ancient Greece, Rome, Renaissance, Industrialisation and Modernity is no longer inexorably linked to the next stage of Western achievement and expression. This is achieved by taking Tocqueville out of the sequence of clearly demarcated Western thought, and resuturing him to a narrative that leads not to the West but to what is presented as its antithesis—Islam in general and the Islamic Republic of Iran in particular. This renarration reveals the contingent nature of the 'Plato to NATO' sequence; it demonstrates the trap of universalism for Westernese. Advocates of Westernese insist on the universal status of their discourse; in other words, the values of that discourse are the ones that have applicability outside any particular frame or context. At the same time, they advocate the Western nature of the universal, that Western values are synonymous with the universal. If we can understand that a truly universal value would be unmarked by any association with any particular cultural formation, what Westernese offers is not universal values, but a suggestion that only Western values are universal (a position that many members of the critical Left end up endorsing by conflating the desire for the universal with ignorance of the 'non-Western'). Khatami's deployment of Tocqueville is a cause for anxiety, since his reading recontextualises Tocqueville in a manner that undermines the Western element in favour of the universal element. Khatami seems to be saying, 'if you want your cultural tropes to furnish the language of universality then you have to give up any special hold or claim over them'. Thus, Khatami's use of Tocqueville is not a source of delight that Tocqueville is being 'universalised,' but rather horror at the way Khatami's interview seeks to rupture the sequence to which Tocqueville belonged. If the president of the Islamic Republic of Iran can find in the mission of a French magistrate to discover the 'elements' that sustain 'democratic stability' in the United States not a critique of the fundamental relationships within Islamist Iran, but a confirmation of the guiding principles of the Islamic Revolution, and if Tocqueville can be read outside the hegemonic teleology of Westernese, it demonstrates the contingent as opposed to the necessary character of the Western enterprise.

The response of the editors of *New Republic* was their way of demonstrating the capacity of Islamist discourses to unsettle the claims of Westernese and to disarticulate the relationship between the universal and the Western. Part of this ability of Islamist discourse can, of course, be traced to the 'scandal of Islam', in other words, the way in which Islam, beginning with a very similar pool of Mesopotamian narratives as Judaism and Christianity, recasts them into what becomes a very different kind of cultural complex. Islam, generating a narrative that includes figures familiar to both Judean and Christian discourses (Abraham, Moses, Jesus, Mary), produces a distinct sense of the sacred, which cannot be simply reduced to being a Jewish or even Christian heresy. The Islamic venture has its beginnings in a space not dissimilar to where we can locate the beginnings of the Western enterprise. Thus Islam, as a constant counter part to the Western enterprise, introduces contingency into the formation of Western identity, which continues to require Islam's expulsion to sustain its integrity. The capacity of Islamism to disrupt and disturb Westernese is not, however, simply due to the accidents of history: it is mainly due to the continued way in which the articulation of Islamism presupposes another future for the world, a future that cannot simply be contained within the prospect of the Westernisation of the planet. Islamism does not necessarily seek to reject the elements that Westernese would consider to be beneficial, what it does more radically is to reject the association between those elements and Western identity. It is at the level of contesting genealogies, at the point where foundational discourses are articulated, that Islamism—by insisting on its ability to renarrate and recast Westernese discourses in such a way that threatens to dissolve the Western identity of these discursive elements—challenges Westernese with universalisation.

One could read Khatami's interview and his deployment of Tocqueville as another forlorn effort by which those located outside the Western enterprise attempt to have a one-sided dialogue with Western interlocutors whose ignorance is only exceeded by their arrogance. One only has to read the column in *New Republic* to see how it trades on Orientalist fantasies through the use of terms such as 'mullah' and 'jihad' in order to establish a metonymic and metaphoric chain with terrorism, fanaticism and Islamic fundamentalism. Rather than engage with Khatami, the editors resort to claiming ownership of Tocqueville, not due to their scholarly mastery of his work—that is, not ownership based on labour—but based on the assumption of ownership and cultural heritage. In the end, Khatami cannot read Tocqueville because Tocqueville is Western and Khatami is not.[7]

One could also see the similarities between Khatami and other instances of apologist discourse in which Islamicate intellectuals attempt to demonstrate the compatibility of Islam with Western civilisation (Sayyid, 2003: 113). It would appear that Khatami has succumbed to the double bind of universalism. As it has been pointed out:

Universalism is a 'gift' of the powerful to the weak which confronts the latter with a double bind: to refuse the gift is to lose; to accept the gift is to lose. The only possible reaction of the weak is neither to refuse nor to accept, or both to refuse and accept—in short, the path of the seemingly irrational zigzags (both cultural and political) of the weak that has characterised most of nineteenth— and especially twentieth-century history. (Wallerstein, 1991: 217)

While there are some similarities between Khatami's dialogue of civilisations and these previous attempts, there is also a very crucial difference. Khatami's use of *Democracy in America* occurs in the context of the 'decentring of the West', it occurs when the assumption of a synonymous relationship between the West and the universal is being eroded. Thus, the manner in which Tocqueville is deployed is not to authorise the Islamic Republic, but to critique the official US representation of

Iran as a fundamentally illegitimate presence within the world system. The recasting of Tocqueville as an analyst of US democracy rather than as an analyst of the Islamic Republic blurs the distinction between the West and the non-West, and thus undermines its capacity to be the grammar of world order. Thus, Khatami's intervention demonstrates a level of skilled reading (that, of course, Bush and Blair and most Western politicians with their rather trite and unconvincing 'interpretations' of the Qur'an are unable to match) of *Democracy in America* that threatens to turn Tocqueville from the authoriser of American democracy (and thus critic of its antithesis) to a supporter of the possibilities of the Islamic Republic. Tocqueville is turned, in the hands of Khatami, from a defence witness for the American enterprise to a witness for the prosecution of US policy towards Iran.[8] As Khatami says: '[P]olicies pursued by American politicians outside the United States over the past half a century, since the Second World War, are incompatible with the American civilisation founded on democracy, freedom, and human dignity'.[9] By universalising Tocqueville on his terms, Khatami sets a trap for Western supremacists. While on the one hand, his deployment of Tocqueville shows that Western tropes can be found within the rhetorical armoury of an Ayatollah and must therefore demonstrate the reach of Western thought, on the other, the use of Tocqueville to admonish American policy and to transcend the 'West and the Rest' divide also demonstrates the weakness of the Western enterprise: its own figures cannot be relied on not to be 'hijacked' and put into the service of those who are considered to be outside of the West.

The price, however, of universalising Tocqueville is that Khatami cannot mount a postcolonial deconstructive reading. He is unable to demonstrate the intrinsic links between liberalism and imperialism, a complicity that was already being reworked during the period preceding Khatami's intervention, but which has come into further focus with the global War on Terror, in which connections between liberalism and imperialism have become explicit. One of the primary reasons Khatami uses Tocqueville is because he sees religion in the United States as a source of solidarity and strength. Thus, Khatami argues that the religious temper of the Islamic Republic of Iran should also be seen in a positive light. It is not, however, altogether clear that the French Tocqueville would necessarily endorse such a conclusion, for when writing about Algeria he sees it as a source of weakness (Richter, 1963: 365;

Pitts, 2000). The Iranian case would more likely approximate to the Algerian case rather than the American case, because both Algeria and Iran can be represented as being more non-Western than Western. This colonial difference is crucial. Tocqueville allows his belief in Western imperialism to trump his belief in liberalism. In other words, the frontier between the West and non-West exerts a decisive role in determining the parameters and possibilities of Tocqueville's critical inquiries. It could be argued that Tocqueville (unlike many contemporary liberal supporters of imperialism and the War on Terror) demonstrates a great deal of discomfort and even humility in his support of the French conquest of Algeria in particular and of Western imperialism in general. It remains the case, however, that he is either unable or unwilling to deploy his critical analysis as he crosses the colonial divide from the Western to the non-Western.

It is important not to simply dismiss Tocqueville's support for the French colonisation of Algeria as nothing more than a reflection of the milieu in which he found himself. This is a fairly common stratagem of those who want to defend historical figures against apparent criticism from what they consider to be anachronistic arguments. Tocqueville's 'turn to imperialism' is neither a transformation that stems from a change in thinking, nor is it a 'turn' that sometimes characterises intellectuals—for example from 'early' work to 'late' work—rather the difference can be fairly described as part of the phenomenon by which thinkers often end up taking positions that they oppose in one context but support in another. The change of context here is one that is occasioned by the movement from the West to the non-West. Thus supporters of liberty elsewhere can articulate support for tyranny in the form of colonial governmentality (John Stuart Mill). Opponents of women's suffrage in England can champion female emancipation in the form of a campaign to end the veil in Egypt (Lord Cromer). Those who argue for the equality of all men (sic) possess enslaved Africans (Jefferson). These instances cannot be reduced to acts of individual hypocrisy. Nor can they be treated as minor personal exceptions, for they have structural features that transcend the human failings to which most of us can, and often do, succumb. In the case of Tocqueville, the colonial turn was clearly not merely biographical but also cultural. The cultural shift did not mean, however, that Tocqueville did not have contemporaries and peers who disallowed the allure of empire to override their condemnation of arbitrary and unjust rule (Pitts, 2005).

Tocqueville's reflections on Algeria are absent from both Khatami's intervention and the reaction of most of his critics. One way to understand this refusal of Khatami to broaden his recontextualised reading of Tocqueville is to suggest that it may have been tactical. For such a broadening would have aligned Khatami in a decolonial critique of the Western canon. Juxtaposing Tocqueville's *Democracy in America* against Tocqueville's reports on Algeria could establish a ground for such a critique. This would allow Khatami not only to use Tocqueville as a translator for 'intercivilisational' dialogue, but also to transform the terms of that dialogue by providing a counter-reading. To do this, however, would have meant that Khatami would have to align his dialogue of civilisations with a critique of Westernese, and criticising those with whom you wish to have a dialogue is not always the best way to proceed. If Khatami's hope was that, with Alexis de Tocqueville as his guide and interpreter, and eschewing the polarising language of Ayatollah Khomeini, he would be able to make ordinary Americans aware of the 'real' Iran and thus begin the slow process of liberating US policy towards Iran from the thraldom of 'Persian' exiles, ultra-Zionists and neo-conservative crusaders, then he had to disarticulate his commentary on Tocqueville from a generalised Iranian revolutionary critique of 'the Great Satan'. As a consequence, Khatami's critique of American hegemony remains limited.

IV

Western supremacists respond to Khatami's trap by pointing out that not only is Khatami a translator and student of Tocqueville, but that he also translated Machiavelli into Farsi. Khatami is also a student of 'Old Nick' and therefore cannot be a trusted interlocutor since, in the act of translation, Khatami may have picked up some of the devil's tricks.[10] His offer of a dialogue was not sincere; what Khatami seemed to be offering is not dialogue but a continuation of the struggle by other means. Is it not the case that there can only be a conversation within a civilisation and never a conversation between civilisations, since the possibility of conversation assumes a ground that only common cultural codes can provide? Khatami's misreading of Tocqueville could only fake such a ground, since to use *Democracy in America* as an intercultural bridge meant rupturing the link between it and its normal attachments. To have a conversation, Khatami had to commit an act of violence that was a prerequisite to his attempt at dialogue.

Identity is relational and contrastive, therefore differences are not mere obstacles to be overcome but are rather constitutive of identity itself. Difference is the condition of the possibility of identity. Thus, to resort to dialogue as a means of transcending differences would imply the erosion of the identities constituted by the articulation of those differences. The erosion of identity cannot escape being a violating act; the more deeply etched and fundamentally drawn the identity, the more likely its loss would be felt as a violation. The existence of differences, however, also points to the possibility of conflict. Conflict guarantees the construction of a world that can always be unravelled to demonstrate its ignoble beginnings. In other words, the presence of conflicts and the inability to reconcile differences prevents structural closure; it keeps a space open in which the struggle for a new construction of the world can take place. This struggle carries with it the possibility of transforming social relations by making explicit their moment of founding, the options that the founding forecloses and the possibility of articulating those social relations in a different way. Conflict provides an opportunity to escape one's socialisation and to remove oneself from the current order by refusing the subjugations and subjectification that are on offer. Some would argue that it is possible to escape ethnocentrism by embracing the universalism of reason. Reason, however, is not external to the exercise of power. Most forms of power have legitimated themselves through claims that they represent the truth, the good and the reasonable; there is no guarantee that the claims of Enlightenment fundamentalists are not just another ruse on behalf of power.

V

For Khomeini, his claim that the United States was the Great Satan came from his understanding of the way in which the American empire established its control over Muslimistan, violating Muslims' identities as Muslims. This, for him, was sufficient to establish the demonic credentials of the US ruling elite, even though the exercise of US power was veiled in the language of prosperity, peace and freedom. Khomeini refused to accept the benign nature of US power, a refusal that enabled Khatami's US critics to question his overtures as being part of a campaign of deceit and deception: that is, in the guise of having an open dialogue with the American people, Khatami was trying to hoodwink them regarding the true nature of his regime. Khatami could have rejected the idea of a clash of civilisations by demonstrating how such conceptualisations see conflict as inherently primordial and cultural rather than contingent and political. He could have used the contrast between Tocqueville in America and Tocqueville in Algeria to show how the 'violent hierarchy' associated with the colonial divide undermines claims of Western universalism. Instead, Khatami opts for a notion of a dialogue of civilisations that is homologous to the idea of a global public space devoid of the political; a space in which there is no need to take sides, just as there is no 'us' and 'them', only a belief in the power of unrestricted communication to uncover underlying commonalities (Buck-Morss, 2003: 106). Such a vision seems to offer a metaphorical return to a time before the destruction of the tower of Babel: a world in which particularistic identities do not hold 'us' apart (Buck-Morss, 2003: 103). Those identities that are castigated for holding 'us' apart are also what hold 'us' up.

At the heart of this vision of a world without the structures of cultural or economic domination is the conflation between power as a form of subjectivity and power as a form of repression. The attempt to replace the paradigm of the clash of civilisations with a vision of the dialogue of civilisations risks endorsing an uncritical cosmopolitanism in which an attempt to articulate an alternative vision of the world can be presented as a form of pathology. The War on Terror was not just a product of a neo-conservative cabal wedded to the government that took over Washington in 2000. By distancing himself from the rhetoric of Ayatollah Khomeini, Khatami presents a rejection of a theological reading of geopolitics. This is, however, accomplished by a rejection of the political rather than its elaboration. I do not know much about devils, and I do not know if Khatami has seen *The Usual Suspects* (1995), but if he has, he would have known that the biggest trick the devil ever played was to convince the world that he did not exist.

3

SECULARISM

I

Secularists would rather any talk of devils or angels or God should not be in the public arena, since they often believe that it is the failure to maintain the proper distinction between the secular and religious which is the cause of great violence today, as Akeel Bilgrami writes in an article on secularism and relativism:

> It seems more and more urgent to declare oneself a secularist (and I hereby do so) in a time when wars are waged by a government dominated by the thinking of the Christian Right, terror is perpetuated in the name of Islam, the occupation of territories of continuously displaced population is perpetuated by a state constituted in explicitly Jewish terms and a beleaguered minority is killed in planned riots by majoritarian mobilization reviving an imagined Hindu glory. (2004: 174)

In contrast, Saba Mahmood argues that what is needed are:

> not so much stringent and pious calls for the reassertion of secularism but a critical analysis of what has been assumed to be the truth of secularism, its normative claims, and its assumptions about what constitutes 'the human' in this world. This is not simply because such an exercise is intellectually compelling, but because what we take to be the moral superiority of the secular vision needs to be rethought urgently. Apart from the fact that this secular vision does not command broad allegiance in the world today, I fear that it is premised on a propensity to violence that is seldom questioned (2006: 347).

Mahmood goes on to examine the convergence between the US-sponsored theological reform campaign as an annexe to the War on Terror and the work of a number of 'moderate Muslim' thinkers who seem to be advocating a secularist interpretation of Islam principally through atomised readings of the Qur'an.[1] Bilgrami would probably consider such a convergence to be of coincidental significance, and his attempt to establish an equivalence between the various enemies of secularism (Christian Right, Islamists, Hindutva advocates and ultra-Zionists) suggests an ecumenical embrace that would seem to dispel any concerns that secularism is just another stick with which to beat Muslims. The idea that forces of concerted global anti-secularism are at work in the contemporary world requires a number of elisions and inconsistencies to circulate. For example, if one wanted to see in Israeli occupation and repression of Palestinians a religious legitimacy one would want the Zionist state to be justified in mainly Judaic rather than Jewish terms.[2] Or is it really the case that the 'planned riots' of India are simply an offshoot of the expansion of Hindutva and were absent during the height of Nerhuvian (secular) hegemony? Is it also the case that the instances of large-scale violence (wars, 'terrorism', occupation and riots) are exclusive to religions? Could we not draw up another list in which the starring roles in the perpetuation of great cruelty and violence would be ascribed to secularist actors?

There is, however, another common thread suggested by Bilgrami—that Islam and Muslims feature in all the cases he cites (War on Terror, 'terrorism in the name of Islam', Zionist occupation or pogroms in India). The relationship between Muslim mobilisation and the contemporary world order are expressed as a problem of secularism and its discontents. In this chapter I will explore the way in which secularism is deployed in coping with the mobilisation of Muslims. The aim of my analysis is not to replicate Mahmood, whose insights on the way in which secularism was being used by the Bush regime (and its various supporters and successors) to reshape Islam I found invaluable, but rather to focus on the way in which the question of secularism turns into the Muslim question. In other words, secularism is one of the categories often deployed in discussions about the difficulties of exercising Muslim agency.

II

Secularism in its simplest and most widely circulated form calls for a de facto if not *de jure* separation between religion and politics. The forceful reassertion of Islam in the public sphere throughout the world is currently presented as one of the most significant challenges to the story of progressive global secularisation.[3] Recent debates in Western plutocracies have focused on Muslim minorities as in need of secularisation. The overlaying of issues of secularisation with questions of how to include ethnically marked, often ex-colonial populations has helped to reinforce and, in some cases, reactivate discursive equivalences between national majorities, the current Westphalian world order and secularism. The 'problem' of Muslim minorities raises not only public policy questions about how to manage relations between a national majority and an ethnically marked 'minority' (Sayyid, 2004; Hesse and Sayyid, 2006), but also more general 'ideological' questions about the extent to which the 'final vocabulary' (Rorty, 1989: 73) of the Western enterprise is adequate to the task of including Muslims and at the same time preventing the subversion of that enterprise.

Secularism is presented as being one of the key achievements of Western cultural formations. Its supposed benefits can be grouped in three broad clusters. One set of epistemological arguments centres on the claim that without secularism there can be no scientific progress, which of course undergirds technological advances. In this sense secularism, as an epistemological category rather than a social one, can be described as a shift from an episteme centred on God to one centred on Man (sic). The core of the argument is that secularism delegitimates the claims of religious authorities to control the production of knowledge and creates the conditions for the rejection of ontological claims found in sacred narratives in favour of a scientifically orientated ontology.

A second cluster of arguments emphasises the civic benefits of secularism. According to this set of arguments secularism is necessary to ensure peace and social harmony and to prevent religious passions from getting out of hand. By separating religion and confining it to the private sphere, secularism prevents differences in religious opinions from becoming the source of conflicts that would engulf a society's public space. Religious differences become matters of individual taste and therefore have little impact upon the organisation of social life at large. In addition, secularism prevents contending groups from making appeals to supernatural forces as a way of reinforcing their positions and keeps all parties on a level playing field in which debate cannot be short-circuited by such appeals.

Third, it is argued that secularism presents the necessary precondition for the exercise of democracy; that it prevents the occupation of the space of power by God or those who present themselves as representatives of the Divine, thus helping to keep the space of power empty. The removal of God allows the space of power to be emptied. The claim being that democracy is government that is ultimately based on the idea of the 'sovereignty of the people' (regardless of how this idea is expressed in reality, for example in Britain it is parliament that is sovereign and not the people, however, the power of parliament derives from the people). Popular sovereignty seems to preclude any place for the idea of a sovereign God or sovereign priesthood.

Thus the benefits of secularism help to define modernity itself.[4] Modernity of course, remains a narrative about Western exceptionality, as in this sense secularism becomes a marker of Western identity. The epistemological, civic and democratic arguments for secularism are formulated as part of the narrative of Western exceptionality. Therefore, the articulation of a Muslim subject position within the context of the ethnoscapes of Western countries presents a peculiar challenge to Western identity. Muslims come to represent anti-secularism simply by virtue of the fact that the designation 'Muslim' is interpreted as being religious, and their appearance within the public spaces of Western plutocracies therefore seems to erode the divide that secularism seeks to institutionalise. The reactivation of a translocal Muslim consciousness has the effect of bringing to the fore the counter-factual nature of Islam vis-à-vis the West (Davies, 2006: 203–5). Thus, the lack of secularism in Islam is contrasted with the presence of secularism in the West and this contrast helps to confirm the necessity and importance of secularism if a civilisation is to prosper. Islam does not only exist as a mere counter-history, however. It also circulates among Muslims as a marker of distinct historical and cultural formations in its own right and, as such, the attempt to present the benefits of secularism as being of universal significance flounders. In other words, the shift from Western to Islamicate societies seemingly undermines the universal claims for secularism.

III

It seems to be increasingly the case that Muslim communities are probably the most prominent groups of people who seemingly do not accept the claims of secularism.[5] Partly, this is due to the way in which Western history and Islamicate history have different things to say about the necessity of secularism or otherwise. Specifically, the applicability of the three main arguments for secularism and their relevance for Muslims can be challenged by focusing on the experience of autonomous Islamicate cultural formations, that is, those cultural formations that existed prior to the colonial enframing of the planet.

The problem with the claims made on behalf of secularism is that they are very often conducted through a discourse of Westernese, and thus Western historical developments are seen as having universal relevance. As argued in the previous chapter, with reference to Western history, secularism in the West is not seen as being a contingent development arising out of the specific history of the West, but as a necessary condition arising out of the unfolding of history itself. Secularism then becomes a necessary stage that all cultural formations have to achieve if they are to progress towards modernity.

So, for example, the epistemological case for secularism rests upon a conflict between science and church—a conflict symbolised by the trials of Galileo. The absence of an organised church made it difficult to draw such clear demarcations between the authority of religion and science within Islamicate societies. More importantly, perhaps, the epistemological case for the benefits of secularism rests on the assumption that the understanding of the Divine in Islamic and Nasrani discourses is homologous.

Christological and Islamic discourses on the Divine cannot be seen as essential or foundational, since differences in reflection on the Divine indicate contingent conversations within diverse hermeneutic traditions and not the uncovering of specific essences that are 'hard-wired' within Christianity or Islam. It may be useful to point to the different positions regarding the nature of divinity that can be teased out once all proper qualifications have been made with reference to both the complexity of the topic and the multiplicity of opinions about it. Many of the early Nasrani sectarian disputes often had a Christological dimension such as, for example, the controversies between those who accepted the interpretations of the Council of Chalcedon and those who did not—the Arians,

Nestorians and Monophysites. The dominance of this Chalcedonian interpretation helped produce a Christological conception of the Divine in which the mundane and the Divine occupy the same ontological plane. The conjoining of human and divine spheres as described through the category of incarnation in which divine and mundane fuse in the body of Christ no doubt helps to sustain a perspective in which human endeavour can potentially compete with the Divine. These narratives of divine causality and intervention come to be locked in a zero-sum game with narratives that centre on human agency. As a consequence, science and religion continually collide.

Within Islamic interpretations the distinction between the Divine and the human cannot be bridged. Islamicate reflections on the nature of the Divine have been very consistent in maintaining the gap between human and divine spheres, a gap that is wide and permanent. Therefore, no human enterprise can appropriate or displace the centrality of the Divine, since the human and Divine can be said to exist in distinct ontological realms that cannot be bridged. Therefore, science would be contained within the field of *aql* (reason) and would not question the role or the authority of the Divine.

The case for secularism as necessary for civic peace is largely based on extrapolating instances/narratives from the European experiences of the wars of the Reformation and Counter-Reformation to make a general point about the relationship between civic peace and depoliticisation of religious belief. As has been pointed out, there is no direct analogue to sectarian warfare of such intensity and scale in Islamicate history and thus the idea that civic peace is only possible if religion is confined to the private sphere cannot be read as simply from Islamicate history. There is no doubt that there has often been sectarian conflict of great ferocity, for example, the First and Second Civil Wars (35–40/656–661 and 60–73/680–692) but these disputes were for the most part intra-elite and in general did not lead to large-scale involvement or destruction of the general population.[6] The conflict between the Fatimids and the Abbasids (296–566/909–1171) is perhaps closest to the scope of antagonisms characteristic of the wars of religion that tore asunder Christendom; however, the infrastructural capacity of both Abbasid and Fatimid political orders was not sufficient to produce such an intensive form of violence as experienced in the wars of religion in Europe.

Indeed, if anything, the very opposite suggests itself: the retreat of religion from the public sphere in Islamicate history has been most often associated with the breakdown of civic peace. The oft admired secularist order in Turkey, for example, was imposed from the top upon an exhausted, war-weary population. The secularism of the Turkish republic was not a response to the demands of the Turkish masses but rather proceeded from the authoritarian project of Westernisation of the Kemalists. Secularism in the context of Islamicate communities has often meant de-Islamisation, and has for the most part been imposed either by colonial, communist or Kemalist regimes.[7] Such projects have all served to increase rather than reduce social conflict. Empirically, the scale and intensity of violence in Muslim countries that have been ruled by avowedly secular regimes has been such that it would not inspire much confidence in the association between secularism and civic peace.

The argument that secularism is a necessary precondition for any political system of popular sovereignty ignores the multiplicity of possible ways in which popular sovereignty can be finessed, from the historical examples of diverse constitutional monarchies to the suggestion by Mawdudi and others who re-described popular will as being vice regal rather than sovereign. In other words, the sovereignty of the Divine is an elaboration of the centrality of God to the cosmos, but cannot be a practical sovereignty in the sense that 'the sovereign is who decides upon the exception' (Schmitt, 2005: 5) if for no other reason than that the idea of a monotheistic version of the omnipotent and omniscient God does not allow for the Divine to have any exception.[8]

It would seem that the meaning of secularism is perhaps to be found in its insertion into the 'Plato to NATO' sequence that encapsulates Westernese. Precisely because the articulation of a global Muslim subjectivity contributes to the provincialisation of Europe's 'final vocabulary' it threatens to reveal Plato to NATO as a historiographical convention rather than history. In the context of Muslims living in Western plutocracies the staples of the 'immigrant' imaginary becomes strained, as categories such as religion, minority, 'race' and so on are seen more and more as part of the Plato to NATO sequence rather than as descriptions of objectivity (Sayyid, 2004). This suggests that the validity of this sequence rests upon the exercise of coloniality. Coloniality is to be understood as not being reducible to colonialism, but rather to refer to the logic of governmentality that underpins specific forms of historical colonialism and continues to structure a planetary hierarchy in terms of the distinction between the West and the non-West (and its various cognates) beyond the formal institutionalisation of colonialism (Mignolo, 2005: 7; Hesse and Sayyid, 2006).

IV

An effort to circumvent some of the objections about the ethnocentric nature of the arguments for secularism is to try and broaden the applicability of secularism. There are two ways in which broadening takes place: historically and geographically. Secularism is broadened historically to argue that it is not a Westphalian invention and can be found in instances before the treaty of Westphalia (1058/1648). This means having to show that empires, the most durable pre-nation-state political structures, were secular; for example, to argue Muslimistan in particular has its own inherent secularism. Such a view is bolstered by references to the various hadith which demonstrate that the Prophet (pbuh) himself made a distinction between decisions and actions made as a consequence of divine revelation and those based on the application of human knowledge and reason. Such a division, however, becomes more problematic in the post-Prophetic context, since it would seem to suggest that other than having the Archangel Gabriel speaking to one, everything else is secular. Thus, the division between the secular and the religious would collapse as the secular entirely colonises the religious. Such a position could only be sustained by a circular reasoning in which the division between the religious and the secular can only be articulated by the hegemony of secularism. Religion, in other words, becomes a category generated by secularism. Secularism, of course, has its own history within the Western Enlightenment and, thus, attempts to expand its temporal reach can only be sustained by presenting the reading of this particular history of the West as the history of the world. Rather than making the case for non-Eurocentric antecedents for secularism, then, the introduction of the religion/secular divide into the historiography of other societies only further re-inscribes the supremacy of Westernese.

An approach in which a conception of secularism, culled from European history, is then applied to other non-European cases and (not surprisingly) finds serious anomalies, is not adequate. Such an approach reinforces the idea of secularism as essentially European, despite the intention to subvert this association.

Geographically, secularism can be extended to places which are considered to be non-Western, so that it is argued that secularism is not just to be found in the West but also outside it. Indian secularism seems to provide an example of such a possibility. Indian (liberal-elite) political rhetoric has made considerable play upon the centrality of secularism in India's public life. It is suggested that the durability of Indian democracy, its relative civic peace (give or take the various 'insurgencies' in Kashmir, Nagaland, Punjab) and, since the days of 'India Shining', its rapid economic growth, all point to the way in which the promotion of secularism provides beneficial effects even in a society as different from Western Europe as India. This, then, would seem to offer an example of secularism in a non-Western context being able to provide the benefits that are claimed for it in the context of Western historical development. India's prosperity, democracy and civic peace seem to be associated with the commitment of India's ruling elite to secularism. If secularism can be said to work in India, then it may be possible to restore its universal claims.

Of course, it could be argued that Indian secularism has clear Western roots: modern India as an heir to the British Raj 'internalised' many colonial governmental practices, including the regulation and articulation of distinct religious communities. Nehru, the principal architect of Indian secularism, 'knew' India mainly through Indology (Brown, 2000). The complicated genealogy of secularism in India does not allow a claim for an autochthonous Indian version of secularism, distinct from its Western counterpart, to be sustained. Secularism in India is deployed in three main ways. First, it is deployed as a way of marking India off from Pakistan. The story of South Asia since 1947 is often presented as a study in contrasts in which one of the successor states to the British Raj is presented as a confessional state and the other as secular. This India-Pakistan comparison that is such a staple of much South Asian historiography also doubles up as an argument for secularism and its universal validity. Indian secularism circulates as a marker of the distinctive character of India vis-à-vis Pakistan (especially so within the Nehruvian discourse that was hegemonic in India for at least the first fifty years after Partition), in which India as a democratic and normal state is contrasted with Pakistan as an Islamic and failed state. The study in contrast conceals a degree of homologies between these two successor states, as Ayesha Jalal argues, that behind the façade of 'largest democracy in the world' and the persistent praetorianism of Pakistan a complex authoritarianism holds sway, which is neither transparent nor unaccountable (Jalal, 1995).

Second, it is deployed as a means of preserving the Nehruvian settlement from the onslaught of Hindutva. Here secularism does not mean a separation of religious institutions from governmental institutions, but rather the establishment of a hierarchy between those faith traditions that are described as Indic and thus authentically part of contemporary India, (Hinduism, Jainism, Sikhism) and those that are considered to be non-Indic (Christianity, but primarily Islam).[9] Secularism in this context is seen as being a badge of Indian compatibility with fundamental Western values through its capacity to demonstrate a tolerant society that corresponds to the images Western plutocracies have of their own societies.

Third, secularism is considered essential to preserving civic peace in India, primarily in defusing tensions between the Hindu majority and the Muslim minority. Secularism in India, then, essentially manages the relationship between a Muslim minority and the nation-state majority. Other issues also enter the ambit of Indian secularism, but it is the management of Muslim populations that is of central concern.

Indian secularism, however (along with Indian democracy), coexists with an institutionalised system of communal violence in which the primary victims tend to be Muslims (Brass, 2003). Secularism allows Hindu-Muslim violence to be represented as exceptional rather than as intrinsic to contemporary India. A careful analysis of Hindu-Muslim violence and the institutionalised riot system through which it is exercised suggests that the discourse of Indian secularism has not so much defused the violence but rather worked to render it largely invisible (ibid.: 377–80).[10] It could be argued that secularism in India along with 'planned riots' are part of the institutional ensemble by which Muslims in India are disciplined and domesticated.

It is this disciplining as much as the virtues of Indian democracy that may account for the presentation of Indian Muslims as being largely immune to jihadi influences. Such a presentation, of course, can be made only if one discounts the events taking place in Kashmir, where the Indian security establishment have maintained one of the highest force-to-civilian population ratios in the world for many years as the means of holding down Kashmiri Muslims. The focus on the relationship of India's Muslim minorities to its national majority is something common to both Indian and Western accounts of the necessity of secularism.[11]

The underlying assumption behind attempts to equate secularism with civic peace and dialogic possibilities is that religion is dangerous because its ability to incite hostility is unparalleled. Thus, secularism actually operates as a name for the commitment to anti-dogmatism. Why should religious passions be more violent than other passions? The response to this question usually takes the form that if someone thinks that they are on 'a mission from God' they are unlikely to be dissuaded by objections on more mundane grounds, nor are they likely to see themselves as being participants in 'ideal communicative' dialogue. This response, however, is not really about religion but about claims that a higher authority is validating one's position. This higher authority, moreover, does not have to take the form of God or gods, it can (and has) taken the name of History, Science or Reason. In this regard it could be argued that secularism helps to hide the higher authority claimed by some groups against claims made by other groups, and does so by reproducing the colonial drama in which the West has science and the non-West has superstition.

V

So far I have discussed the case for secularism largely in relation to claims made on its behalf. I have suggested that most of these claims are not as strong as often suggested. It seems that the two most prominent cases of secularism—Western and 'Indian'—are currently deployed in relation to the emergence of a Muslim identity. Islam is certainly not alone in not organising the sense of the selfhood of its subjects along a religious/secular divide. Hindus and ancient Romans, among others, similarly made little distinction between religious duties and obligations, and other forms of identification. Today this is most clearly expressed in the case of Jewish identity, which continues to refer to ethnicity as well as a set of religious beliefs and practices. In the Jewish case, notions of 'racial' identity seemingly trump notions of identity derived from Judaism: thus it is possible to be a Jew while having no belief in the Divine.

Muslims are multi-lingual, multicultural subjects; therefore, to what extent can we speak of a unified Muslim identity? Clearly, the dominant markers by which collective identities (nationality, class and 'race') are expressed would seem to exclude a Muslim subject position as significant.[12] Muslims do, however, share the possibility of telling stories about themselves; stories that begin with the revelations received by the Prophet (pbuh) and continue with the addition of many discursive threads through time to create a tapestry that can be signified as being distinct, with its own system of signifying practices. Individual Muslims are often thrown into this complex web or choose to become part of it so that the many aspects of their biographies resonate with a privileged meaning within this historical sequence. From the names that they take, or are given, to the way they comport themselves, the story that begins with the revelations delivered by Archangel Gabriel and runs through the formation of the Islamic state in Medina, the circulation of the Qur'an and the expansion of the Islamicate order progressively encompassing ever larger parts of the Earth's surface, help situate those who call themselves Muslims. This situating can take many forms, from uncritical affirmation to total rejection fuelled by self-loathing through all kinds of positions in between and at various stages in one's biography. The articulation of a Muslim identity, however, points to a historical community. And for a variety of contingent and specific reasons (some of which will be discussed elsewhere in this volume) the history of this community has come to embody a counter-history to the dominant Plato to NATO sequence. As such, the articulation of a Muslim subject position becomes political in two senses of the term. First, it is political in that it occurs as an interruption of the dominant discourse and its emergence draws attention to the 'ignoble' institutionalisation of the dominant discourse. Second, by interrupting the dominant discourse it subverts the mechanism that exists for transforming political antagonisms into social differences, and thus it is political in the sense that it is caught up in a field sustained by the distinction between friends and enemies.

The current debate about secularism within Western plutocracies takes place in the context of mobilisations of Muslims in the name of Islam. The potential for Muslims to generate transnational mobilisations puts into crisis one of the major building blocks of the Westphalian system, which produces ethnicised minorities in opposition to national majorities by drawing up boundaries that construct certain populations as national majorities and others as ethnicised minorities. For example, the 1.6 million Muslims in a UK population of 60 million are normally and unproblematically described as a minority. Seen from the perspective of 1.6 billion Muslims in relation to a UK population of 60 million, however, potentially changes the relevance of the minority-majority distinction. As a consequence, the articulation of a Muslim subject position is not merely international, in that Muslim can be found in many nation-states; it is also diasporic in that the scattering of Muslims continues to take place in the contexts of deterritorialised political subalternity.[13] These mobilisations continue to be seen and to be constituted as a problem for a host of reasons, including the shift in power that they signal between national majorities and ethnic minorities, and between coloniality and post-colonial effects.

In this context, secularism then becomes a means of dealing with the articulation of Muslim identity. So while the literature on secularism tends to focus on its merits, what is decisive about it are not the benefits that may or may not accrue from its endorsement, but rather that its endorsement becomes an affirmation of Westernese. The various citizenship tests, the attacks on the veil and its prohibition and the demands that Muslims conform to Western values can be read as arising from the way in which the quest for a Muslim autonomy implicitly (and in some cases explicitly) interrupts the Plato to NATO sequence and, in doing so, undermines the legitimacy of Westernese. Secularism is deployed not to ensure civic peace or epistemological advances, but rather to maintain Western historiographical hegemony. The current debate about secularism, in other words, turns less on its avowed concern with separating religion from politics but rather with the depoliticising of Muslims.[14] Secularism as a discursive regime deals not with 'objective reality' but with a specific constructed version of its object. It generates Muslims as permanently transgressive subjects, whose religious essence is constantly being undermined by the temptations of the political. As a consequence, Muslim politics becomes either a purely empirical designation or an illegitimate articulation. The proper Muslim is religious—where religion is a sign of the pre-modern episteme. It follows that the Muslim who is political is not properly a Muslim. Being political means being modern, it also means being a people with history.

By policing the boundary between the religious and the political, secularism also becomes another means of policing the boundary between the pre-modern and the modern, and the Western and the non-Western. As Talal Asad argues, the distinctions between secular and religious are not invariant but are reconfigured at different times for different purposes (Asad, 2003: 25–6). The meaning of the concepts of secularism and religion are to be found through their insertion in a world history dominated by the distinction between the Western and the non-Western. It is often argued that the religious is not only a secular category but also a Western category—not only ontically but also ontologically. That is, the secularist determination of what constitutes the religious is perhaps the answer to the question posed by Asad as to why there is no anthropology of secularism (ibid.: 21–2). The assumption of the default condition as being secular means that it is religion that needs to be accounted for. The default position of being secular arises from the default assumption within Westernese that being Western is being human and therefore it is the condition of not-being Western that requires explanation.[15] Currently, the sharpest skirmishes on the frontier between Western and non-Western identity are those that involve the Muslim awakening. The deployment of the category of secularism and its associated tropes is one of the key means by which the resistance to the affirmation of Muslim autonomy and agency is expressed. So when Mahmood (2006) points to the various ways in which secularism has been deployed by the US (and also by other Western plutocracies), what is at stake is the primacy of the Western over the non-Western. This primacy is articulated both philosophically and geopolitically, and defended economically, culturally and, of course, militarily.

4

RELATIVISM

I

Ziauddin Sardar, in his typically robust and uncomplicated way, asserts that post-modernity is nothing more than the continuation of Western cultural imperialism by other means (1998: 8–9). He seems to reprise a common theme among many who feel that post-modernism, with its promiscuous play of words and meaning and its fancy invitations that proclaim that 'anything goes', stands in stark contrast to the absolute certainties of Islam. Post-modernism is a very slippery concept. In general, there seems to be a consensus that what it means is a 'suspicion towards meta-narratives'. In other words, post-modernism encourages us to be sceptical of the claims made by various humans to have discovered the royal road to wisdom. Another way of seeing post-modernism is to see it as the 'decentring of the West'. That is, post-modernism is a (belated) recognition that claims made by modernity are, in many ways, less like reflections of universal truths and more like narcissistic fantasies. Post-modernism reveals the limits of modernity's intellectual, moral and cultural mastery. It puts into question the idea that the West is best.

In general, people who are apologists for the West favour the first definition, since it seems to obscure the second. It is difficult, however, to imagine how one could be suspicious of meta-narratives without a decentring of the West, since the most powerful narrative of the past 200 years has been the one that told the tale of the West's destiny. The recent heightening of Muslim sensibilities is a testimony to the way in which Islam can no longer be held back by a belief in the inherent superiority of the West. There are those, who would say: 'Yes, yes, it's all very well to talk about the effect of post-modernism on the relationship between Islam and the West, but what if post-modernism attacks the very foundations of Islam, what happens if the "suspicion of meta-narratives" turns into cynicism towards the Qur'an itself? In other words, what if anti-essentialism associated with post-modernism attacks the foundations of faith of Muslims?'[1] There are, however, three responses one could make to calm these fears. First, to assume that post-modernism would have the same effect in the Muslim world as it is supposed to have had in the European world is unfounded. Not only is there a difference in terms of the unequal distribution of global power, or different historical habits, but also in terms of deep foundations. Just take two examples: the New Testament and the Qur'an are both central sacred texts to the traditions that they founded; despite this similarity, however, they are very different. The New Testament can be seen as a kind of biography of Isa's ministry; the Qur'an, while containing some biographical details of the Prophet (pbuh), cannot be read as his biography. So reading the Qur'an or reading the New Testament is not the same kind of exercise and requires different skills and different critical strategies. There are, of course, many other examples of different histories and different traditions; all these examples point to the way in which one could not automatically assume that what happens in the West will happen in Islam with similar effects. Second, it is not possible to legislate against cynicism; if Muslims become cynical and opportunist towards their faith, it will not be because of post-modernism. Cynicism is a product of political disempowerment; it arises when one cannot imagine a future that is better for all, so one tries to work only for oneself and one's families. This retreat from public participation in society to private concerns is what breeds cynicism. Social problems are depoliticised and presented as ethical challenges. The search for 'a good society' is sacrificed for the cultivation of 'good Muslims' who can do without society. This ethical replacement of politics leads to the emergence of Muslim monks who find the *ummah* irredeemably corrupt. This monasticism is strange considering that Muslims tend to proclaim that 'Islam is a total way of life'—but the life that is envisioned seems hollow: full of rituals, empty of ideals and often cut off from reality. A total way of life that does not have room for public participation and contestation and that does not recognise the rich tapestry of its own past is neither total nor even a way of life. Rather than railing against post-modernism, it may be more useful to invest our energies in reclaiming Islamicate history. It is knowledge of the past that allows you to build hopes for the future, and the only antidote to cynicism is the idea of a hopeful future. Having said all this, it is important to remember that we should not be precious about post-modernism. I am not praising post-modernity or defending post-modernity for the sake of post-modernity, post-modernism should be seen as a set of tools that may be useful in helping to clear the ground and create the space for articulating Islam with the future. Now Sardar is one of those writers who argues that despite the claims made, post-modernity's valorisation of cultural hybridity remains mired within Western cultural practices. This position is in contrast to the one that sees post-modernity as making possible so-called 'identity politics', that is, forms of political mobilisations that seemingly reject universal verities of the Enlightenment, and make narrow exclusionary political demands based upon the cultivation of a cultural identity.[2] In other words, according to this view post-modernity endorses cultural relativism and consequently promotes the abandonment of universalism. Islamism is often seen as one form of identity politics, and its proclamation of Muslim autonomy is presented as extreme particularism that cannot be conjoined with any wider movement of social transformation that would elicit the support of other groups.

How is it possible to see in post-modernity a challenge to modernity's intellectual, moral and cultural mastery, while also seeing it as a means of exercising that mastery? The inclusion of contradictory views such as cultural relativism and cultural imperialism within the swirl of ideas and attitudes that are perhaps too imprecisely described as post-modern can only partly be explained by this imprecision. While it is often the case that post-modernity is used by the fashionable of a certain era as a badge of pride, by the doggedly down-to-earth as a term of abuse and by the thoughtful only in quotation marks, it is also the case that what is at stake is something more than the correct meaning of the term. How is it possible for one epistemological position to be marshalled in such contradictory ways? Perhaps the answer can be found in the structure of what can be (with all possible caveats) broadly described as post-modern thought consisting of two strands: a critique of essentialism and a critique of universalism. The critique of essentialism supports the political, intellectual and moral positions that reject expressions of Muslim identity. This is because Islamism appears as a manifestation of essentialism. The critique of universalism, however, supports positions that reject expressions of Western cultural supremacy. Thus, attempts to articulate universal values from non-Western histories and cultures are considered to be made possible by the rejection of the Western claim for universal validity. This is because of the claim that Western cultural authority is most often associated with claims of universalism.

The debate around the post-modern condition (and its cognates) hinges on the relationship between Western histories and societies, and universal values. The question of the meaning of modernity retains its importance even if it is inflected by a different set of registers, as ultimately the nature of modernity is a question about the destiny of the West. Dominant descriptions of modernity saw it as intrinsically Western (Sayyid, 2003: 84–126). Thus, mobilisations that occur around a banner that cannot be described unproblematically as being part of the West cannot but help raise questions about the possibility of multiple forms of modernity; and implicit in such an undertaking is the 'normalisation' of the West—the subversion of its claims to be the only embodiment of universal values.

Islamism is the most prominent political discourse that seemingly rejects the claims of Western exceptionality. This rejection is represented by three distinct views regarding the relationship that Islamism is said to have with modernity. There is the view that asserts that Islamism is anti-modern. This is a view that is widely held in popular circles in which Islamists are seen as being determined to bring about some form of 'medieval' restoration signified by forms of punishment (amputation and stoning, for example), political institutions (caliphate) or social practices (gender segregation). This view has increasingly been replaced in many expert circles with a view that sees Islamism as being based not on the rejection of but a capitulation to modernity (Schulze, 2000; Roy, 2002). In this view Islamism is another form of totalitarianism, akin to fascism or Leninism (Gray, 2004; Tibi, 2007). The position that I wish to explore is one that sees Islamism as conditioned by a breach in the relationship between modernity and the West. That is, one of the consequences of the 'decentring of the West' (Young, 1990) is that this decentring transforms our understanding of modernity, thereby disarticulating it from discourses of Western exceptionality. It is a view that allows us to understand the sense of 'moral panic' that Islamism seems to produce in Western plutocracies, and the way in which the question of Muslim presence in Western societies has become a battleground for ever-widening *kulturkampf* in which Western identity is forged in opposition to the perceived threat of Islam(ism).[3] The anxiety associated with the loss of Western centrality has increasingly taken the form of a defence of universal values that translates into an attack on any suggestion of distinct Muslim political identity and an attack on those philosophical positions considered to have enabled such Muslim mobilisations to thrive, specifically the policies of 'multiculturalism'.[4]

One of the key strategies deployed in defence of the Western appropriation of the universal is to harness the critique of essentialism to undo the critique of universalism.

II

The work of Aziz al-Azmeh provides a convenient example of this strategy. Not only is he scornful of Islamist pretensions, he is also someone who is reluctant to accept that cultural differentia has any significance, apart from legitimising fascistic tendencies (1993: 5–6, 21). Thus, we see the development of two sets of arguments that have characterised opposition to Islamism: the idea that it is a form of totalitarianism akin to communism and Nazism, and that expression of Muslim political identity in Western plutocracies is enabled by 'culturally relativist' public policies. While al-Azmeh's 'deconstruction' of claims of Islamism took place in the context of early panics about Muslim mobilisations, that is, prior to their institutionalisation in the state of a seemingly permanent War on Terror and the attendant reconfiguration of the structures of governance of Western plutocracies, his arguments illustrate a genre of writing against Islamism that has come to be fairly widespread (see for example, Scruton, 2003; Goves, 2006; Karsh, 2006; Manji, 2006; Kepel, 2006). This genre sees in the myriad mobilisations that articulate a Muslim political subjectivity as essentialism that cannot be sustained and this charge of essentialism denies the legitimacy of the quest for Muslim autonomy.

Islamism is presented as being a discourse 'conjured' around a fantasy of an authentic essence (al-Azmeh, 1993: 7). That is, what the Islamists claim to be their discovery of 'real' Islam is nothing more than the fabrication of an Islamic tradition, which denies its diversity. According to this line of argument, cultural forms such as 'Islamic dress' or 'Islamic way of life' are recent inventions and not the recovery of sacral traditions (1993: 21). The effect of arguments like this is to try and discredit Islamist claims for being legitimate expressions of a Muslim desire for autonomy and deep decolonisation of the world. The rejection of an Islamic essence, as an invariant core that could generate the Islamist project as the internal working of its innate logic, seems eminently sensible. The conclusion, however, that essentialism is necessary for Islamism, does not follow. As I will demonstrate in subsequent chapters, the case can be made that Islamism is not only compatible with anti-essentialism, but that anti-essentialism is the very condition of its possibility. The anti-essentialism that inspires the opponents of Muslim autonomy is based around a (post-modern-inspired) critique of essentialism, which purports to break with Orientalist accounts, which would see in the appearance of Islamism the culminating expression of a continuous Islamic essence. Accordingly not only is Islamism fabricated, it is also a fabrication that is derivative and therefore inauthentic. In other words, when Islamists construct their identities, they do so by using materials that are not intrinsic to Islamic culture. The derivative nature of Islamist discourses, it is argued, arises from their dependency on Western categories (al-Azmeh, 1993: 39, 41, 79). Islamists have to resort to the language of the West to make their demands and thus it is argued are showing their intellectual incoherence: denigrating the West and dependent on it at the same time. The use of conceptual categories of the West demonstrates the universality of the Western enterprise. This rejection of the West takes 'place either in the name of ideologies of the Western province—such as national independence and popular sovereignty—or substantially in terms of these ideologies, albeit symbolically beholden to a different local or specific repertory' (al-Azmeh,1991: 481). The suggestion is that when Islamists demand an 'Islamic state' or proclaim that 'Islam is the only solution', they are using the vocabulary of the West. This then means that protests against the Western order can only be carried out in the language inaugurated and enforced by that very same Western order. The Western discourse of self-determination, popular sovereignty and so on provides the means by which those who are subject to the West have been able to check or disrupt their subordinate status. Even in circumstances in which resistance to the Western order is couched in a language different from that sanctioned by the Western order, the signifiers are different only tokenistically (al-Azmeh, 1993: 35).

This insistence on the universal nature of the West is only matched by equally strident claims for the particularity of Islamism. Surely, it is no coincidence that throughout Muslimistan some of the most virulent opponents of Islamism have often taken positions of a most narrowly based, racially conceived nationalism. For example, the Northern Alliance in Afghanistan used differential treatments for their Taliban opponents depending on whether they were considered to be indigenous or foreigners (Pakistanis, Uzbeks, Peninsular Arabians). The attempt to demonstrate the absence of any wider claims on behalf of Islamist groups in general do not see their projects as being restricted to any specific society, location or ethnos. Islam is meant for all. There may be practical reasons why, at a specific moment in time, an Islamist group may have to confine its activities to a particular arena, but this should not be understood to mean that Islamism does not have universal ambitions (Qutb, 2000; Khomeini, 1981). The opponents of Muslim autonomy claim that the threat from Islamism is precisely its refusal to accept the Westphalian division of the world, and its attempts to draw in Muslims across national boundaries and thus weaken the commitment of Muslim communities to the nation-states that contain them.

The belief in the particularity of Islamism has the effect of positing only the West as a region capable of generating the universal. The conflation between what is Western and what is considered to be universal is what allows an analysis which sees that the partaking of the universal is also the internalisation of Western categories. Thus the Islamist articulation of their position as being anti-Western is presented as intellectually incoherent or disingenuous. In other words, the Islamist rejection of the West can only (it is argued) be undertaken through the language of the West (which is the only universal language), thus when Islamists reject the West they do so by deploying Western categories which supposedly undermines their critique of the West and at the same time rather conveniently shows the hollowness of their declarations of authenticity (al-Azmeh, 1993: 34). This argument is one of the most common tropes found in the commentary on the Muslim Awakening. Its use ranges from those who express a strong antipathy to Islam itself, to those who claim to express a strong antipathy only to Islamism. The conflation of Islamism with a particularity is matched by an unremarked conflation of universalism with the Western enterprise, and the systemic denial of Western particularity. The puzzle of course is that if the universal is based on the dissolution of all particularities then how is it possible to uncover the Western elements in the apparently universal language used by Islamists?

III

To avoid this consequence of such a monocultural reading of universal values Enlightenment fundamentalists make half-hearted gestures arguing that the universal is actually a pooling of all cultures and civilisations. If universalism is a pooling of various cultural formations then it is difficult to describe Islam and the Islamicate as being a particularity that is the other of universalism, unless one is content to exclude Islam from being one of the constituent elements of this universal civilisation.[5] If one sees in the universal the dissolution of all particularities then one cannot claim that the Islamists deploy Western devices (for example influence of totalitarian ideologies associated with fascism and communism). Claims that the Western and the universal are equivalent can only be made by positing a Western essence. These difficulties come about because an anti-essentialist analytic is being married to an affirmation of the universalism of the Western project. Anti-essentialism then becomes merely another weapon in the armoury of Western enterprise

The undermining of any possibility of a 'multi-vocal universal civilisation' continues as al-Azmeh goes on to inscribe universalism as mere Westernisation. Thus his multi-vocal universalism is strangely monological: there are no references to the influence of Indian or even 'Arab' voices. So, despite being multi-vocal, the universal civilisation seems to speak in one voice only. Multi-vocal, apparently, is only another name for the voice of the West. Such a conception of universalism proclaims universality while drawing on only one particularity. The linkage of the West with the universal in such a consistent manner establishes a privileged relationship between one particularity and what is counted as universal. This, of course, implies that the inclusion and dissolution of particularities within the universal are uneven: rather than universalism consuming all particularities as al-Azmeh thinks, universalism comes about by one particularity consuming all other particularities (1993: 34). This consumption is only possible in a situation of gross power imbalances. What makes a particularity universal is not simply its content but its power. In other words, universalism is intimately linked to the exercise of empire (Fowden, 1994; Mazrui, 2001: 11; Crossely, 2002).

IV

Advocates of Westernese are keen to rearticulate the global hegemony of the West in the wake of the incomplete and inconsistent decolonisation of the world. Westernese can be seen as a response to the postcolonial condition. In this regard, what was distinctive about the attacks on US economic, political and military centres on September 2001 was precisely their unmistakable postcoloniality. A postcoloniality that the War on Terror is directed towards eradicating. Part of the rolling back of postcoloniality can be seen in the direct colonial rule over Iraq and Afghanistan.[6] Part of it can be seen in the way in which suspected 'terrorists' have been incarcerated in the American gulag, treated as uppity colonials rather than as proper enemies. Part of it can be seen in the so-called battle for 'hearts and minds' by which neo-conservative crusaders are supposed to elicit the support of 'moderate' Muslims to defeat the ideological appeals of 'extremist' Muslims, by refusing to acknowledge the political nature of Muslim demands for autonomy. As annexe to this, there is clear incentive for Western supremacists to rule as 'out of order' those who oppose their authority and any claim that does not capitulate to Western notions of good and evil. In other words, Western supremacists do not want the non-West to be able to appeal to its heritages as a way of saying that it is incommensurable with Western values. More specifically, they do want proponents of Muslim autonomy to be able to reject the legitimacy of Western primacy by appealing to their Islamicate heritage. Allowing Islamists to deny certain values as being alien and artificial would, to al-Azmeh, be tantamount to appeasement. This charge of appeasement has become another key element in the discourse of those who oppose mobilisations in the name of Islam. Appeasement has an international character in which it is seen to refer specifically to the failure of Western governments to confront 'rogue regimes' and 'terrorists'.[7] This is a view most bellicosely associated with the now virtually defunct Project for the New American Century, which came to define the neo-Reaganite (or neo-conservative) position (Lustick, 2006: 48–70). Appeasement also has a domestic currency, which refers to the way in which Western plutocracies have allowed themselves to give in to demands from 'minorities'. Minority demands for justice and dignity are vilified as 'political correctness', or seen as a direct assault on the 'core' values of Western plutocracies. The charges of appeasement arise as a means of preserving the privileged relationship between Western cultural enterprise and universalism. The figure of the mobilised Muslim is the point of convergence around which these two forms of appeasement have increasingly entwined. The assault on multiculturalism has become one of the features of Islamophobia and the so-called counter-jihad movement.[8] A number of commentators continue to argue that Islamism has been enabled by misguided policies of multiculturalism which they represent as a form of cultural relativism.[9]

A number of 'ex-Muslims' or 'refusik Muslims' are among the most vocal advocates of this position: they see in mobilisation of Muslims not a challenge to Western privilege but rather a subversion of the Enlightenment.[10] This is why al-Azmeh's critique of Islamism has a certain exemplary quality: his fear that the loss of (Western) universalism means the ascendancy of cultural relativism is one shared widely within those who identify with the defence of Western supremacy. Thus, al-Azmeh foreshadows a critique of multiculturalism both in content and style of exposition.

For example, the idea that the assertion of a Muslim subjectivity in the ethnoscapes of Western plutocracies is akin to 'apartheid' is often heard (al-Azmeh, 1993: 40).[11] Again this seems, at first, to be a rather parodic understanding of apartheid. The suggestion seems to be that Muslim settlers in Western plutocracies are analogous to the Boer Trekkers, setting up their own versions of Boerstats in Bradford, Marseilles, Rotterdam, and so on. Al-Azmeh (like many others) seems strangely forgetful that the main cause of ghettoes in the postcolonial cities of Western plutocracies has been 'white flight': ghettoes are created when those with money and power do not wish to have black faces across their white picket fences. It is not 'Muslim settlers' who create ghettoes; it is rather that they are ghettoised. This generous reading of apartheid as simply 'separate development' undercuts the elements of race and power that are as intrinsic to apartheid as any notion of closure or separatism.[12] While al-Azmeh denies that racism has much of a part to play in the recent European representations of Muslim settlers (1993: 4), it is rather incredible that he would disassociate racism from apartheid itself. Apartheid may have claimed to be about separate development, but it was only a separate development based on an implicit imbalance between the various racialised groups that were supposed to be guaranteed separate development. Development may have been separate, but was far from equal. Given al-Azmeh's suspicion of Islamist claims, it seems curious that he seems to succumb to the ideologues of apartheid so swiftly, seemingly collaborating with the 'whitewashing' of racism out of apartheid. The idea that Muslim settlers are practising apartheid is now often heard, for example, in the assertion by the former Bishop of Rochester, Michael Nazir-Ali, that extremist Muslims were turning many of Britain's cities into 'no go' areas for non-Muslims, or similar assertions made by Bassam Tibi about the consequences of the failure of Muslims to Europeanise (Pidd, 2008; TIbi, 2007).

The identity of the West comes about not as a working out of some intrinsic necessary essence, but rather as an operation of an articulation that tries to suggest that a contingent correlation of properties is, in fact, necessary. In other words, the West is a hegemonic project. We can only speak about the West because the West marks a particular historical narrative: for example, the sequence from Plato to NATO, which is presented as a necessary progression rather than as a contingent stitch-up without which it would not be possible to identify the West. The properties that most Western accounts associate with the West are most often presented as being intrinsic to the West's identity. What I would suggest, however, is that it is more useful to understand the relationship between these properties and the West in terms of an articulation, rather than as the working out of a destiny inscribed within the essence of the West. The West is the name by which a number of discursive elements are structured, unified and given a destiny.[13]

The critique of Islamism along the lines of its purported essentialism is dependent on a Western essence. The only way to sustain this critique of the essentialism of discourses of authenticity is by evoking an essentialist notion of the West. That is, we can only identify the Western elements in Islamists' discourses by claiming the persistence of Western identity within the vocabulary of the Islamists. But this can only be done by invoking an essential West—a West that remains constant and invariant regardless of its articulations. If we take a position consistent with anti-essentialism then the West is nothing more than a hegemonic project produced by a variety of articulatory practices. The properties that have historically been sedimented as being associated with the West can remain so only in the context of the web of discursive interventions and institutions sustaining those articulations. The problem for Western supremacists is to maintain the legislating performative of the name of the West, when the networks of power/knowledge that sustained the performance are no longer functioning as they once did. As Said's work demonstrated, the ability of the Orientalist to discourse about the Orient was founded on the dense network of political-cultural relations that supported the Orientalist. The Orientalist could speak for the Orient, because he could speak the language of science, rationality, progress.[14] The Orientalist could use a language by which other languages could be translated and transcribed. The Orientalist was part of an *über*-culture reinforced by the facticity of European imperialism. With the breakdown of European imperial systems and the processes of de-colonisation, the notion of a super-culture that transcends all other cultural formations can no longer be taken for granted.

Without the power/knowledge complex that sustained the sovereignty of the West over the non-West, the principle that the 'West knows best', which once used to inspire awe, is now more likely to provoke incredulity. This can perhaps be seen in the way in which the United States and its allies have tried to block the flow of information by Islamicate news sources. Various regulatory frameworks have appeared in Western plutocracies to ward off the threat of extremist propaganda by Islamists. While, to some extent, these measures betray a colonial repertoire of 'mad mullahs' leading the law-abiding Muslim masses astray, they also seem to betray an awareness that perhaps the truth is not on their side, or an anxiety about getting a message across.[15]

If the name of the West can no longer perform legislatively, if it cannot sanction its visions, perhaps a new brand name might do the trick. Increasingly, the universal is used to smuggle in the Western, while making half-hearted gestures to its 'multi-vocal' character. The relationship between the universal and the West is central to maintaining the ability of one cultural formation to be the only legitimate form of knowledge above all other formations. One of the points that Said makes throughout his critique of Orientalism is the constant refrain in Orientalist discourse that the Orient cannot represent itself, but needs the intervention of the (Western) expert to be represented (Said, 1985: 32–6). The conflict concerning the displacement of a Western canon is experienced as a loss by those who are most embedded in narrating and extending that canon. One strategy of sustaining the canon is to claim that when critics of the Western canon voice their opposition, they are actually still using the language of the West. In this sense, the fate of the universal intellectual is tied to a discourse of universalism (Foucault, 1980: 126–7).One way of perpetuating this universalism is to relocate all attempts to resist that universalism as mere extensions of such universalism. This is done, for example, by making genealogical claims for elements of Islamist discourse being Western. The ability to recuperate discourses like Islamism rests on the ability to 'recover' the culturally copyrighted element in the discourse of Islamism. The battle between universalism and what are often described as particular claims of cultural authenticity is really a conflict about genealogies: about how to narrate the future of the world. The Western discourse is a product of several projects that narrate the world in terms of the continuity of the West. The limit of Europe comes when groups of people begin to articulate their position by rejecting Europe's claims to copyright.

In this light, Islamist rejection of the universal in terms of the refusal of the signifier 'Western' does not necessarily imply the dismissal of what is being signified, but rather the rejection of that hegemonic operation that attaches a signifier to a particular signified. What this means is that the denunciation of Islamists for using Western categories is at the same time the reconstruction and maintenance of particular genealogical traces. It is not that Islamists use ideas which are themselves Western, but the description of the ideas as Western retroactively constructs them as such. The contest between Islamists and their enemies is not a conflict between fundamentalists and liberals, but a contest between a Western project and a Muslim project to write itself into the future.

In this regard, Islamism and the Western project are not that different. One may have one's own prejudices for preferring one to the other, but both are attempts to remake the world. Neither is sanctioned by any innate logic, but are themselves grand political projects: projects that aim to transform our cultures, histories and societies. That is, cultures, histories and societies that are crystallisations of previous political projects. Such projects are attempts to draw boundaries. They narrate themselves in terms of their destiny; projecting themselves into the future, but also writing themselves into the past.

It is not only the Islamists who are engaged in an operation of fabrication—such as making up stories about their authentic selves, claiming for example, that the clothes that they wear are 'Islamic'. Those who reject Islamist narratives of authenticity also do so by making up stories about the West. The need to constantly renew the retroactive operation of constitution (naming) means that the 'universal' must be policed and constantly linked to its particular. This means that the link that is established between universal values and the traces of the West, in opposition to other particularities, is difficult to sustain within an anti-essentialist framework, since the identity of those values comes from their articulation, and not from the historical conditions of their emergence. Belief in the uncontested universalism of the West is a consequence of a hegemonic historiography, rather than simply a matter of history.

Clearly, this conclusion would not find favour with those who, while opposing essentialism in general, are willing to support it in the case of the West. This can be seen by the rejection of Islamist essentialism, which takes place alongside an acceptance of Western essentialism, and thus demonstrates how anti-essentialism can be used to underwrite the conflation between the Western and the universal and in so doing contribute to attempts to keep the 'violent hierarchy' between the West and non-West in place.

Al-Azmeh prevaricates about post-modernism and, on occasion, is openly critical of it (1993: 5, 31). Despite this ambivalence, he is happy to use the post-modernists' theoretical armoury to attack what he calls the 'phantasmagoric trend' of Islamism with its talk of 'cultural treason' and 'authentically Islamic temper' (ibid.: 8). Unfortunately for al-Azmeh and opponents of multiculturalism, there are serious limitations to the use of the critique of essentialism as merely a strategy of de-mystification: nothing more than a critique of the superstructural moment—it is on this caricature of anti-essentialism that the critique of Muslim agency is built. Thus, the critique of what is so easily described as Islamist essentialism is made within a context dominated by an unacknowledged Western essentialism. Al-Azmeh's version of anti-essentialism illustrates very clearly the way in which post-modern 'metaphysics of suspicion' is increasingly being used to inscribe universalism and foreclose the possibility of any form of multiculturalism. The critique of universalism, within the emerging post-modern orthodoxy, however, assumes a secondary importance to the critique of essentialism. This is one of the reasons why, despite all their talk of hybridity and valorisation of the other, as Sardar (1999) argues, the post-modern gaze remains fixed on the centre. The post-modern critique of meta-narratives raises questions about the essentialism of some of these narratives, but, at the same time, it sets the limit as to how far a critique of the Western project can go. The expansion of cultural diversity into a fully-fledged multiculturalism would mean abandoning the certitude and comfort of speaking from the centre—it would mean having to learn new language games. This is a task that implies the decolonisation not only of the periphery, but also of the centre itself.

V

The 'violent hierarchy' between the West and the non-West underwrites much of the current debate around themes of cultural difference and absolutism. As a result, anti-essentialism simply becomes another means of trying to defer considering the consequences of multiculturalism. Thus, the critique of grand narratives is slowly brushed under the carpet by the attempts to articulate an implicit universalism from which anti-essentialism can be used to prevent the consolidation of the multicultural moment. It is not surprising that many advocates of post-modernity end up wistfully expressing nostalgia for empire;[16] a nostalgia that is manifested in attempts to rehabilitate various European empires as benign providers of order.[17]

The invocation of cultural hybridity as a solution to a globalising world presents a paradox. On the one hand, it seems to focus attention on the fragmentary nature of the hegemonic cultural formation, on the way its constituent parts were often marginalised and suppressed. On the other hand, at the same time as making possible the weakening of hegemonic cultural formation, cultural hybridity makes it impossible to displace the hegemonic formation, since the critique of cultural absolutism implied by cultural hybridity also makes it impossible to sustain any subaltern cultural formation. As long as the debate on

universalism and particularism avoids the particularity of any universalism it cannot resolve this paradox. Without its anti-universalist
impulse, the critical energies of post-modernity focus on consolidating
the status quo. This is why Spivak suggests that we need a notion of
'strategic essentialism' as a means of allowing subaltern formations a
fiction of essence around which political mobilisations and campaigns
can be gathered (1987: 205–7; Fuss, 1990: 31–2). Fuss also acknowledges that essentialism has differential effects, depending on whether
essentialism is being used to entrench the domination of the hegemonic
order or being deployed by subalterns to subvert a dominant order
(ibid.: 32). The problem with this approach, as Fuss accepts, is that
subalternity or hegemony does not tell us very much about the content
of a political project, and that strategic essentialism may be another way
of reinscribing essentialism. Despite this, Fuss considers essentialism
worth the risk (1990: 32). The difficulty with Fuss's approach is that it
separates essentialism from universalism: this makes it possible to
articulate an anti-essential universalism. What I want to suggest is that
any critique of essentialism that is not also a critique of universalism is
problematic, and should perhaps be understood as likely to serve as
another strategic ploy within the armoury of Western supremacist
discourse. If a critique of essentialism is to be mounted in good faith, it
can be done only by extending the critique to universalism itself. No
doubt Islamists make use of essentialism, but to point this out without
pointing out that the Western project itself is also equally essentialist
seems to be eccentric at best and mendacious at worst. The conflict
between Islamism and Westernese can be seen as a conflict between a
particularity and universalism only if one makes the particularity of the
West unmarked and natural.[18] The only way to avoid this reinscription
of the West as the universal is to take seriously the logic of multiculturalism. This means neither the simple recognition that there are many
cultures, nor that cultures are inherently locked in mortal combat with
each other. The logic of multiculturalism is based on the consequences
arising out of the decentring of the West; in other words it is not an
attempt to close the gap between the West and the centre, rather it is an
attempt to explore the possibilities of widening the interval between the
West and the idea of centre. This is the terrain of the multicultural. The
cost of making a multicultural move is the abandonment of any
investment in the uncontested universality of the Western project. This

is a price that Western supremacists are unwilling (or perhaps more charitably, unable) to pay. Thus they deploy the logic of Eurocentrism as a way of responding to the end of the European age. Eurocentrism is an attempt to resuture the relationship between the West and the centre; one of the key strategies in this project is to use the critique of essentialism while avoiding a critique of universalism. The result is to legitimise the Western hegemonic project with its globalising, assimilationist political thrust (Mazrui, 2001: 13). This is particularly evident in Europe where Muslims are said to constitute the largest 'non-European' presence within the European Union and, as such, the Muslim question is better understood as demanding questions on the nature of Europeanness.

The various attacks on Islamism on the grounds of its purported essentialism are only possible by evoking an essentialist notion of the Western enterprise, which is able to uncover the Western essence even in the most determinedly anti-Western discourse. The conceit in which the West is universal and the non-West is particular animates many of the Enlightenment fundamentalists. The universal can no longer be a euphemism for the Western project, nor can the particular be simply considered nothing more than the periphery of the West. The continuing presence of various Islamist groups (and various other movements) indicates that the West can no longer be the uncontested template by which we give shape to the world. One of the reasons that Islamism is seen as a disruptive force is that it fails to accept this juridical role of the West. Many of the critics of Islamism are often merely content to try and reinscribe a de facto Western hegemony in the guise of universalism, instead of recognising that there is a need to develop different language games that do not presuppose the juridical function of the West, especially juridical functions that come armed with a panoply of colonial violation and violence.

5

DEMOCRACY

I

The language games of Western hegemony are played not only in governmental circles, but also in popular culture; one such example of this is provided by the *Star Trek* franchise. This popular television series was about the crew of the starship *USS Enterprise* on a five-year mission to explore new worlds. The series of seventy-nine episodes was first made and broadcast in the United States in the mid-1960s. Since then it has spanned the globe, being shown in over one hundred countries. It has generated five spin-off series, eleven major Hollywood films, hundreds of items of merchandise and over one hundred novels (Sarantakes, 2005: 74). *Star Trek* depicts a future in which conflict among humans (both personal and social) has been erased and the Earth is a liberal Utopia that is prosperous, democratic and post-racial. From the very beginning *Star Trek* has acted as a mirror of the United States and its role in the world, but a mirror that sees the best of the Western experiment. In an episode of the second season, an onboard malfunction occurs, which transports some of the regular crew of the *USS Enterprise* to an alternative universe. This universe seems identical to 'our' universe, with the same characters and settings. There are, however, subtle differences in the behaviour of the characters, values and practices that characterise this world. The characters in the mirror universe are played by the same actors and hold approximately the same ranks, so the question arises as to how we can differentiate the characters in 'our' universe from those who belong to the mirror universe. The way the question is resolved in *Star Trek* is by using political practices as signifiers of identity. In the mirror universe, the existence of a secret police, torture chambers, assassinations and so on points to the fact that even though it was inhabited by characters and objects that are superficially identical to our universe—we are, nonetheless, in another universe. This mirroring was marked out by the way in which the Federation of Planets, a voluntary association of different worlds, never existed in the alternative universe; instead we find ourselves confronting a vicious militaristic Terran empire. The use of political practices to mark out differences between humans makes sense once we are confronted with the similarity of our common humanity. In other words, the differences in systems of political practices becomes one way of delimiting different human groups.[1] I would like to suggest that this movement from federation to empire is perhaps another way of replaying the distinction between Western democracies and Oriental despotism.[2] This episode of *Star Trek* (called 'Mirror Mirror') can be seen as one of the periodic explorations of oriental despotism.[3] To the extent that our universe is based around a valorisation of democracy, the mirror universe is beholden to racist caricatures framing the depiction of Oriental despotism. Ultimately, a political system points to types of political agents; the empire is the empire because its political agents lack compassion, reason, truthfulness and so forth. Thus, a narrative of fundamentally different political systems becomes a narrative of fundamentally different societies. So what happens when an event occurs which seems to throw into question that relationship between political system and society?

The politics of the *ummah* have been characterised by an overarching antagonism between the forces arranged around Kemalism and those arranged around Islamism. (This does not mean that there are not other groupings—liberals, socialists, conservatives—but rather that the defining frontier in Muslimistan is one between Kemalism and Islamism. But these positions are coalitions in which not all the elements are equally enthusiastic partners.) Specifically, what happens when 'Orientals' revolt and bring down a despotic regime?

When Mohamed Bouaziz set himself on fire he started a conflagration that brought down the decades-long rule of despots like Ben Ali, Hosni Mubarak and Muammar Gaddafi. The key to these regime changes were not American-led military invasions but rather popular mass mobilisations. There are those who see in the so-called 'Arab Spring' proof that the long march of democracy has finally reached the 'Arab street', thus confirming the universal validity of the democratic form.[4] According to this view, the Arab Spring comes about as a result of a Westernised youth wired up via social networking media, and fired up with visions of the democratic life found in the West. This view of the Arab Spring focused on the way in which the demonstrations were a secular rather than religious phenomenon, even though the demonstrators would use slogans such as 'Allah Akbar' and organise rallies around Friday prayers. This narrative has a general appeal among Western audiences as well as the 'westoxicated' in the rest of the world; it inscribes a vision of the continued centrality of the West and its fundamental superiority. It suggests that the Arab Spring means the final end of Islamism and the failure of Al-Qaeda and other armed Islamist groups. For the leadership of the Islamic Republic of Iran, however, the removal of men like Hosni Mubarak is part of a historical sequence that began with the Islamic revolution in Iran.[5] Explanations of the Arab Spring turn upon the relationship between democracy, the West and Islam. In the universe of *Star Trek*, Orientals—whether they are alien species (Klingons, Romulans, and so on) or humans who are Orientalised like in the mirror universe—are despotic. Being Western means being democratic, even though such an assertion belies the impact of colonialism and racism on the subversion of any meaningful notion of democracy.

II

'Democracy' operates in a variety of registers: academic, governmental and popular. It should be clear that what I refer to as 'Democracy' is a retrospective reading of the themes that have historically been designated by a variety of labels, reflecting local contexts (republicanism, liberalism). The category of 'Democracy' that I refer to is an overarching label which has, at least at the level of the non-specialist political theorist, colonised aspects of these earlier labels. Thus, many of the features of liberalism are now considered to be intrinsic features of Democracy. One of the difficulties of discussing a concept like Democracy is that, in terms of the variety of circuits it operates in, none of them are hermetically sealed from the others. This, of course, makes the task of a critic much easier, since they can always cite another circuit, another rendition of Democracy, which apparently does not display the same qualities in the notion of Democracy that are being argued for.

Alongside the narrow methodological definition often found in political science textbooks, there is a more diffused and generalised understanding of democracy, in which Democracy is a metaphor for a political regime. There is considerable slippage between the methodological and the metaphorical use of the term. It is, however, the metaphorical use of the term that draws the boundaries around the technical elements considered to be central to the understanding of democracy and those considered to be marginal.

There are a variety of features that are considered to be constitutive of democracy, such as elections and peaceful transitions of power, and most definitions of Democracy refer to some or all of these features. The presence or absence of these features can be used to determine whether a particular polity is democratic or not. This is the approach that many non-governmental organisations (NGOs) and think tanks follow. Freedom House, for example, has been producing a listing of democratic countries since 1970, thus suggesting that a democracy that lacked these key features would no longer be considered a Democracy. There are, however, a number of difficulties with this conclusion. The literature is replete with various examples in which there is considerable muddying of the democratic waters. For example, was Hitler democratic because he was elected to power? The Enabling Act, which underwrote much of the Nazi takeover of power, was a piece of legislation legitimately passed. Was the United States democratic before the passing of the Civil Rights Acts that guaranteed adult African-Americans the right to vote? Was Switzerland democratic before 1970, when women were given the right to vote? What are we to make of the 'freedom of the press' in an age of oligopolistic media moguls? And to what extent is voting an exercise of autonomous individuals or the product of manipulation through clever advertising? What is interesting about these anomalies is that they do not seem to undermine the democratic status of some countries, whereas other anomalies are considered as sufficient to discredit the democratic credentials of others. It could be argued that the difference is in the nature of the anomalies, or it could be argued that the difference is in the nature of the different countries. The understanding of democracy, which sees it as typified by a list of key features, is inadequate, since the identity of Democracy is not based on substantive qualities, but rather, like all identities, it is relational and contrastive. In the case of Democracy, its identity is derived from its negation of despotism. The elements that constitute Democracy gain their significance from being contrasted with elements that are considered to be constitutive of despotism. This frontier between Democracy and despotism has a long history.

III

Democracy begins in ancient Greece (Held, 1995).[6] This is the hegemonic view of the genealogy of Democracy, but one which immediately calls for a series of caveats. First, it is not certain that the democratic form is not a property of other city-state formations—for example, Sumerians or Phoenicians (Hornblower, 1993; Held, 1995).[7] Second, not all of ancient Greece was democratic; it is principally Athens during the third to the fifth centuries BCE that is typified as democratic, and even in democratic Athens, women, slaves and foreigners were excluded from political participation.[8] The identification of Democracy with the Greeks proceeds not from an enumeration of forms of governance by various Greek communities, but rather from the Greeks' perception of themselves as free in contrast to the enslaved subjects of the Persian great king. Greek freedom versus Persian slavery is one of the first instances of a trope within Western political thought, which is played as a variation on the theme of the opposition between Western Democracy and Oriental despotism (Springborg, 1992).[9] The distinction between Greek Democracy and Persian despotism arises most clearly in the wake of the Greek-Persian wars and is one of the means by which the various anti-Persian Greek city-states forged a common identity, facilitating the formation of a united front against the Persian invasions. The claim that Greeks were free, ruled by their peers, while Persians were slaves ruled by the first Oriental despot is like many of the claims that the Greeks made, taken to be historical rather than historiographical.[10] Many subsequent writers took this division between Greek Democracy and Persian despotism seriously—so that this dichotomy between Democracy and despotism has come to be seen as one of the great divides between the West and the non-West (Bobbio, 1989). Since the 'roots' of the West are most often traced to the formation of Greek civilisation, Democracy thus became a component of Western identity. Democracy is articulated by its opposition to the supposed despotism of the Persian monarch (and behind the figure of the king of kings a metonymic chain of monarchies and absolute rulers: from the pharaohs of Egypt to the great kings of Assyria and, by extension, the 'sons of Heaven' of China and India, the caliphs and sultans of Islam and the general secretaries of the Soviet Union). The other of Democracy was despotism, and despotism is found not in Sparta but in the sprawling Persian Empire. The freedom of the West is guaranteed by its contrast with the slavery of the Orient.

There is, however, another possible reading in which we do not associate the quality of freedom with the designation of a society as being 'Western' or 'Oriental', but rather with a consideration of the ways in which agrarian societies were disciplined and regulated. A comparison of ancient Athens, with a population of perhaps a quarter of a million and a 'police force' of perhaps 600 (Ober, 1996: 148–51), with the Persian Empire, with a population at least ten times larger and a permanent military establishment numbering in the tens of thousands, in terms of their respective capacity to regulate their societies suggests a variance with the popular conception of Greek freedom and Persian despotism. Ancient Athens was a far more tightly disciplined society than that controlled by the Persian king of kings (see also Mann, 1986). The king of kings may have had a permanent administration, a permanent military and have been able to draw on regular tributes; however, in all instances, the imperatives of imperial control entailed co-operation with, and reliance upon, local elites. Prior to colonial European empires, all agrarian empires lacked the skilled personnel to penetrate deeply into the communities they governed. The Persian ruling elite made a virtue of this weakness by developing a discourse that allowed them to preside over complex and diverse groups and societies by following what we could call a multicultural strategy, in which the king of kings ruled as pharaoh in Egypt, the vicar of Marduk in Babylon and so on. In other words, Persian rule was based on a high level of the self-management of its constituent communities. The king of kings ruled over peoples who believed in one God, many gods or no god. His concern, however, was limited to the extraction of general deference for his authority and the payment of tribute.

In contrast, it can be argued that the claustrophobia that often features in small-scale societies in which everybody knows everybody, combined with a highly mobilised citizen body, can produce what can be described as small-town totalitarianism; that is, a disciplinary society in which the pressure to conform to the conventions of that society is insistent and intrusive. The citizens of Athens lived among just such a highly mobilised citizenry.[11] Neighbours could be a combination of informers, prosecutors, juries and judges. A consequence of a population that is mobilised and intensely politicised is to erode any distinction between the public and the private. At the same time, the relatively circumscribed area of the Athenian state meant that there was little respite from snoopy and gossipy neighbours with political axes to grind. One could thus be mischievous and suggest that it is just as useful to see in Athens the dawning of totalitarianism as it to see the dawn of Democracy (Agamben, 1998). This is perhaps one way to understand the assertions made on behalf of the Athenian polis as the place marking the emergence of politics itself (Finely, 1991; Žižek, 1998). The intensified capacity for surveillance, the intense mobilisations, are all considered to be the hallmarks of modern totalitarianism. (The major difference between Athenian totalitarianism and its modern counterparts has to do with the absence of a permanent bureaucracy and a permanent military.) The democratic Athenian polity could not tolerate individuals whose beliefs did not accord with that of the polity itself, as many Athenians (including, most famously, Socrates) found to their cost. Even though the historical record does not support the idea of a clear-cut distinction on grounds of individual liberty between Greek Democracy and Persian despotism, such a sharp distinction has emerged in the form of Western democracies and Oriental despotisms. In other words, the distinction between despotism and Democracy is too complex and too blurred in real life to be made with dogmatic certainty. It is difficult to conclude that Athenian citizens were freer than Persian subjects, simply by focusing on the constitutional form of these two political entities. To make the distinction credible, it requires that despotism and Democracy become over-determined as categories associated with grand cultural formations. Thus Democracy is Western and despotism is Oriental. This demarcation between the West and the Orient may not have been sedimented until the early modern period, but it has its roots in the retrospective construction of Western cultural identity through its contrast with an Oriental cultural formation (Springborg, 1992: 1). In other words, the frontier between Democracy and despotism also maps onto a frontier between the West and the Orient, and while this frontier did not stabilise until the end of what is called the early modern period, its precursors could be found in the beginning of ancient history. Not only does Democracy begin with the ancient Greeks, the West also begins with the ancient Greeks. Democracy becomes a signifier of the West within the narration of Western identity. Thus, from the very beginning, it is possible to see how the discourses of Western identity were intertwined with the discourses of Democracy. As such, there is hardly a period in human history in which the regions considered to be the core of Western patrimony are not also generally considered to be freer than the realms that are associated with the Orient.[12] Western historiography has tended to ensure that the link between the West and Democracy remains unbroken. The narration of Democracy is also the means by which Western identity is narrated. Thus, the instance of the non-democratic government of the Third Reich problematises the membership of the Third Reich as a member of the West. Similarly, the radicalised denial of Democracy in the nation-empires of Britain or France has been made palatable by making the distinction between home and abroad almost hermetic. Thus, one could always claim a democratic status for these countries because of the rights that metropolitan populations enjoyed, while excluding accounts of the denial of many of those rights to their imperial subjects. Nor is it mere coincidence that the emergence of absolutist monarchies in Europe enhances the significance of maintaining the distinction between the Orient and West, hence the introduction of despotism as a term marking out the rule of the Ottoman Empire as being fundamentally distinct from the strong monarchies of Europe (Valensi, 1993: 98).

What is at stake in the distinction between Democracy and despotism is not merely a set of governmental procedures or styles; rather it is a way of life. The content of the difference between Democracy and despotism is based on the way in which the political forms refer to distinct cultural formations. What is important is not that the boundaries of these cultural formations are fuzzy and ultimately have no essence, but rather that they operate as having a 'logical superhardness' (Staten, 1984: 150). Attempts to 'deconstruct' the West and Orient division by, for example, showing how the roots of the West can be found in Mesopotamia or (even) Islam fail to understand that the distinction between the West and Orient is not purely an empirical one that can be corrected by bringing in new data. The West is a discursive object, the identity of which is formed by making it distinct from other discursive objects. The logic of identification imposes the distinction between the West and non-West. Attempts to show the Near Eastern roots of Western civilisation only aim to shift the boundaries between the West and the Rest, rather than to abolish the distinction itself. For example, attempts to demonstrate that the West-Orient divide is reductive, by pointing out elements that supposedly blur these distinctions, are based on essentialist readings of the West and the Orient, for example, arguing that Islam in Spain was Western (Turner, 1989) or that Yusuf Islam (Cat Stevens) is a Westerner who is Muslim (Sadiki, 2004: 138). Such positions can only derive from a sense of the West that is unchanging; thus, Spain or Sicily or Cat Stevens have a Western essence, which can always be located beneath the Islamicate surface. Neither what constitutes the West nor what constitutes the Orient is immutable in itself, what is immutable is the presence of the frontier. In other words, as long as the discourse that specifies Western exceptionality vis-à-vis the rest of the world continues to hold sway, it will always require a frontier to determine what is included and what is excluded from that exceptionality. This is why objections to the specific histories or societies falling on one side of the frontier or the other may vary over time, but it is the frontier that remains and constitutes the identity of both the West and the Orient. These identifications do not exist outside the frontier. The boundary between Western democracy and Oriental despotism can shift (and has shifted) but it cannot by definition be removed without dissolving the West-Orient dyad. The contrast, however, between Oriental despotism and Western Democracy is constant, even if the meaning of democracy as such is not fixed. In fact, it could be easily demonstrated that while various signifiers have denoted the political system of the Western cultural formation, the contrast between the West and the Orient has been key in determining the identity of those signifiers. The description of political regimes in Western political thought is conducted against the backdrop of the constitutive difference between the West and the Orient, and the discourse of Democracy is not an exception to this.

The West is not reducible to machinations of what has been called the 'Western conglomerate state' (Shaw, 2000), although this political entity is often decisive in articulating the frontier between the West and its others. Commentators, who are swift to dismiss the idea of a West as some essentialist fantasy and keen to point to its fragmented nature, ignore the way in which the West is manifested throughout the world in a mundane and almost banal sense. There is often confusion between the nominal unity of the West and its substantive properties. The West, like other collective identities such as Islam or China, is a name that erases differences; to point to the (internal) differences that constitute the West (or any other collectivity) does not diminish the way in which heterogeneous elements that constitute these collective formations are marshalled under one signifier. The identity of signifiers (including, for example, Democracy) arises from inclusion in a system of differences. Thus to assert that the identity of democracy is a function of its contrast with other signifiers is not to engage in essentialism, since we are dealing with logical and nominal entities not substantive properties.[13] Within Western political thought the articulation of the West (what it is, what it means, who is part of it) is a decisive move prior to the articulation of forms of political regimes. The link between Democracy and the West is not purely opportunistic or merely accidental, it is part of a set of sedimented (and naturalised) practices that form the identity of both Democracy and the West.

The conflation between Democracy and the West has important implications for the way the demos is conceived and constructed. Democracy as a political system is often justified (in popular terms) as the expression of the will of the people; this translates, within the conceptual language of liberalism, into the will of individuals. In other words, the rule of the demos becomes the means by which individuals express their own political preferences. Democracy, by providing the means by which individuals can find political expression, becomes the political system that is most in accord with what it is to be human, since it allows individuals to choose their political arrangements and, as individuals, to form the basis of all human social arrangements. The authentic experience of being human can only be discovered within the context of a democratic regime. In other words, Democracy provides the arena in which the essence of being human can be acted out. The significance of this is that the idea of an essential human presupposes that there are humans who are inessential. The universal nature of a human essence is belied by the way in which any set of humans who are chosen to display that essence must do so in a particular way. Humanity, as a general category, only becomes concrete in its culturally embedded form. Within Western supremacist discourse the essence of what it is to be human is clearly identified by the practices of *homo occidentalis*, the idea being that it is only in the West that humans are truly human and everything else is either cultural accretion or a deviation from that norm. Racist ideologies have made this relationship explicit and such racist discourses continue to influence the way in which humans are conceptualised. The idea of what constitutes the authentic essence of humankind has now become related to being the same as what is authentic within Western cultural practices. Thus, Democracy allows true human identity to realise itself— other forms of governance, however, act as restrictions and constraints on human identity. By removing restrictions and lifting constraints, Democracy allows humans to be truly human. Western supremacist discourse claims that universal values are not something that you can find everywhere; they are, strictly speaking, the property of the West. Thus, the universal cannot be generated from every history or from every region. It has a home, it has a particular history, and any cultural formation that wishes to partake of universal values has to make its way to the home of these values, by following a specific historical sequence. Democracy then becomes the way towards excavating these values that are hardwired into the essence of humanity, by establishing a procedure through which the (essential) qualities of being human can find authoritative public expression. It cannot be understood merely as a set of institutional and procedural arrangements. The nature of Democracy is linked to a wider horizon of what the world is like, the question of human nature and ultimately what is seen to be the destiny of the world itself. Over-determining the explicit appeals to Democracy are implicit assumptions that democratisation is only possible via Westernisation. It functions within the contemporary world as a marker of a specific cultural formation. The actual difference between Democracy and despotism is culturally discussed as the difference between freedom and tyranny or any of its analogues; however, it is actually more about the difference between Western culture and its others. Democracy, therefore, operates more as a cultural marker than as a designator of a settled set of procedures and practices, and it is this convergence between Democracy and Western identity that makes it so difficult to imagine a regime that can be generally considered to be both simultaneously democratic and anti-Western. Accordingly, an anti-Western regime cannot be a Democracy regardless of how many elections it may hold, how transparent its governmental procedures may be or how just its legal framework may be. The difficulty of articulating Western despotism and Oriental democracies is not purely empirical, it is also dependent on the way in which Democracy operates as a marker of cultural identity. Democracy is the name by which Western political practices are staged; similarly, despotism is the name given to the politics practised by the Orient. Both the Orient and the West refer not to geographical entities but to complex cultural formations with mobile boundaries that can shift as a result of changes in political practices. For example, Russia can be Oriental during the Cold War, and yet it becomes Western as soon as it introduces electoral politics, engages in the language of Democracy but, more importantly, becomes a de facto supporter of US foreign policy in relation to the periphery (for example Iraq).[14] Democracy is a name for a way of life beyond its specific mechanisms and procedures.[15] The concept of Democracy gains its unity and its coherence by constant implicit or explicit contrast with despotism. Democracy is what despotism is not. Despotism is not, however, a category that is more secure than Democracy, it is also given its identity by contrast to Democracy. This game of mirrors between 'Democracy' and despotism, as being formed relationally and through the negation of the other category, is overdetermined by cultural signatures. It is the relative stability (the *longue durée*) of these cultural signifiers that helps sustain their signifieds, including political systems. Democracy and despotism are marked elements, where the marking takes the form of a cultural prefix: Western and Oriental. The stability of these prefixes allows Democracy and despotism to be partially fixed, as part of the frontier that divides the West from the non-West.

During the period 1945–91, the meaning of Western democracies was given by their contrast to the Oriental despotism of the communist bloc. Thus Democracy began to expand so that it was no longer simply concerned with the political equality of those defined as citizens, but was also concerned (to a greater or lesser degree) with issues of social and economic equality. The identity of Democracy was based on the constitutive contrast with communist totalitarianism, but is in the process of being transformed as a result of the collapse of the communist system of governance, and it is perhaps not coincidental that questions of social and economic equality are considered to be less central to Democracy. The War on Terror has led to further redefinition of Democracy as it has become compatible with torture, rendition, preventive war and so forth.

DEMOCRACY

The constitutive relationship between Democracy and the West presents a problem for cultural formations of the world that find it difficult to be re-described as Western. For in these instances Democracy can be used as a means of violent repression. In the name of Democracy (either actually existing or that is to come) many regimes have excluded and repressed Islamists, asserting that the anti-Western nature of Islamism is a threat to Democracy.[16] A clear example here is the so-called 'postmodern' coup that removed the Refah (Welfare) Party from power in Turkey, as is the military intervention that prevented the victory of the Front Islamique du Salut in the Algerian elections or the opposition to Mohammed Morsi in Egypt. I take it for granted that all of these instances can be seen in various lights, and one should not be surprised that the various champions of Democracy act in their own interests and thus have a rather self-serving definition of Democracy. The politics of the deployment of the concept of Democracy are, however, not merely reducible to opportunism and short-term tactical calculations, rather it is this opposition between the Western and the Oriental that sets the context for Muslimistan's engagement with Democracy.

IV

An alternative to the Eurocentric account of democracy that establishes a privileged relationship between the idea of the West and the democratic form is, of course, possible.[17] Such a decolonial account challenges the hegemonic description of democracy through a series of displacements. A temporal displacement that refers to the existence of democracy prior to the Greeks. An etymological displacement would deny that democracy is a Greek word, by tracing the roots of demos to Mycenaean liner B and from there back to the Sumerian DUMU which translates as 'sons/children of the city' (Keane, 2009: 113). A spatial displacement would include the venture of Islam in the story of democracy as well other cultural formations that are commonly designated as non-Western (for example contemporary India as an illustration of 'monitory democracy'). A decolonial reading liberates the signifier Democracy from its signifieds in the West. The question then arises if democracy can be ripped from its conventional historiographical sequencing, and becomes a metaphor for an ensemble of practices and institutions that are predicated on attempts to regulate the exercise of arbitrary power through assertion of accountability as an act of agency. If the signifier democracy can be detached from its Western signifieds, is it not possible to detach signifieds of democracy from the signifier of the West? In other words, could not another name be a means of articulating practices in which accountability and agency can be marshalled from historical sequence other than that of the West?

It is possible to see in Islamicate political thought five models of good governance in which the exercise of arbitrary rule is restrained. The first model was that of the first Islamic state established in Medina under the leadership of the Prophet (pbuh). This remains the paradigmatic model of benevolent governance for all Muslims. This model could only survive as a horizon, following the death of the Lord of Medina, since it relied upon divinely guided Prophetic interventions. In the absence of such guidance, Muslim political thought focused on the caliphate as the crystallisation of Islamicate benevolent governance, a feature recognised in classical Islamicate historiography as the rule of the four Rightly Guided Caliphs who became the models of benevolent governance. The Rightly Guided Caliphs had to rule without Prophetic abilities (however, their role as close companions of the Prophet provided them with ontological privilege by proxy or in the case of Ali, ontological privilege by blood— at least according to the Shia) and could thus be more appropriate models of benevolent governance. This second model eventually came to dominate what became the majority strand within Muslim political thought. Running alongside this strand was a perspective in which Islamically sanctioned benevolent governance was only possible under the rulership of imams, who could trace their descent directly from the family of the Lord of Medina, via issue of his daughter and cousin. In other words, the descendants of the Prophet (pbuh) are ontologically privileged so that they can implement divine injunctions. This position became dominant within Shia political thought, but also influenced other political positions that remained critical of existing caliphates. With the abolition of the Caliphate in 1342/1924, the idea of benevolent governance within Islamist circles came to be constituted around the provision of an Islamic political order, expressed as an application of sharia law or through the installation of rulers who were conversant with a knowledge of Islam. Khomeini's theory of the *velayat-e faqih* unified Sunni and Shia political thought, by arguing for an interim leader who did not possess sacral authority, but who could work towards establishing an Islamic government that would hasten the return of the Mahdi. Thus, Khomeini's theoretical intervention transformed Shia political eschatology, making it, for all intents and purposes, compatible with Sunni political thought. Khomeini's de facto Caliphate opened up the possibility of reconstructing a Muslim political centre.

In the wake of Khomeini's political thought, and the crisis of Kemalism, it could be argued that we are witnessing the development of a fifth paradigm of Islamicate benevolent governance, one that is based on the attempt to articulate the relationship between Islam and democracy as not only a possibility but a necessity. Implicit in this fifth paradigm is the development of a notion of a moderate Islam (Aktay, 2007) that is compatible with Democracy. This paradigm of Islamicate benevolent governance includes former ideologues of Islamism (for example, Rached Gannouchi, or even Abdolkarim Sorosh) as well as secular liberals (such as Nawal el-Sadawi) and various technocrats. Four main strategies by which democracy is being aligned with Islam can be identified.

First, there is a set of arguments which, by identifying Democracy with a method that gives a voice to the will of the people, seems to give Islamists a way to achieve political power, since they see themselves as being representative of the people, in a way that the ruling elites who oppose them are not. Thus, democracy offers a way for the Islamists to achieve power without having to go through a violent armed struggle which, in many instances, has alienated and frightened many potential supporters. Second, there is a set of arguments which seem to accept that the end of the Cold War signals the superiority of the democratic form of governance and, as the prevailing world order is committed to Democracy and insists (selectively) on its imposition, it makes sense to bow to the inevitable. It is worth noting that many ideologues of the Islamist movements were heavily influenced by the vanguardist model of political power exemplified by fascist and communist parties in the 1930s. Thus, the historic victory of liberal democracies over fascism and communism suggests that such models of power are flawed. Third, there is a set of arguments that sees the failings of the various Islamist movements to achieve power, or, when they have achieved power, the failure to do anything to implement an Islamic order, as a general failure of Islamism as a political project. Fourth, given the degree of torture and repression that many Islamist activists have faced, and given that in the current crusade against Islamism/the War on Terror, the capacity for

Islamists to articulate a distinct vision is increasingly circumscribed. Consequently, the appeal to Democracy offers an alternative way of trying to readdress the gross inequalities and cruelties that disfigure Islamicate societies.

Currently, in many parts of Muslimistan, there is a wide gap between the rulers and the ruled. It is the presence of such a gap that points to the absence of benevolent governance. Islamism attempts to conceptualise a closure of the gap by formulating a benevolent governance in the shape of a rather nebulous vision of an Islamic order. It is this project that an increasing body of commentary seems to think is bankrupt (Sayyid, 2003). Thus, many voices have begun to urge Muslims to accept benevolent governance that works, instead of striving for benevolent governance that does not deliver—that is, accept that only a democratic arrangement can provide benevolent governance in the contemporary world. Advocates of Democracy for Muslimistan use the experiences of the Western countries to illustrate the benefits of Democracy, and this often tends to follow the narratives of Democracy which are based on Westernese. Soroush's tendency to universalise contingent historical development in Western history as necessary is indicative of this trend (Soroush, 2002). This is the discourse that is still dominant within the world order (if not hegemonic). As a consequence, Democracy is considered to be equivalent to a set of descriptions, such as freedom of the press, the protection of human rights, peaceful transfers of power and so forth. Thus, they respond to a definition of Democracy that is produced by particular (Western supremacist) narratives, a definition that tends to be (understandably) hazy about some anomalies of the democratic discourse, for example the persistence of racist governmentalities (Goldberg, 2002; Hesse and Sayyid, 2009).

There are four major difficulties that confront any project trying to install democracy in Muslimistan. First, any project of transformation will be met by resistance from those who seek to maintain the status quo. In the case of Muslimistan, there is little indication to believe the majority of regimes will be more amenable to being replaced by a democratic regime than an Islamist regime.[18] Thus, the question of democracy in Muslimistan cannot be separated from a political question regarding the means and possibility of carrying out regime transformations in polities in which regimes have both external and internal support that limits the possibility of their transformation. In other words, to close the gap between rulers and ruled in many Muslim polities requires not simply a proclamation of the virtues of Democracy but also concrete strategies as to how such a democratic transformation is to take place.

Second, to the extent that the difference between democracy and despotism is also a difference between the Orient and the West, it is difficult to see how any democracy can be established in Muslimistan without a prior Westernisation, even at a superficial level—which means a 'pro-Western alignment'. To the extent that Western and Islamicate identities are articulated in a mutually exclusive frame, Westernisation presents an ontological challenge to societies based around Islam. It could be argued that one way around this problem is to de-link the technical side of democracy from its metaphorical aspect. By using the discourse of Muslim apologia it is possible to re-describe the technical features of democracy as being compatible with, and found within, the practices of the Prophet (pbuh). Such arguments are, however, unsatisfactory, since they take little or no account of the way in which control over democratic discourse is exercised through grossly unequal power relations. The capacity of Muslimistan to disarticulate and rearticulate democracy is circumscribed by the way in which democratic discourse is still an important component of Western identity. Thus the rearticulation of Democracy means a renarration of Western identity—a renarration that many forces in the Western world will (and do) resist. Until it becomes possible to go beyond the dyad: 'the West and the non-West', until a vocabulary develops that does not see the non-Western as a residual category, until it is possible not to refer to the 'non-Western' as 'non-Western', the ability of Islamicate or other societies to narrate Western democracy is going to be limited. The consequence of this is that any attempt to articulate democracy in an Islamicate register will have to take place in a context where the commanding significations of Democracy come from the West. As the gross inequalities in the world order are, to some extent, sustained by a political system that many actors within the West support, the Western capacity to reduce Democracy to a form that makes its compatible with its imperium means that democracy in the 'Rest' can take a form that allows a corrupt and unjust social order to prevail. Democracy can become an obstacle to radical social transformation rather than assisting such an end.

Third, and following from the above point, one of the ways that Democracy works in the post-Cold War world is by blurring the distinc-

tion between friend and enemy, and thus bringing about a depoliticisation of society (Žižek, 2000: 10). Thus, Democracy as a promise of the
end of history has the effect of preventing the recognition of the political
nature of the Islamicate societies and their place in the world. This generalised depoliticisation allows technological thinking to dominate. The
reduction of the political to the administrative means that Muslim governance remains trapped in a mimetic methodology, unable to make
meaning, and unable to construct and perpetuate the Islamicate elements
of their societies, except as a form of sentimental attachment. If government is only about efficient administration then there is no reason why
Muslimistan should not contract out the administration of its territory.
The current articulation of Democracy means a shift from political to
economic governance, which is not only seen in relation to the way in
which state authority is eroded in favour of the market. The hegemonic
articulation of Democracy at the level of the global means accepting the
current socioeconomic order and refusing the possibility of any radical
transformation that challenges the neo-liberal 'consensus'.

Fourth, and most important, the quest for Democracy forecloses the
possibility of articulating benevolent governance within an Islamicate
register. The implications of this not only turn on the possibility of
maintaining a pluralistic world, but also a world in which the postcolonial moment is not replaced by a revamped colonial order with its attendant injustices and cruelties. Unless we believe in the possibility of
articulating theories of legitimate rule from different histories and traditions, the promise of justice, prosperity and peace will remain nothing
more than window dressing on a violent and iniquitous world order.
Accepting Democracy and its Western logo works towards homogenis-
ing the world in a way which counters the appeal of Democracy as an
expression of the demos. If the proper demos has only one history and
one tradition, it cannot be a global demos. The idea that a planetary
humanitarianism could underwrite a global demos would carry greater
weight if it could be demonstrated that such a demos would be truly
global. It is decolonisation not Democracy that promises a global demos,
and without a global demos Democracy will retain all its restrictive and
ultimately xenophobic features.

Some of the ambiguities of the way in which the signifier of
Democracy can be deployed can be clearly seen in the attempt by the US
occupiers to try and impose a democracy on Iraq in the wake of their

conquest of the country.[19] This is not only the function of the way in which the imposition of a US proconsul and an undemocratic puppet Iraqi government, along with the apparent necessity of recolonising Iraq as the foundation of its democratisation, seems at odds with what is commonly represented by Democracy. It is also the function of the way in which a number of writers, including the neo-conservative gurus, see in the democratic transformation of societies not the possibility of the often-repressed people of those societies discovering their voices, their capacity for thinking through their history, but rather a transformation into pro-Western (if not pro-US) subjects. Democratic transformation becomes the continuation of Westernisation through other means. For the neo-conservatives, the reorganisation of Muslimistan around the signifier of Democracy will help inoculate the *ummah* from being antagonistic towards the West. Democracy will allow Muslim societies to see their 'national' interests as being compatible with Western interests.

The expansion of the democratic revolution is limited to the extent that the frontier between the West and the Orient conditions the identity of Democracy itself. Thus, whereas in the context of the regions of the world that can be rearticulated with relative ease as Western, Democracy, with its promise of liberating and empowering the demos, can provide the basis for closing the gap between rulers and ruled. Here one could point to the relative success of democratisation in southern Europe in the 1970s. In parts of the world where the conceptual frontier has been sedimented for a variety of historical reasons, and gives the impression of having a *longue durée*, the importation of the signifier Democracy requires the rearticulation of the importing society as part of the West. In these conditions, where the demos has to be first 'de-Orientalised', the reliance on the signifier of Democracy can expand the gap between the rulers and ruled, with all its attendant repressions. The eighty-year experience of Turkey, and the largely unsuccessful attempt of its ruling elite to reclassify it as Western, at least illustrates some of the difficulties of requiring 'de-Orientalisation' as a necessary prior move to 'Democratisation'. Reformers in Muslimistan may be better employed in trying to articulate the presumed dividend of Democracy (freedom from repression, a demilitarisation of public life, possibilities of non-violent and routinised transformations of government) under another signifier of benevolent governance that does not require the detours of using the logo of Democracy. For what such reformers may gain in support from the Western plutocracies by organising their opposition to repression under the brand name of Democracy they are likely to lose in relation to their genuine aims of empowering their demos. While Western political thought may be content with its ideas of benevolent governance being organised under the signifier of Democracy, it does not follow that all political thought should reach this conclusion.[20]

V

The 'Age of Europe' bequeathed to the world a name for good governance. This name, like other names for benevolent governance, always escaped full realisation; benevolent governance can never be perfect if it can always be called to better itself in the name of itself. The initial baptism of Democracy as the political form of the West at its most Western, means that the good governance that Democracy nominates is too often blind to the way in which Western cultural regimes have been supplemented, if not formed, by disparate assemblages of power—liberalism and colonialism, human rights and racialised governmentality (Hesse, 2004).

Those who seek in Democracy for a more just world need to let go of Democracy as the signifier of the West, and dare to imagine a world in which various societies and histories can produce notions of good governance that are commensurate with the fundamental pluralism of this planet. This means abandoning the colonial discourse of Westernese that sees the future and past of human endeavour in terms of the distinction between the West and the Rest (and their cognates). The idea that tools for a better life can be found in any particular set of social practices ultimately means rejecting the idea that the salvation of humanity only lies in Westernisation under whatever logo, and allowing the emergence of discourses that might even exclude the Western ratio (Diawara, 1990: 87).

There is another narrative also in play that sees in the Arab Spring not a flourishing of people power but rather another chapter in an American-inspired 'colour coded regime change' (Massad, 2011). According to this view, part of US strategy has been to use apparently popular mobilisations to try and weaken regimes that the US considers to be hostile. Those who hold this view focus on popular mobilisations in the former

Soviet Union—the rose revolution of Georgia and the orange revolution in the Ukraine—that weakened Russian hold over the region, as well as the abortive cedar revolution in Lebanon and the Green Movement in Iran. They point to the level of material support the United States has given to those involved in these mobilisations as an indication of US conspiracy. They also point to the way in which Syria and the Baathist regime is being threatened with a regime change and also to the US silence that has allowed Saudi arms to put down an uprising in Bahrain while supporting those in Syria and Libya.

From 1492 to the world of *Star Trek* is almost a thousand years. The appropriation of the 'New World' that inaugurated the Age of Europe is replayed in the way in which *Star Trek* colonises the future, by projecting forward the 'Age of Europe'. The beginning of each of the original episodes of *Star Trek* announced that the final frontier was that of space; but perhaps the fault-line that really matters is not in the stars but between the Orient and the West. Maybe in another parallel universe there is another series of *Star Trek* that is a mirror, not for Western exceptionality but rather the fundamental pluralism of history. Of course, to deny such a possibility or denigrate it as a descent into relativist chaos is not only a failure to imagine that others may also dream of better worlds, it also demonstrates 'we' are resolutely unwilling to live in the dreamscapes of others, while continuing to expect that 'others' will only find well-being in playing extras in 'our' dreams. Writing the history of the future is not only the province of science fiction but, as we shall go on to see, one of the possibilities of the political.

6

FUTUROLOGY

I

Apart from the *Star Trek* mythos, one of the most popular attempts to tell a history of the future is the series of films and novels inspired by Frank Herbert's *Dune*. The *Star Wars* saga, David Lynch's 1984 film version of *Dune* and the television mini-series *Dune* and *Children of Dune* are the most well-known examples of science fiction directly indebted to Frank Herbert's tale set in the distant future. Even though this future is distant (although in the case of *Star Wars* it is stated as being 'a long time ago in a galaxy far, far away') and the different workings of the same basic story are obviously related to the social, cultural and historical context of their production, the future is determinedly still dominated by a West and non-West dichotomy. In the mini-series *Dune*, there is a scene in which Paul Atreides finds himself hailed by the Fremen—the indigenous desert-dwellers of the planet Arrakis—as the Mahdi.[1] Paul raises his hands to silence the crowd and proclaims: 'You say I am the Mahdi, I say I am your duke.'[2] There could be a number of reasons why Paul Atreides would refuse the title of Mahdi in favour of the title of duke. It could be that, given this series was made for a mass audience, the reason for this reluctance is purely to do with the banalisation necessary for popular entertainment. Thus, by refusing the unfamiliar Mahdi for the familiar duke, the makers of the series were simply making a concession for a mass audience. For example, it is easier to deal with a feudal lord as a hero rather than as a cosmic deliverer. This is unlikely, given that science fiction often deals with realities that involve all kinds of cosmic beings. Is a saviour really that difficult to grasp? Surely, the various Biblical epics have inured an audience into knowing how to watch stories of divinely guided redemptive figures. Furthermore, science fiction often requires its audiences to master new worlds with new languages and new customs. Why would the idea of a Mahdi be more difficult to comprehend than the existence of Klingons? There is little reason to assume that the concept of a divinely guided saviour figure is more problematic for a sci-fi audience to understand than the figure of hereditary leader. Science fiction often deals with concepts that are not familiar or commonplace, for example time travel, non-human life forms, exploration of alien cultures and so forth.

Perhaps the film-makers were deliberately emphasising the title of duke as a subliminal homage to John Wayne, an icon of Americana, whose popular nickname was the Duke. Thus, perhaps it was a way of reassuring the audience that although we may be in another 'galaxy far, far away', we still have the spirit of John Wayne to tame this alien environment. By calling himself duke, Paul is thus making a gesture to the audience that he is the John Wayne figure—and despite the exotic trappings of the story, underneath it all Paul is the rugged individual destined to win the fight for freedom and what would more commonly be called the American way. Furthermore, as Paul's father was also a duke (Duke Leto), by proclaiming himself a duke, Paul could also be paying homage to his father and gesturing towards the continuation of the Atreides genealogy. This burst of filial loyalty (perhaps to both Leto and John Wayne) still does not explain why Paul Atreides would use the title, given that he is leading the Fremen in rebellion against the forces of the empire. Why would he accept a title that forms part of the imperial order of privilege and inequity? It could be that the makers of *Dune* wanted to express the reluctance of Paul to be a messianic figure. In this they would be illustrating his humility by his reluctance to play the part of a great historical figure. Such an interpretation of Paul Atreides, however, seems to mark not the refusal of leadership itself, but rather the rejection of a particular form of leadership; that is, the leadership entitled by being the Mahdi rather than that entailed by being a duke.

The following section explores this rejection in more detail, for if one way of understanding popular science fiction is to see it as a dramatisation of political theory (Vzw, 2006) in which issues associated with political thought are explored in a mass medium, given the mass popularity of the *Dune* world (both the novels and the mini-series),[3] it is worth asking what sort of political theory is being articulated by *Dune*.

It could be argued that science fiction remains as a popular genre of literary and cultural production that is heavily focused on the West.[4] For example, there are hardly any sustained productions of science fiction films by non-Western countries with large cinema industries (Sardar, 2002). This is partly due to the nature of science fiction. This is not a purely accidental development, but rather reflects the way in which Western culture was the first (and perhaps the only culture) to be organised around technology—'technology' meaning a way of being that transforms the world into a resource that can be deployed and controlled through the application of calculative reasoning. Technology refers not simply to a set of complex tools, but rather to the instrumentalisation of the world,[5] so that technology comes to denote the transformation of human problems into algorithmic solutions. The political is mastered by transformation into a mere form of administration, where resources are deployed to find equilibrious solutions to conflicts. The encounter between technology and humanity generates conditions of the possibility of science fiction. Specifically, science fiction emerges from the exploration between technology and the political.

The political should not be confused with politics, or a specific domain of life; it is not reducible to the activities of governmental agencies, political parties or movements. The political is an ontological category. It arises in the context of any situation in which it is possible to make a distinction between friends and enemies; that is, a situation in which social relations have not been institutionalised into a seemingly natural order (Schmitt, 1996). In other words, the political is a process that inaugurates an ensemble of social relations so that their constructed nature, and/or their beginning as exercises of power, is erased. The political demands that decisions be made between contending alternatives that cannot be placed upon a common scale by which experts determine the correct solution (Mouffe, 2005). In contrast, technology promises a neutralisation of social strife, since it suggests that all societal conflicts can be resolved by the application of its method—in other words, rational ordering can eradicate strife entirely (Gray, 2004: 42).[6] One could argue that ever since the wars of religion that ripped

Christendom apart—in the confrontations between the force of the Reformation and Counter-Reformation—there has been a desire within Western thought to find a means of overcoming civic conflict, and with the advent of modernity, increasingly technology and its cognates have been thought capable of guaranteeing that neutralised social sphere (Schmitt, 1993). Technology would seek to transform the antagonistic nature of the political into conflict-free routines, it would turn the political into mere administration. Thus, the political and the technological have an antithetical relationship.

Science fiction, by juxtaposing the technological and the political, establishes a way of thinking the relationship between the political and its domestication. An investigation into the decision of Paul Atreides to reject the mantle of the Mahdi in favour of being hailed as a duke raises questions about not only the relationship between technology and the political but also, as will be shown, the relationship of the West and the political.

II

The world of *Dune* offers a vision of a future universe dominated by Islamicate themes. A casual glance at Frank Herbert's creation immediately brings this forth. It can be seen in the subtle and not so subtle use of Islamicate terms (jihad, *padishah*, *aql*, and so on).[7] Apart from these lexical influences, there is also the adoption and translation of concepts associated with Islamicate cultural practices: for example, in *Dune* there are specially genetically engineered human computers called *mentats*— one could draw parallels with the existence of *hafiz* (those who committed the Qur'an to memory) within Islamicate cultures. Further, the commodity that enables interstellar travel is spice on Arrakis—compare this with oil and its centrality within the contemporary world economy. There is also, of course, the major theme of *Dune:* the poverty of desert-dwellers who become holy warriors. For Frank Herbert, *Dune* was an exploration of the messianic impulse in humanity and the dangers of religious and political intermingling.[8] Given the themes that he set out to explore it is not surprising that Herbert culled fragments of Islamicate history to flesh out his vision.[9] For the themes of the messianic impulse and the conflation between religion and politics, fatalism and fanaticism are often described, by Western accounts, as being intrinsic to the world of Islam.

One way to describe the representation of Islam within Western discourse is Orientalism. As Edward Said's work maintained, Orientalism provides accounts of Islam and associated phenomena that are organised around three main themes: one, that there are ontological, systemic and persistent differences between Islam and the West. Second, the world of Islam is a counter-image of the self-representations of the West, so that the world of Islam is generally considered to be static, and uniform. Third, the world of Islam is to be either feared or mastered (Sayyid, 2003: 32). Orientalism provides an account of an alternative vision of a society in which politics, social change and philosophy are all marked as being exotic. Though Said never explicitly drew the relationship between Orientalism and science fiction (in particular its subgenre, science fantasy) one can see how it is possible to think of science fiction as a form of Orientalism: that is an exploration of hostile, strange worlds. While many types of science fiction as Orientalism are able to keep the Islamicate influences and references either discreet or hidden, Frank Herbert's *Dune* series is far more explicit in its gestures towards an alternative distant future over-determined by Islam.

Dune can be seen as a relatively sophisticated space opera in which the crude and casual 'Yellow Peril' inflexions of Flash Gordon are replaced by an elaborate and studied 'Green Peril' of Islam.[10] No text, however, can be contained within the intentions of the author. *Dune* in many ways exceeds Herbert's reach.[11] A Muslim reading of *Dune* is confronted with the structural ambivalence of the text. On the one hand, the text is populated with Orientalist tropes and caricatures. From the valorisation of the European man leading the Muslim masses, to the ability of the Western man to disguise himself as a native, to the primitive superstitious nature of the Muslim masses, to an idea of Islam as a simple religion—all of these can be found in *Dune* represented through the figures of Liet Kynes, Paul Maud'dib, the Fremen and so on. What transforms these Orientalist stereotypes and introduces the structural ambivalence is that they are located in a narrative set in an alternative future. By taking all the Orientalist themes and making explicit the references to Islam, and then placing them in the future, *Dune* seems inadvertently to project Islam into the future. This in itself is a bold move, since popular science fiction rarely makes space for non-Europeanness to exist in the future, unless it is expelled from the category of human, in other words, when alien beings denote non-Europeanness.

It can be argued, however, that despite being in the future the quasi-Muslims of *Dune* are still in the past of the future. This is because they are found at the edges of the civilised world, living poverty-stricken lives on a harsh desert landscape. To that extent, the primal construction of Western identity is in relation to the negation of Islam. A zero-sum relationship is established in which Westernisation and Islamisation are only possible at the expense of the other. Thus, if Islam is in the future, then it suggests that the West has been left behind in the past. The binary structure of *Dune*, in which the West and Islam are spatialised as being represented by the world of empire and civilisation and the world of tribes and barbarism, would seem to preserve the hierarchy between the West and the Rest. Even if there are 'Muslims' in the future, they are still in a subordinate position and the hierarchy between the West and the non-West is preserved. Thus, the relationship between quasi-Muslims and the civilised world can still be contained within the idea of an Islamicate inheritance, perhaps like Andalusia, where the monuments and achievements of the Islamicate civilisation are all present, but Muslims are considered to be absent. This allows the past to be incorporated as part of the common heritage without the payment of moral reparations. A gift from a dead past without any living descendants does not need to be acknowledged.

At the beginning of *Dune* we see a setting that can be interpreted as a world like the European Renaissance—that is, a world populated by an Islamicate inheritance that it largely disavows. This is the world of civilisation and empire, of the Houses of Atreides and the Harkonnen. What changes the balance of forces, what turns the Islamicate from an inheritance to history, is the mobilisation of the quasi-Muslims in choosing the lexicon of power not derived from the history of the West. It is not the slogans of the French or Russian revolutions that herald the Fremen storming of the (winter) palaces of the empire, but the return of the Mahdi. It is the centrality of the Mahdi within the *Dune* universe that turns the story of *Dune* into a history of the future, one that breaks with popular science fiction conventions in which the future continues to be colonised by the Western enterprise. The Mahdi is not just the expression of the messianic interruption of a naturalised social order, he is the unravelling of the process of naturalisation as Westernisation. The appearance of the Mahdi demands a double negation, of both the naturalised social order and the order of the West.

III

The significance of the Mahdi requires an appreciation of the way in which the advent of Islam impacted on the construction of political imaginaries of late antiquity. While it is the case that the founding dichotomy of Western political thought between Occidental democracy and Oriental despotism predates Islam, this dichotomy has been deployed to incorporate Islam into parameters set by Western political thinking.[12] What this shows is that Western political theory is not immune to Orientalism. Rather than replay the representations of Islam found within Western political thought, let us explore the way in which Islam articulated its categories of power. There are distinct repertoires through which power is expressed. These expressions of power include rituals, narratives, tokens and titles. It is the lexicon of power as articulated through the construction of categories of power-holders that allows us to understand the implications of the deployment of terms such as duke and Mahdi.

Islam's appearance as a major geopolitical force occurred in a landscape dominated by two imperial imaginaries: the Persian and the Roman. From the Mediterranean Basin to the eastern edges of the Iranian plateau two rival imperial traditions faced each other for over half a millennia. The Persian lexicon of power could be traced back to Mesopotamian antecedents, specifically the Assyrians and Babylonians. The Roman lexicon of power was based on its Republican heritage, but through the tropes that characterised *Imitatio Alexandri* to Persian imperial imaginary. Thus western Afro-Eurasia was dominated by two distinct lexicons of power: one Persian and the other Roman.[13] The early Muslims were based in a region that was on the periphery of these empires and lacked an imperial imaginary of its own, thus, it would seem very likely that the Islamicate polity would represent itself in a lexicon based either on Romans or Persians. It is strange that, for the most part, the Muslims did not do this but rather forged a new semantic order.[14]

The Muslim leadership was aware that the scale and rapidity of their conquest contributed to the creation of a political entity that was practically *ex nihilo*.[15] The empire of the Muslims was not the rejuvenation or continuation of a previous state (mythic or historical). Thus, there was no prior lexicon of power that the Muslim leadership could draw upon without reservation.[16] Hence, the Muslims developed a distinct lexicon that eventually consolidated itself into a more or less coherent hierarchy of supreme ruler, rulers and petty rulers: caliph, sultan, emir (Findley, 2005: 69). This hierarchy underpinned a political, social and economic order—an order that was Islamicate, largely because the ruling elite of that order was Muslim—and its Muslimness was partly manifested by the use of its specific lexicon of power(-holders). Islam bequeathed to the world a distinct nomenclature of political titles as part of a new semantic universe inaugurated by Islam. The acquiring of these Islamicate titles indicated an entry into the Islamicate order. It is within the context of these political titles and entitlements that the category of the Mahdi has to be located.

The Mahdi does not mark a specific rank within the Islamicate convention of power-holders, for the Mahdi emerges with the development of an Islamic eschatology. The return of the Mahdi marks the rupture of the existing order of privilege and injustice and cruelty—thus the Mahdi is the disrupter of all hierarchies except those based on virtue. The Mahdi (the one who is divinely guided) is expected prior to the Day of Judgment; his return would enable the restoration of the world to justice and order, prior to God's judgment. While the Mahdi is not explicitly mentioned in the Qur'an it emerges as a significant figure within Islamic thought. Among the Shia schools of thought, the Mahdi has an eschatological significance, and is regarded as the saviour that will restore the world prior to the end of time. Among the Sunni traditions, the Mahdi does not initially have the same eschatological significance, but nonetheless is an important title used by several caliphs as part of their regal name. Over time, however, the Shiite view of the Mahdi started to influence the Sunni interpretations and the Mahdi was increasingly considered a figure that transcends social and political categories.

Historically, a number of figures have been associated with the title of the Mahdi, most famously in Sudan in the 1880s, in which a Mahdist state was established as a result of a movement lead by a Muslim claiming to be a Mahdi. Upon his death, the head of the state took the title of Caliph, thus signalling that within the Islamicate lexicon of power the title of the Mahdi transcends that of even the canonical title of the supreme ruler. The Mahdi trumps any lexicon of power-holders—for his authority transcends all mundane authority.

In contrast, the title of duke derives from the Latin *dux*, which was the rank of senior officer of the later Roman army in charge of a frontier district.[17] With the collapse of the Western Roman Empire, the title of duke becomes incorporated into the system of European peerage. The duke was the second-highest rank just below royal titles; often dukes exercised sovereign powers (for example the Duke of Burgundy). If the title of duke does not connote a feudal order—since the power of European peerage extends beyond the feudal era—it certainly connotes an established order of privilege in which hereditary rather than ethical or moral values predominate. If the Mahdi's appearance marks the transvaluation of all established values, the appearance of the duke symbolises those established values—values and privileges that are naturalised and their ignoble beginnings erased from memory, if not history.

Thus, the contrast between Mahdi and duke is not only a contrast between the established and the revolutionary, between the divinely guided and the mundane, between the anti-hierarchal and the hierarchical. It is also a contrast between Islam and the West,[18] for the presentation of the messianic through the figure of the Mahdi translates the messianic into an Islamicate category. This translation has a number of consequences for the way in which Islam (and its cognates) have been represented within the discourse of Orientalism. This is because within Orientalism the contrast between the Orient and the Occident is always predicated on the relative superiority of the Occident vis-à-vis the Orient, and the possibilities of transformation remain inherent to the West. The West has History, whereas the Orient is organised around a system of differences that change only in a cyclical fashion. The concept of the messianic is inherently historical, in that the messianic signifies the possibility of history as a teleology and this teleology is what gives history a meaning. In other words, history becomes not simply a record of the past, but an account of significant transformations that will lead to the end of time: history becomes History. The deployment of the Mahdi within *Dune* threatens to disrupt this Orientalist schema in which Islam is essentially static. *Dune* makes it possible not only to think of Islam as part of a history of the future, but more importantly, to think of it as History itself. If, however, Islam is History, then the West that has been constructed in opposition to Islam can have only a secondary role. This would reverse the hierarchy upon which the colonial vision of the world ultimately rests, that is, the hierarchy of the West over the Rest.

The significance of the reversal suggested by *Dune* can be illustrated by contrasting it with another popular American science fiction series.

In the episode of *Star Trek* called 'The Omega Glory' a conflict rages on a planet divided between two civilisations: the Khom and the Yang. The Yang are a primitive freedom-loving people subjugated by the oppressive Khom. As the episode progresses we discover that the Yang civilisation is based on the United States, in that not only is their name derived from Yanks, but their holy book is the US Constitution and their most sacred relic is the US flag. The Yang are also racially marked as being Caucasian. The Khom, on the other hand, are clearly identified as being related to communists and racially signified as being East Asian.[19] The episode concludes with the victory of the Yang and their commitment to make real the 'holy words' found in the US Constitution. The end of 'The Omega Glory' signals the restoration of the hierarchy of the West and the Rest. It is precisely because the Mahdi cannot be seen as a proto-American or as a quasi-Western figure that the reassertion of this hierarchy is prevented.

The closure of the possibility of overturning the hierarchy of the West and the non-West requires the erasure of the double negation of a naturalised unequal social order, and of the future expansion of the Western horizon. One way of doing this is by demoting the Mahdi, by turning the Mahdi into a shaman, so that the Mahdi no longer connotes an eschatological figure and is no longer the representation of the full stop of history but a mere 'witch-doctor' of a primitive superstitious people. When Paul asks to be known as the duke of the Fremen and not their Mahdi he is asserting not only the primacy of a category culled from the Western lexicon of power, but also the idea that only under the leadership of Western categories is it possible to become an agent of transformation. The price of demoting the significance of the Mahdi in favour of the duke is, however, the depoliticisation of the world.

Politics is a rule-governed activity which, of course, always has the possibility of being turned into a contest without any rules (that is, a fight). Normally, however, the players of the game of politics exercise restraint. For a variety of normative and pragmatic reasons they try to prevent the game from turning into a fight. This distinction between a game and a fight is similar to the distinction between politics and the political. In a game we have opponents—those who we want to defeat by the rules of the game, and those who will concede that they have lost by the rules of the game. So, for example, chess players are governed by the rules of chess, and victory and defeat in a chess game is clear enough.

In a fight we have enemies—those whom we want to defeat by any means we think necessary and where the terms of defeat and victory are themselves not very clear. In *Dune* politics is represented, for the most part, by the intrigues of various noble houses (Atreides, Harkonnen) and the emperor. The appearance of the Mahdi threatens this 'politics as usual' by introducing the political into the world of *Dune*.

Given that the political marks a space of contestation and the institution of social relations, any stable social order depends on the degree to which it can master the space of the political. There are three means by which the political can be kept in check. First, the political can be controlled by the process of domestication. That is, when the space of the political is occupied by politics, enemies are reduced to legislative opponents and the game between government and opposition is installed as a means of regulating the political. Second, the political can be overcome by the cultivation of what has been described as cynical reason (Sloterdijk, 1998). Cynical reason insulates the social order by making it immune to any critique of its values or any attempt to demonstrate its ignoble beginnings and exclusions. This is done by representing such critiques as the already-known, as platitudes and clichés, without any force. Third, the political can be mastered by an act of displacement, that is, by expelling the space of the political to the exterior. This means that the frontier between the interior of the social order and its limits becomes a frontier between order and chaos, between civilisation and barbarism, and between stable society and the deconstructive tendencies of the political. The consequence of the successful pursuit of these strategies is depoliticisation. Depoliticisation promises the end of History, based on the establishment of neutral, conflict-free social relations.

By having Paul Atreides proclaim himself a duke rather than the Mahdi, the *Dune* mini-series does two things. First, it reasserts the hierarchy of the West over the Rest. For Paul Atreides to prefer the second-rate title of duke rather than the Mahdi it suggests that a second-rank Western power-holder is superior even to a non-Western eschatological figure. Second, it reasserts the social over the political, because it establishes the preference for privilege over a revolutionary change.

The duke offers stability, and a society in which positions of respect and distinctions are fixed. The Mahdi implies an overturning of such hierarchies and a questioning of the distribution of respect and distinction to be found in the existing social order. A consequence of favouring the title of duke over that of Mahdi is then the displacement of the political and the inscription of *Dune* as a recolonised future of the world. Popular science fiction as exemplified by the mini-series *Dune* becomes part of the colonial frame, beholden to the hierarchy of the West and the non-West, and committed to its projection infinitely onwards and outwards.

IV

There are many ways of reading the story of *Dune*. Most conventional interpretations refer to the contrast between being a duke and being Mahdi as an opposition between earthly power and heavenly power, but my preference is for what Borges calls 'rabbinical explanations' (1999; also Sayyid, 2003: 1). Staring into the abyss of a decolonised history of the future, the makers of the mini-series *Dune* turn back and in proclaiming the duke continue to articulate the future within the terms of coloniality. The presentation of a 'complete' story arc within the limits of a mini-series for a mass audience means that *Dune* the mini-series becomes the text upon which the Orientalism of mainstream science fiction risks being undermined by the construction of *Dune* as a history of the future, and the use of the Mahdi to represent the messianic impulse. In this context, the Mahdi becomes a signifier for the political, for Islam and for History to be restored to a people without history. Thus, for *Dune* the mini-series to prevent this over-determination of the symbol of the Mahdi, to relegate once again Islam and Muslims to a cycle of Orientalist narration, there is a need to articulate the possibility of transformation within a recognisably Western register. Hence, when Paul Atreides proclaims he is a duke, he is going back to the hierarchy between West and the non-West which underpins the colonial configuration of the world. In that utterance one can see the attempt to restore the violent hierarchy of the West and the Rest and all that entails. Even when imagining a distant future, the makers of *Dune* are unable to imagine it without coloniality. They would seem to suggest that it is better to be a Western feudal lord, than the Muslim 'Lord of Time'. The cost of privileging the duke over the Mahdi means endorsing the status quo over the possibility of a better world to come, but in this age of neo-liberal 'consensus' it should not surprise us that it is a cost that so many are willing to bear. One implication of this is that popular science fiction continues to defer the decolonisation of the future.

This deferral of decolonisation takes many forms: cultural, philosophical as well as socioeconomic and military. In previous chapters we have seen how the deferral is played out through the policing of the frontier between the Western and non-Western and part of this policing is prevention of the creation of a third space: the inability of the spatial ordering of political subjectivities contributes to the maintenance of the violent hierarchy that characterises coloniality. The Mahdi as a metaphor for a transformative cultural event that would overturn the prevailing inequitous order becomes banalised in *Dune* into the idea of earthly political order that reconfigures the status quo. The quest for the Islamicate polity can be seen in general terms as a quest for an instrument of decolonisation but, more specifically, it has to be seen as an attempt to address the fragmentation of Muslim agency.

7

DIASPORA

I

Sayyid Qutb made the uncompromising declaration that: 'There is no nationality for a Muslim except his creed which makes him a member of the Islamic Ummah in the abode of Islam' (1989: 48). At one level, of course, many Muslims, if not most, would not quibble with this statement; there is a vague sense in which the idea of being a Muslim ought to transcend other commitments and loyalties circulating throughout the *ummah*. Such a stark declaration, however, immediately raises two questions: can being a member of the *ummah* be the same as belonging to a nation, and what about Muslims who live outside the 'abode of Islam', whatever its precise boundaries may be? In this chapter I want to address these two questions. I want to explore the significance of thinking about Muslimness as being akin to being a member of a nation-state and what the limits of that nation-state would do to Muslims who find themselves on the wrong side of the border.

Even though the nation-state was invented perhaps only over 200 years ago with the French Revolution, as an invention it has proved to be fairly durable and highly mobile. Its durability is manifested by the way in which it has continued to undermine empires and other forms of political community. Its mobility is shown by the way in which it has spread to cover all parts of the planet. Despite its apparent success, however, there are reasons for thinking that the days of the 'nation-thing' are numbered. The idea of a 'clash of civilisations' sums up the anxieties about the nation, by arguing that nations are being replaced by quasi-primordial constructs such as civilisations (Huntington, 1998). Despite the problematic nature of defining a civilisation, what is clear is that these entities are the manifestations of an a-national logic. Civilisational cleavages are the source of post-national conflicts—in other words, inter-civilisational conflict takes the place of international conflict.

The political, as I have mentioned previously, is founded upon the distinction between friend and enemy (Schmitt, 1996: 28). This enemy is a collective enemy. The reason for this is that for the friend-enemy distinction to operate, there must be a capacity for combat (Schmitt, 1996: 32). This capacity means that within the political there is the possibility of war as a means of negating the enemy. War is a group activity and since the invention of the nation, it is an activity restricted to the national. This notion of the political does not necessarily involve the nation. Since the invention of the nation, however, most political conflicts have taken a national form. The friend-enemy distinction not only constructs the political but also helps to necessitate that the political takes the form of the national. Thus, any attempt to contest the logic of the nation implies a transformation of the political. In other words, the relationship between the Westphalian model of political order and contemporary identity formation requires an examination of the nation and its future.

The nation was conceptualised as a homogenous indivisible body. Recent critiques of the logic of the national have highlighted its empirical deficiencies (multiplicity of identities), its ethical difficulties (the possibility of genocide and totalitarianism) and its theoretical limits (the impossibility of eradicating difference) (Bauman, 1989; Smith, 1991, Anthias and Yuval-Davis, 1992; Held, 1995). These studies have been very important in undermining the logic of the national and suggesting a multicultural alternative that is a normative stance arising out of the recognition and celebration of the variety of cultural forms and practices that exist within the body of the nation. Critics of normative multiculturalism point to the way in which such valorisation may lead to the Balkanisation of the nation. In the rest of the chapter I want to examine this implication by focusing on contemporary Muslim subjectivity.

II

The assertion of Muslim subjectivity presents a serious challenge to the idea of the nation. It is argued that: '[F]or a Muslim, the fundamental attachment is not to the *watan* (homeland), but to the *ummah*, or community of Believers, all made equal in their submission to Allah' (Castells, 1997: 15).[1] I want to explore the implications of this *watan/ummah* distinction in the next section. Castells' reading of Muslim subjectivity reproduces Orientalist and neo-Orientalist accounts of Islam. As a consequence, he positions Islam as an anachronistic presence in today's world, almost a monolith in a world of flows. It is also interesting that Castells perceives Muslim identity as articulated in terms of a diffuse Islam rather than as a spatially bounded unit. The effect of this is to include Islam as a reaction to the world of flows characterised by globalisation. It is often argued that an uncertain world produces crises that require the solace of 'primary identities', be they religious, ethnic, territorial or national. This is interesting because the way in which we have talked about collective identities has relied on the use of stable bounded spaces. The general argument is that for a variety of reasons we are now living in a world of flows, and that these flows are unsettling because they disrupt the continuities that allowed collective identities to be formed, maintained and projected.[2]

Globalisation is one way of summing up the transition to this world of flows. It is a process that is intrinsically linked to the formation of dislocated communities; populations that no longer fit within the Westphalian 'container'. The container is unable to accommodate them, not only because of increased mobility but also because its own walls are becoming blurred. The 'spatio-temporal dimensions of globalization' include a stretching, intensification and speeding up of social relations (Held et al., 1999: 14–16). The effect of these processes has changed the global landscape in five major ways:

1. The rise of cosmopolitan centres such as London, New York, Tokyo, Paris and the like provides the terrain where many of the trends associated with globalisation can be manifested. Not only are these world cities nodal points in the international economy, but they are also the spaces from which attempts to articulate a global culture are sited. These global cities are, to a large extent, cut-off from, or at least have an exceptional relationship with, the nation-states in which they are situated and are more connected to other global cities (Sassen, 2001).

2. The development of nascent global civil society (Keane, 2003). Not only do we have a proliferation of NGOs that operate across national state boundaries, we are also seeing the beginnings of an attempt to construct a 'consensus' on issues such as human rights, economic management, gender issues and so forth.

3. The emergence of supranational state-like formations such as the European Union also points to a way in which the Westphalian container is being superseded. One can note similar tendencies in the formation of North American Free Trade Agreement (NAFTA) and the Association of Southeast Asian Nations (ASEAN). These 'super-state' structures serve to undermine the relationship between national forms and sovereignty. In the European Union we see the attempt to articulate a pan-European identity that subsumes, to some extent, the national identities of member states, and the impact that this has upon the distinction between the national majority and the ethnic minorities that organise the ethnoscape of Western plutocracies.

4. The generalisation of the experience of distant travel (whether it takes the form of labour migration, the compulsory movements of refugees or tourism) has created a situation in which very large numbers of people are on the move or have moved. In this moving, one can trace the implosion of Western colonial empires (including the fallout from the collapse of the Soviet system) as well as the imperatives of the world economy. While there is dispute as to the extent to which contemporary international migration is of the same scale as that which characterised the nineteenth century (Hirst and Thompson, 1996), there is little doubt that long-distance travel and tourism have become a mass phenomenon. The development of cheaper means of information flows (internet, cable television) also contributes to the destruction of distance and the transformation of the contours of social activity.

5. The development and increasing integration of the world political economy acts to suture disparate economies and societies and, at the same time, limits the ability of nation-states (with a few powerful exceptions) to regulate their economies. This integration has been enabled by the breakdown of the communist-style autarkic command economies and subsequent global domination of the belief in neo-liberal understanding of economic management (Rupert, 2000: 42–64)—a belief that continues to hold sway among elite policy

making circles of Western plutocracies despite the global financial crisis of 2008/09.

It is in the context of these processes of globalisation that the need to find a vocabulary to describe the political/cultural communities that transcend the limits of the Westphalian model becomes necessary. One such community is that of the Muslims.

III

The *ummah* refers to the sum total of all adherents of Islam, regardless of whether they are located in Muslimistan or elsewhere. There are three factors that point towards the formation of a globalised *ummah*. First, there is the phenomenon of the assertion of an explicit Muslim subjectivity. This process has reached all Muslim communities. There are no significant Muslim communities in which more visible indicators of the assertion of Muslim subjectivity are absent. Second, Muslims are heavily represented in various migrant communities throughout the Western plutocracies. This has occurred partly because of integration that has been attended upon decolonisation, but it is also the case that since the 1980s a large percentage of refugees have been Muslims. Third, like most recent migrants, Muslims have tended to concentrate in urban areas. These areas are in the nodes of the new developing planetary networks (Castells, 1997). The net effect of these developments has been to produce situations in which Muslims from different traditions converge around commonalties. This juxtaposing of various Muslim populations has the effect of producing the conditions for the articulation of a *ummah*. Islam interrupts the logic of the nation by highlighting the problem of integration; that is, how to include various populations within the boundaries of a nation, while at the same time focusing on the problem of their loyalties to an edifice larger than the nation. In other words, Islamism undermines the logic of the nation at the same time as it seeks to transcend the logic of the nation. How can we conceptualise this collective? What kind of a structure is the *ummah*, that is a community of believing women and men unified by faith and transcending national state boundaries?

The *ummah*, however, is not the nation writ large. One of the main qualities that distinguishes the nation from other forms of collectives is its limited and restricted nature. The nation is exclusionary. It is a bounded and limited entity, not open to everyone, though its boundaries may be drawn tightly or loosely. Thus, the problem of integration has poignancy for the nation in a way that it does not for other groupings. Unlike other formations, the nation rarely imagines itself to be a composite or mélange. The only universalism that the logic of nation can articulate is one that is based on exclusion rather than inclusion. The universal nation can be an exceptional grouping, an incarnation of all that is considered to be great and good; it can be infinite in a temporal sense, but spatially it has to be bounded, it cannot expand forever. The idea of the *ummah* rejects all such limits and its universalism and implicit expansionism is constantly reiterated. Clearly, the *ummah* is not a nation.

Nor is the *ummah* a common market. It has been pointed out many times, despite pious statements that occasionally emerge from bodies such as the Organization of Islamic Cooperation (OIC) that we cannot conceptualise the *ummah* as a structure arising out of economic integration. The unity of the *ummah* is not built upon trading contacts and global networks of labour and capital flows. This is not to deny that such flows exist, as clearly the relationship between the Gulf states and Muslim labour-exporting states (such as Egypt, Bangladesh, Pakistan and Yemen) is clearly based on such flows. These linkages are not, however, strong enough or extensive enough to suture the *Ummah*.

Nor is the *ummah* a common way of life or a linguistic community. There is no doubt that once upon a time an argument could have been made for the *ummah* to be seen as a collective based around a fairly integrated elite culture. Books of *fiqh* collected in Delhi would be commented upon in madrassas in the Maghreb. Arabic functioned as the lingua franca. There are still some practices that are uniform among Muslims (for example all Muslim pray towards the direction of Makah), which constitute the unity of the *ummah* as its uniform way of life. Of course, it is precisely this idea of an Islamicate civilisation that animates people such as Huntington, but like all attempts to conceptualise a civilisation as a unit, these flounder since it is difficult to conclude from the examples that they rest upon anything but an eclectic collection of observable and generalised features.

If the *ummah* is neither a nation, nor a common market or a civilisation—is it anything at all? Does not the difficulty of identifying the *ummah* suggest that the idea of a Muslim identity is nothing more than a chimera? Analysts have tended to treat 'Muslims' as an epiphenomenon of other, sturdier bases of identity formations (such as class, kinship, caste and ethnicity). This analytical tendency is not only the product of Orientalism, but also of the way in which nationalist discourses within Muslim communities have served to undermine the idea of a distinct Muslim identity. If Muslim identity is so fragmentary, how can we conceptualise it? One way might be to think in terms of a Muslim diaspora.

Diaspora may be used in a descriptive manner to refer to an empirical situation in which settler communities are relocated from their ordinary homes. Extrapolations from the experience of the Jewish and African diasporas have become templates for the understanding of what constitutes a diaspora. Both involve the forced mass removal of people(s) from a homeland to a place of 'exile' and the construction of cultural formations premised on territorial dispersal and political fragmentation. The notion of diaspora rests on three coordinates: homeland, displacement and settlement. In other words, a diaspora is constituted when communities of settlers articulate themselves in terms of displacement from a homeland. The homeland acts as a horizon around which the community articulates its collective sense of self. A diaspora is formed when a people are displaced but continue to narrate their identity in terms of that displacement. For example, the Jewish diaspora is possible because, unlike other groups that were deported by various ancient conquerors, the Jews managed to maintain their collective identity even when they were territorially displaced and politically subordinated. The pre-condition for diaspora is the articulation of a demotic ethnos (or if you prefer, nationalism) that is a mechanism to bind a community in terms of its vertical linkages. This is the reason why diaspora refers to Jewish experiences because it is one of the first instances when a demotic notion of ethnos was circulating (Armstrong, 1983; Smith, 1995). The Jews were not the only people deported en masse by the Assyrians and the neo-Babylonians, but what distinguishes their experience is that they continued to hold on to their 'Jewishness'. The Jewish diaspora is made possible by the development of a proto-nationalism, which prevents their assimilation into other cultural formations.

The idea that a nationalism of sorts is a pre-condition for the construction of diaspora is given added credence by the way in which diasporas tend to take the form of the nation (for example, Palestinians, Armenians, Assyrians). In other words, diaspora refers to a nation in exile. The boundaries that the discourse of nationalism draws around a community are that which prevents the dissolution of that community once it is displaced from its locality. Nationalism constitutes both nations and diasporas—that is, a peoplehood which is territorially concentrated (nation) and territorially displaced (diaspora). Such a view of diaspora, however, would only be partially adequate to account for the African diaspora. Of course, there are many examples of nationalist or proto-nationalist discourses among the African diaspora, which correspond very closely to the 'classic' definition of diaspora (narratives that are organised around the coordinates of a homeland [Africa, Ethiopia], a displacement [the slave trade]—and a horizon of return either as a redemptive gesture or as an empirical possibility). There remains, however, the suspicion that in the case of the African diaspora we are dealing with a process that is not simply a nation in exile. Paul Gilroy's (1993) notion of a 'Black Atlantic' suggests a more complicated cultural formation that cannot be adequately described in such terms.

Attempts to broaden the notion of diaspora usually take the form of trying to include another population group alongside the classical exemplars of diaspora. So, for example, there is an attempt to speak of an Irish diaspora or a Greek diaspora and so on. While these accounts seek an empirical enlargement of diaspora, they do little to extend it theoretically. It is the case that the most common notions of diaspora are continuations of the ethnic framework, but it does not follow that other identity frameworks are somehow more real and more permanent than ethnicity. How populations are classified and formed into particular clusters is ultimately a political process. All social identities are heterogeneous since they do not have an essence that can guarantee their homogeneity. Thus, it would be impossible to empirically ground the homogeneity of social identities, and the various ethnographic studies within the field of ethnic relations will always be able to point to divisions and diversities. Homogeneity is an effect of articulatory practices, an articulation that rests upon exclusion and not on the uncovering of some deep underlying essence. Having said that, one should not confuse the existence of social identities as being necessitated by some essence. The recognition of the inessential character of social identities does not demand that we reject the possibility of all social identities. Or, more problematically, that we maintain the social identities that we do not agree with are mere fictions, or that we argue the only social identities that take particular forms (ethnically-based) are essentialist.

Just because a group of people hail from a particular place does not necessarily mean that they then constitute a 'valid sociological category'. The validity of sociological categories cannot be the product of a practice external to the process by which identities are articulated. Diasporic identities have significance to the extent to which they appear in different discursive practices. One has to recognise that diasporic imaginings can have an empowering effect, for example, Marcus Garvey and Malcolm X saw in the possibility of diasporic connections a way of 'outflanking' some of the constraints on African-American communities (Tyner and Kruse, 2004). For example, Malcolm X's establishment of the Organization of Afro-American Unity (with echoes of the Organization of African Unity) explicitly set out to 'internationalise' the African-American liberation struggle (Malcolm X, 1965: 76; see also Tyner and Kruse, 2004). Similarly, the idea of Muslim subjectivity within Western plutocracies owes its significance to the possibility of making links between and beyond the sites in which Muslim settler communities have been ghettoised and thus transforming the balance of power between national majority and ethnic minorities.[3]

A useful distinction can be made between diasporas that are simply extensions of ethnic frameworks, and diasporas as a condition. What is required is an attempt to articulate diasporas as political formations in the context of the erosion of the Westphalian order. In the case of the Muslim experience (which like the experiences of all collectives, is riddled with division and diversity) the category of diaspora as extended ethnicity is inadequate. While it is the case that there are many Muslims living as minorities throughout the world, the idea of a diaspora demands both a displaced population and a homeland—the point from which the displacement originates. Such a homeland is clearly lacking in the Muslim case. We Muslims do not have a Zion—a place of redemptive return. Also, the universalist urge within many Muslim discourses makes it difficult to privilege a particular locale as a homeland, imagined or otherwise. In addition, there is no founding act of displacement. For the *ummah* is not only reducible to displaced population groups, it also includes the Muslim population in Muslim countries. It is for this reason, therefore, that the notion of diaspora seems an unlikely metaphor for describing the *ummah*. Thus, to read the Muslim experience as diasporic requires the reconceptualisation of the notion of diaspora from the demographic to the political. Given these limitations I would like to suggest another way of understanding diaspora. It is possible to expand the idea of diaspora beyond its descriptive core. There are a number of notions implicit in the descriptions of diaspora that would allow us to reconsider the idea of diaspora as a political formation.

Earlier, I made the point that diasporas were dependent upon the discourse of nationalism. Without a form of nationalism it would be difficult to construct a diaspora. The idea that a diaspora is a nationalist phenomenon is, however, not the only way in which this phenomenon has been described. Diasporas have also been considered anti-national phenomena. Unlike the nation, with its homogeneity and boundedness, diaspora suggests heterogeneity and porousness. Nations define 'home' whereas diaspora is a condition of homelessness; in the nation the territory and people are fused, whereas in a diaspora the two are disarticulated. The diaspora is not the other of the nation simply because it is constructed from the antithetical elements of a nation, it is, rather, an anti-nation since it interrupts the closure of nation. The existence of a diaspora prevents the closure of the nation—since a diaspora is, by definition, located within another nation.

The Jewish experience of diaspora acts as an illustration of the anti-national character of diaspora. Hannah Arendt shows how the parvenu/pariah distinction underwrote Jewish integration into European society during the period up to the Second World War and its aftermath. Arendt (1958: 66) argues that Jews had two main subject positions open to them. One was based on assimilation; that is, the Jew became part of the 'host' society as an exceptional Jew. Somehow, one was a Jew in an exotic sense but, at the same time, one was not a Jew. The other option available was that of total alienation. A Jew who was totally distinct from the 'host' did not belong to that society. The figures of parvenu or pariah both have problematic relationships with the idea of the nation, as both suggest that the nation is not home. The nation is not the place wherein one's identity finds affirmation through the daily mundane rituals of life. The parvenu as a figure of obscure origins and recent recognition is a figure who is not settled. She arrives from an unknown place, gains prominence without a trace and is clearly an exception to the rest of her 'race'. The pariah, as a figure, is clearly and unambiguously someone who is not at home—an outcast. Arendt's reflections on the relationship between identity and belonging after Nazism point to the importance of a notion of home as a way in which the nation sutures the subject. It is the nation as home that acts as an arena for our everyday practices, practices that give focus and meaning, if identity is 'a way of life', then by providing a home the nation is the stage upon which a particular way of life is enacted.

Those without homes face the prospect of trying to enact their 'way of life' off-stage. This is a task that they can only accomplish by using either a strategy of alienation and thus becoming a pariah, or by using a strategy of assimilation and thus being considered parvenu. Members of a diaspora have an undecidable relationship with the idea of nations and homes. For example, Arendt's opposition to Israeli statehood stemmed from the privileging of 'Jewish homelessness', which allowed Jews to escape the blinkers of belonging to a single nation. In other words, the condition of homelessness is seen as a way of escaping the limits of ethnocentrism. Similarly, Gilroy evokes the 'Black Atlantic' as countering both what he perceives to be the cultural absolutism of black nationalism and the closure of the Western project (1993). The Black Atlantic emerges as the name of a space that inhabits the West and that also transcends it. This use of diaspora as anti-nation, as a presence that subverts, hyphenates and hybridises national identity, points to the impossibility of constituting a nation.

It is this undecidability that Arendt privileges in her account of the Jewish experience. Similarly, Gilroy in his description of the Black Atlantic makes an appeal to the experience of the African diaspora as constituting a marginal (undecidable) position within Western modernity—being in the West but not of the West. Both Arendt and Gilroy see in the possibility of 'not-quite being a nation' a position that subverts absolutism. There is a certain pathos in these notions of homelessness. Homelessness suggests the possibility of being hyphenated and hybridised. If we understand a diasporic formation as being an anti-nation, then it becomes clear that what is involved in a diaspora is the deconcentration of power and subjectivity. In other words, the concept of diaspora disarticulates the relationship between the political and the national. The nation focuses power and subjectivity; it makes the national subject the locus of power. Diaspora problematises the possibility of establishing a relationship of coherence between power and subjectivity. What is of critical importance in the formation of a diaspora is the extent to which power and subjectivity are dispersed. This suggests that, in many ways, diasporas do not require the trinity of displacement, settlement and homeland. From this perspective, it would be possible to conclude that we are living in an age in which nations are being replaced by diaspora—that is, the dream of homogenous, hermetically contained spaces is being replaced by the idea of hybridised, porous collectives that flow and overflow through any attempt to contain them. I would suggest, however, that such an understanding fails to acknowledge the nature of diasporic logic and fails to acknowledge the unevenness by which nations are transformed into diasporas.

The logic of diaspora is paradoxical. On the one hand it emphasises the possibility of a nation in even the most difficult circumstances where the Westphalian order does not apply. On the other hand it suggests the impossibility of a nation—by preventing the nation from being fully formed, by deferring the moment of closure and absolutism. If diasporas are nations without homes, then the process of homelessness is not generalised; some nations are less likely to be homeless than others. If homelessness is a consequence of the way in which relations of power and collective subjectivities are disarticulated, then this process is intrinsically political. It is a reflection of broader global struggles. A flavour of these struggles can be gleaned from publications such as *Jihad Vs McWorld* (Barber, 1996).

In this book, a distinction is made between the forces of global disintegration, captured in the banalised idea of jihad and the idea of global integration represented by the metaphor of an American fast-food chain. This dichotomy tends to suggest two different conceptions of the articulation of power and collective subjectivity. One, the road of jihad suggests the prospects of 'retribalization' and Balkanisation: a global Hobbesian war against all, in which narrow particularities rage against modernity, against technology, against pop culture and against integrated markets—against the future itself. The road of jihad seems to point to an attempt to assert nationhood (ideas of collectivities bound by cultures of authenticity and the exclusion of the possibility of heterogeneity).

In opposition to the idea of jihad, we have McWorld, a place of:

shimmering pastels, a busy portrait of onrushing economic, technological and ecological forces that demand integration and uniformity and that mesmerise peoples everywhere with fast music, fast computers, and fast food—MTV, and McDonald's—pressing nations into one homogenous global theme park, one McWorld tied together by communications, information, entertainment, and commerce. (Barber, 1996: 4)

Although this global theme seems to promise heterogeneity, the form that this globality takes excludes that very possibility. In other words, the homogeneity associated with McWorld is culturally marked and, as such, it is more like the homogeneity associated with 'narrow particularism' writ large rather than an escape from particularisms. In this sense, McWorld is the latest trope in the history of the exclusionary universalism that has characterised the Western enterprise. McWorld is based on the domestication of difference and its subservience to the universalism and exclusion that has underwritten the West's relationship to the non-West and reduced the latter to superficialities. Underlying the diversity of surface effects is the idea of homogeneity founded upon the recognition that underneath our cultural skins we are all the same. The form this sameness reflects is our common unity based on our being humans. This makes possible our concerns for the 'starving' in the Third World, it makes possible our demand and extension of human rights across the planet. It is only by focusing on our common humanity that we can avoid the tribalism promised by the advocates of jihad. The snag with this comforting vision is that the notion of what the common human is, what constitutes those values and beliefs that arise from our common humanity and those that are incidental to essential humanness, also tend to correspond with the boundaries of the Enlightenment project. In other words, features that arise from common humanity too often become conflated with features associated with a particular cultural formation. Thus, the West becomes the only place where a human can be truly human, freed from the veneers of superstition and retrograde cultural practices: humans can express their humanness only in the West. This conflation between what is essentially Western with what is essentially human excavates heterogeneity from the globalisation of McWorld. McWorld emerges, not as a 'rainbow' formation where all human cultures find a home, but rather, as an attempt to make the whole world a home for one way of life, one cultural formation. The difference between McWorld and jihad comes down to matter of scale rather than content, for both projects seem to be about making the world familiar. Making the world a home.

IV

If, as a Believer (female or male), you go on hajj, you may travel to the Red Sea port of Jeddah, and from there you will take the road that has taken many Believers before to the Holy City. The road leads up to the Haram, and opposite the Haram there is an air-conditioned shopping mall—inside the shopping mall, the weary pilgrim who comes from far away will find a McDonalds fast-food restaurant. Like any other shopping mall in any other city, you are never far from a McDonalds. If the city that will not admit any others than believing women and believing men, will admit a McDonalds, is not the world already lost to the Believers?[4]

Of course, it is possible to argue that the establishment of a fast-food chain does not really tell us very much about the ways in which global, cultural identities are being transformed. If chicken tikka masala can emerge as one of Britain's most popular dishes (Ahmed, 2006), then the appearance of a McDonalds chain in Mecca is equally insignificant. Why consider McDonalds to be more a sign of cultural imperialism than General Motors or Sony? Is it really possible to make such sharp distinctions between those goods that are considered to be the carriers of cultural values and aspirations and those that are seemingly mute on this point? Surely, we have seen that even the Taliban came to recognise that it was not 'television' that was demonic or Western, since once they captured Kabul, they began to broadcast their own programmes, and their attitude to television had changed.

The most common way in which a particular form or cultural object is given a specific identity is by postulating an origin and then tracing its trajectory from that privileged moment of origin. The problem with such an approach is that it tends to confuse historiography with history. For example, as we saw previously, most accounts of democracy see the process beginning in Ancient Greece (Athens being the model), developing in Europe and finally reaching its fullest form in the Western plutocracies (see Chapter 6). Such a sequence ignores the arbitrariness of constructing an origin from among many beginnings and it ignores the possibility of other kinds of narratives that could reconstruct democracy as originating from other sites (for example, Sumerian city-states).[5] I want to suggest that one sign of being at home is that the narratives that tell tales of origins are also narratives that project one's identity backwards. In other words, being at home means that the world is familiar to us, because its institutions, rules and its complex web of relations are the same discursive productions that articulate our identities in terms of being 'at home'. There is then a sense of belonging that is produced through various hegemonic discursive practices. That is, we are at home when the world around us seems to be our mirror.

What I am suggesting is that being at home is no longer simply an empirical experience of the kind that is produced as international movement becomes further restricted due to tighter immigration controls. Just because the movement of people is becoming increasingly difficult, it does not mean that more people are settled, and are more at home.[6] The process of globalisation is an attempt to make a home for some. This settlement implies that others have to be unsettled. In other words, does the redeployment of the Westphalian order and notions of diaspora on a planetary scale transform the rules by which we could conceive of diaspora as merely 'ethnic minorities' harking back to the lands of their origins? Diaspora is a condition of being homeless—that is, of being displaced and territorially diffused. But if this process is global then the only way by which one can maintain the idea of a diaspora is to make the effects of global displacement specific, rather than general. Global displacement is not a culturally neutral activity: the process of globalisation imposes displacement upon some cultural formations by settling other cultural formations. This means that the logic of diaspora has a cultural specificity (arising out of current historical circumstances). The logic of diaspora includes those who are articulated as homeless in this world. That is, for whom the global hegemonic order is not an echo of their subjectivity. The logic of diaspora is then not simply an interruption of the logic of the nation, it is also an interruption of the global hegemonic order: the logic of diaspora is culturally marked. It is this cultural marking that prevents the logic of diaspora becoming simply a synonym for an anti-nation. The logic of diaspora is not only anti-national, but in present circumstances, when a particular national formation takes a global form, it also becomes anti-global.

In other words, the logic of diaspora cannot escape the most fundamental distinction: that is the distinction between the West and the non-West. It is this distinction that underpins all the forms of coloniality. Attempts to overcome the West/non-West distinction by pointing to an empirical multiculturalism (that is the existence of many cultures and the impossibility of a fully homogenous culture) and valorising hybridity (the normative celebration of multiculturalism) fail because they ignore the way in which the West/non-West distinction is played out as the distinction between the hegemonic and subaltern, and between the culturally unmarked and the culturally marked. In the rest of this chapter I want to see to what extent this diasporic logic can help us understand Muslim identity.

I have earlier argued that with the dominance of the nation-state, national identities are the principal way by which the political tends to be thought. Clearly, there is no single Muslim nation-state that, through its institutional ensemble (schooling, common administrative framework, standardised practices), could be said to be producing a specifically Muslim subject. Muslims appear in spite of the nation-states, not because of them. This is the case even when we consider the example of the handful of states where it could be argued that national identity is synonymous with Muslim identity (in Chechnya, Bosnia, Algeria, Pakistan or Saudi Arabia). For even in these cases Muslimness transcends the boundaries of the states, as none of these states declare in a serious and sustained way that there are no Muslims outside their borders. In addition, their discursive practices (criteria for citizenship, passport controls and so on), tend to privilege not Muslimness but membership of the particular nation-state. This becomes very clear if one considers the neo-Apartheid regimes in the Arabian Peninsula, whose economies are sustained by (mainly, although not exclusively) Muslim helots. The Muslimness of these workers is not sufficient to allow them to overcome the institutionalised social exclusion common to Westphalian-model states. Nor is it sufficient to overturn the internalised global racial order that is constituted by privileging Europeanness (whiteness) over non-Europeanness. Rather, the petro-economies of the Arabian Peninsula are perversely happy to pay the wages of whiteness as a marker of their prosperity and 'modernity'. The emergence of a Muslim subject position, even within nation-states in which Muslims are subordinated and marginalised, reinforces the idea that being a Muslim is not part of the process of nation-building.

By seeing Muslim identity as diasporic it is possible to affirm its political nature, while accepting that it is without a state. Since it is not a specific empirical group of Muslim population that is diasporic (for example Palestinians), but it is being a Muslim itself that is in a condition of diaspora.

The notion of diaspora that I am advocating for the *ummah* is not based on racialised notions of ethnicity (in the form of a common descent from an originary homeland or ancestor), nor is it merely metaphoric in the sense of trying to come to terms with the mismatch between peoples and places. I do not make the claim that Muslim identity is organic, but I do argue that for various reasons it is the subject position that currently has greater prominence than other forms of identification for those who describe themselves or are described by others as Muslims.

I am also aware that there are many among those who would be constituted as Muslims who would reject the political significance of that appellation and who would refuse to accept the idea that there is a *ummah*. The idea of the *ummah* as a diaspora is an attempt to come to terms with the limits and the crisis of the nation-state. As forces and developments associated with globalisation have weakened the institutional rigidity of the Westphalian-type state, cracks and gaps began to appear in the international state system that provided the terrain for politics. Given the mobile and constructed nature of social identities, these fissures within the dominant institutional forms of the nation-state have allowed different kinds of collectives to be articulated, taking advantages of these gaps. These formations seep through the Westphalian edifice, creating political formations that are neither in nor out of the nation-state, but that have an undecidable relationship to it. In this sense, diaspora is the name of this undecidable political formation.

This logic of diaspora suggests an attempt to create a full subjectivity in the form of the nation in the context wherein the nation cannot be completed. One way of thinking of the *ummah* is to see it as the remainder of an incomplete political project which, if it had been successful, would have produced a cultural formation that would have been as remarkable or unremarkable as the Chinese one. The processes associated with globalisation have led to the denationalisation of peripheral nation-state forms at the same time as the expansion of the central nations. The division of Muslimistan into nation-states has made it difficult to sustain a distinct Muslim identity. The process of globalisation has meant, at least for peripheral states, the erosion of the Westphalian type of state, which has helped open up the possibility of the reconfiguration of Muslim subjectivity in a way that is less and less particular and more and more universal. The inability of the *ummah* to fully articulate itself as universal means that it is caught in the logic of diaspora. The *ummah* interrupts and prevents the nation from finding closure and, at the same time, it points to another nation that will come into being at some point in the future. In this, the *ummah* is a becoming—it is a horizon as well as an actuality. The current world is characterised by two types of decentring. There is the decentring of the West that marks the end of the Age of Europe and there is the decentring of the peripheral nation-state that is associated with globalisation. It is in this nexus between these two forms of decentring that we can locate the *ummah*, and it is this location that gives it its diasporic form.

8

CALIPHATE

I

According to Faisal Devji (2005: 70), the contemporary notion of the caliphate should be understood as a metaphysical category rather than a political vision, since there is no viable strategy that could see its restoration. I am not convinced that such a sharp distinction between the metaphysical and the political is particularly useful in helping us understand the significance of the caliphate. I tend to read in such distinctions another instance of the idea of the scandal of Islam. Such a distinction betrays a notion of politics that is derived from liberalism and, as such, it confuses politics with mere administration. The idea that political visions are the same as administrative blueprints circulates in commentaries on the politics of Islamism and does not really accord with many historical studies, which seem to show that political transformation and struggle are waged through the medium of contending visions and not opposing detailed administrative blueprints.[1] The caliphate may well only be an ideal, but that is precisely what makes its articulation a political act. The question that needs to be asked is why should the caliphate be idealised almost eighty years after its demise? Why is it that the idea of the caliphate has begun to circulate in public discourse? How are we to understand the appeal of the caliphate in the contemporary *ummah*? I would like to suggest an answer to these questions by contextualising the caliphate in terms of the diasporic condition of Muslims.

In the previous chapter I suggested that it might be helpful to think of the *ummah* as a global diaspora, because Muslims are homeless in this world. The assertion of a Muslim subjectivity when there is no overarching political structure that can represent this subjectivity at the global level creates a condition in which a substantial group of people are increasingly alienated from the world order. Perhaps one of the reasons why the plight of the Palestinians resonates among the *ummah* is precisely because it is a metaphor for Muslims everywhere: the exercise of coloniality over the *ummah* finds its brutal dramatisation in the Palestinian struggle for justice. The diasporic condition of Muslims, however, does not admit a spatial redemptive return, as they are not connected to any specific territory, and, because the homelessness of Muslims is global, there is no specific place to return to.[2] Thus, for Muslims redemption lies not in a return to a homeland but a rooting in the world. That is, a resolution of the discrepancy created by assertive subjectivity and its marginalisation within the world order requires an overarching political structure able to suture Muslims as Muslims to the so-called international community. The caliphate seems to promise such a rooting. The growing prominence of the idea of the caliphate among Muslims can be seen as a dawning recognition that the institution of the caliphate may provide an escape route for Muslims from a world of constant subjugation and marginalisation.

This helps account for the way in which the caliphate has started to appear in public debates about matters Islamicate. A number of statements from Al-Qaeda have alluded to it (Lawrence, 2005), political movements such as Hizb ut-Tahrir have campaigned for its restoration for many years and one could even argue that Khomeini, who saw in the caliphate the means of restraining the Great Satan, became a de facto caliph, even if he was unable to institutionalise the caliphate in the office of the *velayat-e faqih* (Sayyid, 2003: xi; Sayyid, 2013).[3] The idea that the caliphate may empower Muslimness, however, is no longer found only in Muslim circles. Non-Muslim policy and opinion makers have expressed their concern that the caliphate-to-come may play an empowering role in the not so distant future. From 2006 onwards, senior members of the Bush regime began to speak of the caliphate as the objective of Al-Qaeda and similar groupings. For them and their allies among the commentariat the caliphate stands for a revanchist 'totalitarian Islamic empire' embracing much of Muslimistan. The emergence of the caliphate as part of the chitter-chatter of Western geopolitical discourse can be seen in the way in which it is deemed to be one of the possible futures of the world. A study by the National Intelligence Council commissioned by the US Department of Defence outlined eight scenarios for the world in 2020, and one of these scenarios included the establishment of a new caliphate by the grandson of Osama bin Laden (2004: 83–91). The caliphate has also been used as a way of differentiating the current quests for Muslim autonomy from past anti-colonial struggles, which are presented as being compatible with Western values. The contemporary quest for Muslim autonomy, in contrast, is considered to be antithetical to such values. The restoration of the caliphate appears as one of the quartet of principles that drive mobilisations in the name of Islam and which cannot be conceded under any circumstances by the West.[4] So, even though it could be argued that since at least 1342/1924 the shadow of the caliphate has hung over the deliberations and discussions of many Muslim intellectuals,[5] the Western discovery of the salience of the caliphate in the contemporary world owes a great deal to the War on Terror and the reaction, in the first place, to the pronouncements of Al-Qaeda and subsequently to other Islamist movements.

It is, however, often pointed out that Al-Qaeda's references to the caliphate are not as central to its political project as has often been suggested (Pankhurst, 2010). There is good reason to believe that Al-Qaeda did not make explicit references to the caliphate. It can, however, be shown that Al-Qaeda had some background awareness of the caliphate and its role within Islamicate notions of political authority. For example, Al-Qaeda saw itself as establishing an Islamic emirate in Afghanistan, a polity theoretically subordinate to, and thus compatible with, the caliphate-to-come. Al-Qaeda's initial programme tended to focus on issues like the eradication of Western support for tyrannies in Muslimistan, demands for effective sovereignty for governments of Muslimistan and the end of the occupation of Muslim lands. To a degree, these claims can be encased within the morphology of the Westphalian order, and as such can be seen as being analogous to anti-colonial national liberation struggles, in which the place of the caliphate would appear to be rather marginal. For organisations like Hizb ut-Tahrir, on the other hand, the caliphate is far more significant, at least in explicit formulations. For them and similar organisations the caliphate is the only legitimate form that an Islamicate polity can take. The caliphate seems to have a far greater resonance than was expected by many who, guided by Orientalist readings, saw its demise in 656/1258 with the sacking of Baghdad by the Mongol Hulegu Khan.[6] For good or ill, the caliphate has been released into the general field of discursivity.

II

It is possible to think of the caliphate as having five different meanings. It can mean a polity in which the boundaries of the *ummah* correspond exactly to its frontiers. In other words, the caliphate would be coextensive with the totality of the world's Muslims. Such a conception, however, has no historical analogy since it can be shown that even in the time of the early Islamicate state (10–132/632–750), and despite pronouncements of many prominent *ulama* that Muslims should not live outside the borders of an Islamicate polity, there have always been such communities (Muslims in Ethiopia, for example). A conception of the caliphate based on an isomorphic insistence on the limits of the *ummah* would seem to consign it to the realm of human impossibility. This reading of the caliphate is often used by those who are critical of its appearance: for them, the caliphate was never able to unify the *ummah* and therefore it cannot be expected to do so in the future. Underlying these arguments is the assumption that political unity can only be established on a basis far more sturdy than that afforded by religious affiliation.

A more plausible conception of the caliphate would understand it as a sole Muslim polity. This would approximate it to the situation that prevailed from the successful conclusion of the wars of Ridda (10–11/632–633) to the establishment of the Abbasid regime in 132/750 CE. Such a conception of the caliphate would be able to accommodate the discrepancy between its frontiers and the boundaries of the *ummah* and, at the same time, it could assume for itself the political leadership of the *ummah*, since there would be no other Muslim political entity. This would imply that the bulk of Muslims would be citizens of this state.

Another way of thinking about the caliphate would be to see it as a polity that exercises leadership over Muslims. A caliphate understood in these terms would only require a piece of territory sufficient to house a caliph and his (or perhaps even her) staff. It could even be a mini city-state as long its leadership role was acknowledged.[7] In this version of the caliphate it would be similar to the Pope and the Vatican city-state.

A fourth take on the caliphate would emphasise its internal coherence rather than its external relationship with the rest of the Muslim community. In such an understanding the caliphate would be an arrangement of institutions and practices like those found in historical manifestations of caliphates. In which case, the caliphate would refer to the abstraction of these arrangements, so that the caliphate would exist wherever such approximations of governmental practices could be found, regardless of scale or situation. Thus, the caliphate would simply refer to an authorised version of a legitimate 'Islamic state'.

The fifth way to understand the caliphate is to see it as a metaphor for an Islamicate great power. This would be similar to the situation that has existed since the time of the battles of Yarmuk (15/636) and Qaidassasy (15/636) and the demise of the Ottoman caliphate, a period when it could be argued the world has nearly always known an Islamicate great power.[8] That is, the caliphate does not need to represent the entirety of the *ummah* or the exclusivity of a solitary Islamicate polity; but it does, at the minimum, need to have the capability of a great power. This conceptualisation of the caliphate appears to be the most fruitful, for an Islamicate great power could end the marginalisation of Muslims qua Muslims from the world. In other words, the redemptive return of the Muslim diaspora would be established not by a territorial but rather a political gesture. In other words, the end of the diasporic condition of the *ummah* means not a return to a homeland but the restoration of a great power.

The term 'great power' belongs to the European politics of the nineteenth century,[9] specifically to the concert of Europe inaugurated in the anti-Napoleonic coalitions, and the desire by the ruling elites of Austria, Russia, Britain and Prussia to avoid another hegemonic war in Europe (Holsti, 1992: 30–57). Even if the vocabulary of what a great power is focuses on Europe, there are reasons for thinking that the category has wider relevance and is a function of any ensemble of interacting polities and uneven distributions of capabilities between those interacting units. Great powers are polities that have significantly greater capabilities than the other units they interact with, and thus they are able to pursue policies with much fewer constraints than other states in an international system. Examples of great powers abound: New Kingdom Egypt, the Hittite Empire, Assyria and Babylon in the so-called Amarna system of 1000 BCE (Cohen and Westbrook, 2000); Zhou and Qing in Spring and Autumn China; the jostling Janpadas of pre-Mayauran India. It is the relative rather than absolute distribution of capabilities that determines great power status. For example city-states like Uruk and Lagash, Sparta and Athens, Milan and Venice could all be considered as great powers, even if their resources and capacities were dwarfed by other contemporary polities. The boundary of an international system is as crucial as the uneven distribution of capabilities in determining great power status. The expansion of the European state system of the sixteenth to eighteenth centuries to encompass the planet means that great powers cannot be merely specific to a region. It means that the resources and capabilities required to sustain great power status have to be on a continental scale.

Great powers are the strongest participants in an international system that they often guarantee and lead (Schmitt, 2003: 190–1; Waltz, 1979: 194–5). The exercise of leadership means the capacity to make decisions, a capacity that is linked to questions of sovereignty. In other words great powers are those polities who are able to make the rules of international order rather than simply obey them. Their capacity for action is far greater than that of ordinary polities. To have this freedom to manoeuvre means that, ultimately, a great power must be able to insulate itself from threats to its existence. A great power must have sufficient military strength to deter coercion from other great powers. The centrality of military capabilities to great powers is not simply a conceit of realpolitik, but arises from the primacy of the political itself.[10] In other words, to the extent that the political is determined by the intensity of the distinction between groupings of friends and enemies, it follows that the ability to wage war is inherent to any manifestation of the political. There is an ever-present possibility that a dispute between two groupings could reach such an intensity that the conflict could become an existential struggle. This possibility of an existential conflict ensures that the military, as the means of waging such a struggle, has an organic relationship to the political. The recourse to armed, organised violence is a standing reserve that can be called upon when conflict goes beyond a particular threshold. Great powers without the potential to wage war can only come about when there is no possibility of making a distinction between friends and enemies: a completely pacified world in which there is no possibility of warfare would be a world without politics (Schmitt, 1996: 35).[11] Thus, great powers have military capabilities that are in a class beyond other states, which enables them to contemplate large-scale warfare (Bull, 1982: 201–5; French, 1990: xii).

Great powers contribute to the norms and values of an international system whose interests and identity are principally supported by the routine functioning of the system (Gilpin, 1981: 29). They are expected to exercise special obligations and rights in relation to the rest of the international system, and this exercise of special prerogatives has widespread legitimacy within the international community (Bull, 1977/ 1982: 201–5). Weak states—those with a low level of 'sociopolitical cohesion' arising from their failure to integrate civil society and government—tend to follow the leadership of great powers and accept their legitimacy (Buzan and Little, 2000: 254–5). The capacity of weak states to alter the 'rules of the game' is restricted and therefore they tend to work within the terms of the current spatial order, partly because their capabilities are limited and also because, as a consequence of low sociopolitical cohesion, their ruling elites very often identify their interests and values with those of the great powers (Gilpin, 1981: 31). The socialisation of local elites into the values and norms of the great powers helps to restrict the capacity of weak states to make decisions about their fate. This socialisation is often achieved by reconfiguring the divisions in the societies of weak states to produce a grouping that identifies with one or more of the great powers.[12]

Great powers help sustain and anchor political subjectivities, especially in hostile environments. Examples include not only the support provided by the Soviet Union or the People's Republic of China to communist groups throughout the world, but also the way in which the United States, United Kingdom and France also made possible certain political positions. In very broad terms and making allowances for all kinds of local contingencies and caveats, the political positions underwritten by great powers are easier to sustain than those that are continually opposed by all great powers. Therefore, conflict between great powers is most likely to produce conditions in which political projects that great powers oppose can be established. For example, the October Revolution in Russia was pivotal in breaking what Du Bois (1989) described as the international colour line, thus allowing colonised subject populations to leverage sustained support from the exterior as a means of challenging colonial rule. Political projects that are opposed by all the great powers are likely to require major upheavals to give them space to develop. This surely is the case with Islamism, where there is an informal concert of great powers that oppose the Islamist project of establishing autonomous Islamicate political structures. It is relatively easy to see how the United States and its Western 'allies', China, Russia and India share for purely contingent historical reasons what they would consider to be irredentist challenges in which Muslims feature strongly: Palestine, Eastern Turkestan, Chechnya and Kashmir to name the most obvious examples.

An Islamicate great power would need to have both the capacity and the willingness to represent Muslims globally. The question of capabilities rests upon the caliphate's status as a great power; the question of its willingness depends on its Islamicate character. In the rest of this chapter I shall focus on the question of its capabilities, and in subsequent chapters I will address the question of its willingness to represent Muslims globally as a function of its Islamicate identity. What capacities would be necessary for an Islamicate great power?

III

Imagine a country larger than Russia, more populous than China, with an economy bigger than Japan's. Would not such a country qualify as a great power? This country is not purely an exercise in imaginative speculation: it would emerge if the fifty-seven current members of the Organization of Islamic Cooperation were able to turn their ramshackle body into an overarching political structure. Such a polity would have enough agricultural resources to feed itself, and it would have sufficient capital resources to finance its own socioeconomic development. The marriage between capital surplus and labour shortage regions and labour surplus and capital shortage regions would help stimulate rapid economic growth. The combined military capabilities of such a state would be formidable. It would be a sovereign entity able to make decisions on behalf of Muslims and channel Islamic norms and values into the international system. It is hard to imagine the reasons why such an entity would not be a major force within the international system. Why is there no such state or even a state approximating such dimensions? The existence of regional blocs such as ASEAN or Mercosur puts into sharp relief the failure of effective regional integration among Muslimistani states. The existence of other continental-sized *grossraums* (for example the Russian Federation, the United States, China) suggests that there are no necessary geographic, demographic or economic factors that would prevent the formation of an Islamicate state on such a scale. Therefore, the question why no such state exists is worth considering.

One way to account for this failure is to argue that Muslimistan is not a viable entity. In other words, what is common to Muslimistan is Islam, and that is not sufficient to provide the degree of homogeneity that would allow Muslimistan to be a *grossraum*. The idea that being a Muslim is a rather fragile and superficial basis upon which to build a political structure is, as we have seen in previous chapters, a fairly wide-spread trope. In other words, identifying oneself as a Muslim in matters of devotional practices may be fairly sturdy at the individual or congregational levels, but it is assumed that such practices cannot be translated into the stuff of great power formation.

The break-up of united Pakistan in 1391/1971 has almost become a clichéd illustration of arguments that Muslim identity is not strong enough to sustain a contemporary polity.[13] It is asserted that, because Pakistan was founded on the notion that Muslims of British-ruled India constituted a nation and therefore deserved a polity that reflected that, the blood-stained separation of Bangladesh from Pakistan is not only a specific failure of the 'two nation' theory but in general, points to the inadequacy of Muslim subjectivity as a means of underwriting polities. If these differences between the west and east wings of a state formed on the basis of a Muslim political identity could not be overcome, it is unlikely that Islam could be a meaningful way of identifying any possible *grossraum*, given the differences it would be called on to bridge would be far greater.

The claims for the fragility of Muslim political identity are based on a disregard for the actual working of political identities.[14] As I argued in previous chapters there is no specific form of identification that is preordained to be the building block of a meaningful social group. The assertion that Muslim identity is less sturdy, less authentic and far more fictional than ethnicity or class and is therefore incapable of constituting and sustaining a collective identity is little more than a reflection of the idea that the political is impossible for the non-West.[15] Different forms of identification can emerge as various demands are mobilised and coalesce into collective agents. The emergence of a Muslim subjectivity makes it possible to conclude that societies in which the prevailing culture is informed by the venture of Islam can constitute a distinct and viable spatial order. The example of the break-up of Pakistan, if it demonstrates anything, demonstrates the failure of Westphalian notions of political community. Despite the mobilisation of the Muslims of South Asia to identify with Islam, the institutionalisation of that movement into the state of Pakistan was organised on Kemalist principles, which emphasised national cohesion in terms of linguistic and ethnic homogeneity. Thus the attempt to downgrade Bengali as an official language, the internalisation of colonial racial discourses around the 'martial races' and restrictions on citizenship that prevented even Muslims from South Asia becoming Pakistani citizens indicate not that Muslim identity was insufficient to bind the two parts of Pakistan, but rather that it was abandoned in favour of a project of building a Westphalian-style nation-state with its insistence on linguistic, cultural and ethnic homogeneity as necessary for high 'sociopolitical cohesion'. The break-up of united Pakistan should be seen as another failure of this Westphalian-inspired Kemalist model of nation building, rather than an illustration of the inability of Muslim political identity to sustain a unified state structure.[16]

IV

The question of why there is no Islamicate great power requires answers that do not begin by asserting that Muslimness is inherently incapable of being a sustained source of political cohesion. Being a Muslim is no more difficult or easy than being Chinese or British—what makes it difficult is its articulation in specific institutional contexts. One can trace four sets of often overlapping arguments that are made to account for the inability of Muslimistani states to effectively pool their resources and energies.[17] First, the nature of Muslimistani economies, geared as they are towards North-South rather than inter-Muslimistani trade, is used to explain the failure of Islamicate attempts at economic integration.[18] It is assumed that without prior economic integration, projects of political unification will face insurmountable hurdles.

Second, some maintain that the petty nature of governing elites of Muslimistan precludes selfless cooperation among them. It has to be pointed out that the venal nature of such elites, however, does not prevent them from cooperating with each other when needs must, for example, as co-participants in the War on Terror. Nor is it obvious outside classical historiographical accounts (in Thucydides, Livy or Tabari) that virtue (in a moral sense) is a necessary requirement for successful political endeavours, and certainly it does not follow that Western European elites, who managed to fight two world wars in the space of thirty years, were any less driven by jealousies and rivalries than Muslimistani elites.[19]

Third, the lack of success of Muslim projects of unity is also blamed on the degree of heterogeneity of Muslimistan and, in particular, on the deep sectarian and ethnic divisions that are said to exist in those societies. This line is also fairly popular among Muslim opinion makers who cite 'fitna' as a perennial problem for the *ummah*. Some of the more theologically inclined tend to see such divisions as arising from the incorrigible nature of humankind. Others, who have internalised discourses of racialised governmentality, see it as a product of cultural/biological factors that are hardwired in the human persona: the inability to deal with ethnically marked differences. Even if one was to accept any value in such reasoning (and there are a good many reasons not to do so) it is far from clear why the degree of heterogeneity in Muslimistan is considered to be more divisive than heterogeneity in Europe, India, Russia or China.

Finally, there are the panoply of arguments that consider the artificial nature of most Muslimistani states as being an effective barrier to any sustained coordination and cooperation among those states. Specifically, because the boundaries of most Muslimistani states reflect the priorities of European colonial administrations and intra-European international agreements, the states contained within these colonial borders lack any deep organic roots with the populations they govern. This is seen as a major impediment to the national cohesion that could allow such states to pursue policies of integration without risking disintegration. The notion of 'artificial' states is a fairly pernicious way in which ex-colonial racially marked polities are often represented. Such accounts have a certain amnesia about the so-called natural states of Western Europe, where the Enlightenment-inspired narrative about 'natural borders' has helped to confuse cartographic exercises with geographic expressions (Lustick, 1996: 657). The 'natural' frontiers of UK or France are no more 'natural' than those of Pakistan or Iraq, and the process of creating Britain and France and their seemingly organic national majorities out of disparate societies, cultures and histories was a process of naturalising the contingent and often arbitrary crystallisations of forces. These countries were not the discovery of some underlying national essence; they were (and are) invented, like Western countries. For example, the British state did not find a British nation; it invented it. The problem confronting Muslimistan is not that its polities are artificial per se, but rather that they seem to have found it difficult to manufacture national majorities from the poisoned inheritance that European colonialism often bequeathed them, either directly or indirectly.

These responses to why there is no contemporary Islamicate great power are at best partial and at worst misleading. They assume that the proper unit of analysis is the nation-state of the post-caliphate universe. (This, of course, is one of the key features of Kemalism.) The fundamental problem with these arguments is that they fail to bring a historical or comparative perspective into the equation. Great powers are formed in the context of successful contestation with other states, and these contestations often crystallise into bouts of sustained major military conflict (Gilpin, 1981). Successful 'state-building wars' have been the main mechanism of state and great power formation (Tilly, 1975; McNeil, 1982; Mann, 1986; Porter, 1994: 11–20; Lustick, 1996: 646). For example, the United Kingdom as a great power was built upon the foundations laid by Plantagenet and Tudor monarchs who fought a series of wars to establish English rule over the 'Atlantic Archipelago' (Davis, 2000). The transformation of Muscovy from one of the tributaries of the Golden Horde into Russia involved a sustained series of military conquests that brought under its control various Khanates of steppes to the east and south, as well as Slavic territories to the west and north. Crucial to the emergence of Russia as a great power was its military ability to overcome challenges posed both by steppe and agrarian warfare (Lustick, 1996; Lieven, 2001; Stevens, 2007). The unification of Germany required Prussia to win a number of wars between 1864 and 1871 (Showalter, 2004). The struggle to absorb smaller political entities led these centralising regimes to fight recalcitrant notables, heretical sects, rebellious provinces and other potential rival centres of power. Such successful military campaigns required a mobilisation of resources and expanded state regulation and supervision.

A number of post-caliphate Muslim states have, at various points, been touted as possible candidates for an Islamicate great power to come: united Pakistan, Nasserite Egypt, Saudi Arabia, the Islamic Republic of

Iran, Saddamite Iraq, even 'moderate' Turkey. The reason for including a country in this list is often the half-hearted rhetoric of various leaderships of these countries or alarmist projections of the potential of these states to exercise a leadership role on behalf of the *ummah*, or sometimes the requirements of Western interests for a regional gendarme. Currently, in terms of GNP (measured in terms of purchasing power parity), the ten leading states in Muslimistan are: Indonesia, Turkey, Iran, Saudi Arabia, Pakistan, Egypt, Bangladesh, Malaysia, Algeria and Nigeria.[20] In addition, two out of every three Muslims in the world lives in one of these countries. It is likely that if the core of an Islamicate great power was going to emerge it would emerge from the ranks of these countries.

Any potential Islamicate contender for great power status that was seriously tempted by the success of Piedmont or Prussia or Muscovy or the American thirteen colonies would, however, have to overcome a series of legal, strategic and political barriers that foreclose the military path to achieving great power status (Lustick, 1996: 675). As this has been historically the most successful means of establishing great power status, its exclusion from the repertoire of Muslimistani states means that their ability to become great powers is greatly circumscribed. Any attempt to integrate the current plethora of Islamicate states into a larger union is likely to encounter strong resistance from forces (both internal and external) wedded to the current world order. Thus, the most significant factor impeding the possibility of an Islamicate great power is the international system itself, which not only embodies a generalised antipathy towards state-making warfare, but also specific geopolitical and cultural contexts that impose further challenges.[21]

Overcoming these obstacles would require reforms that seek 'to increase economic capabilities, to increase military strength, to develop clever strategies' and diplomatic 'moves to strengthen and enlarge one's alliances or to weaken or shrink an opposing one' (Waltz, 1979: 118). The content of such a judicious mix of policies is provided by conventional statecraft. A world order consists not only of the arrangement of polities, but also the institutionalisation of particular forms of knowledge and belief. It offers a 'postivisation' of the world in which particular background understandings are taken for granted and institutionalised. Thus, what constitutes economic capabilities and the policies needed to enhance these capabilities, would have a very different content if understood within terms of the neo-liberal hegemony or a non-capitalist framework.

Great powers often emerge in the context of a hegemonic crisis in the world order. Such a crisis not only displaces or weakens existing great powers but also undermines the prevailing intellectual-moral certainties that sustained and supported the world order. In such situations, the paradigm of conventional statecraft is disclosed as being inadequate to the exigencies of the times. The 'latecomer' status that has hindered the possibility of a post-Ottoman Islamicate great power also means that what Muslimistani states can aspire to is heavily constrained by a statecraft steeped in coloniality and unable to imagine a post-Westphalian and post-Western world order. Not only does the quest for Muslim autonomy collide with the interests and integrity of many existing major powers, it also interrupts the paradigm of conventional statecraft.[22] As long as the countries of Muslimistan remain within the horizon of conventional statecraft they are unlikely to escape from their fate as subordinated actors in a violent and hierarchal world order. In terms of conventional statecraft, Muslim aspirations for the caliphate are both dangerous and impossible.

Given these obstacles, it seems self-evident that the caliphate cannot be realised and Muslim aspirations on its behalf are either foolhardy or tragic. The desire by Muslims for a caliphate seems to be unmatched by the ability of Muslimistani governments acting alone or in concert to meet such popular demands. This lack of delivery is not surprising and simply emphasises the declining legitimacy of most governments that rule over Muslimistan. If the barriers, however, to the caliphate are so great, then surely the failure of these governments to pursue a forlorn policy should be admired as an act of prudential statecraft, rather than despised as an abrogation of their duties. Even if Islamists were to acquire state power, the state would need to operate in an international environment that would quickly limit its capacity to enact policies that entrenched Muslimness in strategic areas. The fate of Somalia beckons. The Union of Islamic Courts, which after seventeen years of stateless violent strife brought order to Mogadishu and allowed the society and economy to function, was overthrown by a US-backed Ethiopian invasion. As consequence of that invasion, Mogadishu once again became a playground for various warlords. This illustrates the difficulties faced by any polity that wishes to follow a different script. If it is successful it can face very grave pressure to go back to the usual repertoire of statecraft.

The absence of the caliphate represents the lack of a mechanism by which Muslims as Muslims could become at home in the world. It means that the obligation to defend Muslims has fallen increasingly upon Muslim individuals and organisations.[23] The involvement of Muslimistani states in these mobilisations has been too often fragmentary, fissiparous or cynical. In this context of coloniality the articulation of the caliphate as a great power becomes necessary for the continuation and deepening of decolonisation. It would contribute to the fundamental pluralism of the world; it would allow the diasporic condition of the *ummah* to be redeemed as a political structure that is able to promote and protect Muslim autonomy. The problems that Muslims face stem not from cultural inadequacies or individual pathologies, but from political weakness. This weakness ultimately comes about because there is no Islamicate great power. The restoration of the caliphate as a great power threatens the continuation of coloniality, providing Muslims with a means by which a 'people without history' are able to become 'world-historical'. It would deepen the process of decolonisation, and could have the potential to erode Western hegemony and coloniality. The caliphate as a great power would be both a voice of the *ummah* and its echo, the expression of Muslim autonomy as well as its engine. The caliphate would make space for the cultivation of Muslim autonomy, represent the *ummah* and restrain the 'Great Satan'.

Given all the difficulties of realising an Islamicate great power, the question still remains whether the 'restoration' of the caliphate is possible. Furthermore, even if it was possible to imagine an Islamicate great power, what guarantees are there that it would be able to maintain its Islamicate character? What would prevent an Islamicate great power being a xenophobic authoritarian entity, a sort of Saudi Arabia on steroids? Even if an Islamicate great power could avoid the fate of a narrowly conceived and dogmatically exclusionary citizenship, there is a danger that it would become just another state, and its Islamicate character would only be of cosmetic significance. In other words, what would prevent the caliphate from being recuperated into the romance of realpolitik? This problem is continually faced by the current states of Muslimistan; however, the problem becomes starker in the case of an Islamicate great power, since such a state will have a representational role for the *ummah* and Islam. In the next chapter, I will examine how the Islamic(ate) character of any Islamicate great power could be established and maintained, and the possible pathways to achieving such a political entity.

9

ORDER

I

A group of worshippers wait impatiently for the appearance of the Mahdi. They are however, confronted by a disturbing realisation:

Because the Imam is hidden and must not be found by his enemies, we must be ready to recognize him in the most unexpected disguises. He who will one day inherit all the world's riches might come in rags. He who is the wisest of the wisest might appear in the form of a madman. He who is all piety and devotion might commit the worst sins. (Maalouf, 2002: 32)

In this story we see echoes of the way in which many Muslims currently await the establishment of an Islamic state that closely approximates the virtuous order established by the Prophet (pbuh) in Medina. The problem, however, is not only pragmatic and strategic—how could such a structure come about? It is a more basic one: what would an Islamic order look like, how could we identify it, in what way would it be different from other orders that exist? The difficulty of recognising the Mahdi in this fictionalised account echoes the difficulties of identifying an Islamic political order. This becomes a pressing issue in the wake of the dismantling of the caliphate, for the caliphate could provide a sense of historical continuity in which Islamic(ate) identity was a product not of any specific sets of practices or behaviours, but rather of a more or less accepted genealogical sequence. European colonial rule and the advent of Kemalism helped to institutionalise a rupture within this autonomous Islamicate past. Nor can the application of the view of classical Islamicate scholarship on the practices that constitute a legitimate Islamic order provide authoritative answers, partly because the expansion of the activities undertaken by public authorities exceeds what was considered possible in this scholarship. More importantly, the conditions of reception in which Islamicate learning functioned no longer apply. In other words, the rhetorical and regulatory performance of classical Islamicate political philosophy has become decontextualised and subject to contestations that do not allow Islamicate scholars to play an authoritative role in the deliberations on the future of the *ummah*.

The problem of discerning the Islamic character of any political entity can be illustrated by a consideration of the decision made in January 1991 by the then autocrat of Iraq, Saddam Hussein, to add *takbir* to the Iraqi flag (rumour has that it was written in his own hand).[1] The decision was made in the context of impending Iraqi defeat at the hands of the American-led invasion. Saddam Hussein's decision signalled a number of very obvious attempts to establish the Islamic rather than the purely nationalist or secularist credentials of his regime.[2] Must we conclude that Saddam Hussein had, by this gesture, confirmed his and his regime's Islamic credentials? The obvious answer many Muslims would give is that Saddam's record over a thirty-year period did not accord with the policies and values that they would consider to be Islamic. They would see Saddam's gesture as a cynical ploy showing the way in which Islam can be used by tyrants for their own purposes. These responses are fairly common; however, they do not actually help us understand why Saddam would make that gesture. In other words, even as we concede the instrumental nature of adding a *takabir* to the Iraqi flag by such a brutal regime, it does not explain why that instrumentalism would take such a form. When I say that it does not explain the reason, I mean that it does not explain it in a universe not dominated by essentialism. For those who accept that Iraq is part of Muslimistan and thus Islam is always there, it does not apparently require much analysis as to why Saddam or other rulers try and purchase legitimacy by using the currency of Islam. In fact, it would be rather odd if they did not. The problem of course, is that if this was the case it would have been the case in the 1970s, in the 1960s, in the 1950s and so on; but we know that the place of Islam and its ability to act as the medium of legitimacy has fluctuated in intensity over time. Why Saddam Hussein made an effort to establish the Islamic character of his regime, even if it is a superficial and cynical gesture, is nonetheless interesting. It tells us something about the salience of Islam in the *ummah* after the abolition of the caliphate and inauguration of the Kemalist repertoire of governance throughout Muslimistan. Given that all those who govern Muslimistan now attempt to claim a legitimacy derived in large part from Islam in some shape or form, the problem of identifying a proper Islam and a correct Islam becomes intensified. If all those who rule Muslims can claim to be representing the virtues of Islam, how is it possible to conclude that such and such government is Islamic or more Islamic than others? What exactly would be the policies and values that a contemporary state adopts to ensure its Islamic character? In previous chapters we have seen how the question of what Islam is and who Muslims are cannot be answered through a focus on the ontic. An enumeration of the qualities of being Muslim or the iterations of Islam and local inflexions in various locales is inadequate. The Islamic character of an Islamic great power cannot be arrived at by simply listing the various descriptive features of such an entity. I will expand on this point later in this chapter, but next I want to consider two major attempts to pin down the Islamic identity of sociopolitical arrangements. In the post-caliphate universe it is possible to discern two main attempts at institutionalising a collective Islamicate identity: Islamic economics and the Islamic state.

II

One of the most sustained attempts to articulate a distinct Islamic identity to matters of socioeconomic organisation has been the project of Islamic economics. For almost eighty years many well-meaning Muslim economists have struggled to formulate an Islamic economics as a distinct academic discipline but, more importantly, as an alternative means of organising a national economy. An Islamic system of production and consumption would be one in which Islamic mores regulate the economy. Islamic economics emerges by attempting to consolidate Qur'anic injunctions and hadith literature into a comprehensive economic system. The beginnings of a distinct Islamic economics that could be differentiated from both capitalist market-led economies and socialist command-economies can be traced to the 1930s and to the work of

Sayyid Abul-Ala Mawdudi. In 1947, Mawdudi published *The Economic Problem of Man and its Islamic Solution* in which he sketched out what became Islamic economics. Mawdudi saw the economic problem in terms of the disruption of social harmony. He rejected communism for its economism. For Mawdudi '[t]he fundamental mistake of communism lies in the fact that it treats the economic problem and then tries to revolve the whole of human life around this axis' (Mawdudi, 1992: 32). Islam offered a holistic solution to the economic problem (Khan, 1994: 52). Mawdudi argued that an economy informed by the moral precepts of Islam would ensure the absence of the extremes of prosperity and poverty, and would assure the dignified livelihood of all.[3] Thus, not only would Islamic morality domesticate and discipline the excesses of modern economy and its effects on social harmony, it would also become a platform for disseminating Islam.

Such a project highlights the relevance of Islam in the contemporary world, given the place of the economy in the way in which ordinary lives are imagined. It demonstrates that the only role for Islam to play is as the source of private morality, but it can also be an instrument for engineering a greater degree of social justice and cohesion. If it was going to be argued that Islam was a total way of life not confined to the mosque or Fridays, it would need to show a relevance to people's lives beyond matters of moral education and spiritual well-being. Islamic economics was to be part of an overall Islamic system. According to Mawdudi such an 'economic system has a deep relationship with the political, juridical, legal, cultural and social system of Islam' (Mawdudi, 1992: 43).

The recognition of the importance of economics is something that Mawdudi sees as a function of modernity. It is likely, however, that it is not modernity but the success of the Bolshevik takeover of Czarist Russia that helped to establish the importance of a distinct economic system as a marker of distinct political, cultural and social formation. The October Revolution suggested that an intense geopolitical rivalry necessitated a radically distinct approach to the organisation of economic activity. Prior to that, it had been possible, even within the European sphere, to entertain the most intense form of international conflict without demanding that the conflict represent alternative economic systems. For example, the enmity that defined the sides in the French Revolutionary and Napoleonic Wars (1792–1815) did not have a rival economic system as a major distinguishing feature. Similarly, in the First World War (1914–1918) the conflict between the Central Powers and the Entente powers did not include contending visions of economic systems. It is possible to argue that, from the advent of the Soviet Union in 1917 until its unravelling in 1989–1991, all alternative political orders had to provide a template for economic management that sought to transcend capitalism, to demonstrate that they were actually an alternative rather than simply a continuation of capitalism. The attempt to reduce global conflict to conflict about alternative visions of economy had the consequence of obscuring the political nature of conflict and the possibility of different constructions of conflict other than fundamentally that of class, between the bourgeoisie and the proletariat. For the supporters of Islamic economics, if Islam was to play a public role, it would need to present itself as offering an alternative to capitalism, fascism and communism. To make good on this offer, there needed to be a distinct Islamic method of organising the economy.

The project of Islamic economics is based around three major claims. First, it is claimed that the absence of *riba* (interest) is the hallmark of an Islamic economy, thus, its elimination is vital to the establishment of such an economy and such an establishment would have a beneficial and transformative effect on the rest of society. Second, Islamic economics positions itself as a third way between the free-market excesses associated with capitalism and the authoritarianism of socialist central planning. Islamic economics would facilitate social equality without resorting to the authoritarianism of statist programmes of economic distribution. Third, the project of Islamic economics maintains that an Islamic economy would be based on a holistic sense of well-being, including material and spiritual elements, and it would not be simply driven by profit maximisation. In other words, an Islamic economy would be 'free of interest rates and would provide social justice, equity, and harmony' (Nasr, 2001: 122).

There is no country in Muslimistan that has reorganised its economy along the lines dictated by Islamic economics. Countries like Pakistan, Sudan, Iran and Malaysia have made some attempts in the direction of Islamising their economy but the process has been piecemeal and the results have fallen far short of the standards that the advocates of Islamic economics envisioned (Tripp, 2006: 125). There are three areas that the development of Islamic economics has focused upon: the prohibition of *riba*, the establishment of an Islamic banking system and the state provision of *zakat* (alms). Moving to an interest-free economy has been the cornerstone of Islamic economics.

The efforts to ensure an economy shorn of *riba* have been a major impetus for the development of an Islamic banking sector. In the Islamic banking complex, profit-loss sharing arrangements replace conventional interest payments for provision of various loans and financial services. The provision of sharia-compliant halal financial products runs alongside other forms of economic activity. Islamic banking has proved to be sufficiently lucrative for many major international non-Muslim banks to also become involved in the provision of sharia-compliant banking services.

A number of countries have experimented with state-led systems for the collection and distribution of *zakat*. Nasr sees in the imposition of *zakat* in Pakistan a very modest intervention by the state into provision of welfare functions. He makes the point that while the figures involved were miniscule as a percentage of GDP (amounting to less than 1 per cent), they were still significant in relation to what existed before. The significance of the *zakat* system, however, is not only in terms of the resources distributed as a percentage of GDP. It also involved the recruitment and staffing of large administrative cadres to implement and service the *zakat* system. In the case of Pakistan, the machinery of *zakat* has a number of important effects in terms of supplementing the income of the underemployed. In Malaysia, it is argued that the compulsory collection of *zakat* by the state has had an adverse effect on wealth distribution (Tripp, 2006: 125).

As an overall project of transforming the societies of Muslimistan, the results of Islamic economics have also been disappointing. For the most part, the economies of Muslimistan lag behind the tiger economies of East Asia.[4] As an intellectual field, Islamic economics grew substantially during the 1960s and 1970s as disenchantment with both socialist and liberal economic imaginaries coincided with the transfer of immense financial resources to Muslim oil-exporting countries. As an academic discipline, Islamic economics has not yet developed analytical tools for the explanation of the behaviour of Muslims, it has remained confined to the prescriptive domain (Khan, 1994: 32; Nienhaus, 2010: 95). Islamic economics has not established itself even intellectually as an alternative to capitalist orthodoxy or its socialist rival. Nor can it be said to have made significant contributions to 'Islamic' economic policies

(Nienhaus, 1982: 92). Islamic economics has so far failed to address the fundamental issues that affect most of Muslimistan.

Timur Kuran, one of most trenchant critics of Islamic economics, concludes that the significance of Islamic economics lies not in the economy but in politics as a means of bolstering the place of Islam in society (2004: 5). Kuran argues that Islamic economics has retarded development of Muslimistani countries (ibid.: 121–48) and promoted Islamism. This project of moralising the economy too often ends up being the effective sum total of 'Islamic economics', and mainly consists of a range of economic activities that are considered reprehensible and are the focus of corrective measures, while the major issues of economic structure are ignored. For example, most of the Islamist parties have not been consistent or principled advocates of land reform, minimum wage or other innovative measures to widen the access to capital, even in situations in which these issues are major contributors to inequalities in Muslimistan. Kuran (2004) sees the failure of Islamic economics as not merely empirical but conceptual: there can be no distinctly Islamic way to manage an economy, build a bridge or cure an epidemic.[5]

There is however, a difference in how a bridge would be built in continental Europe or the United States. The difference may not be the most obvious one, in the actual engineering requirements of the bridge; but it would be clear in relation to the mix of private and public finances available for the bridge, the level of consultation allowed, the administrative apparatus available, and the size and roles of the various stakeholders would all be different. At a certain level of abstraction, such details would be irrelevant as the purpose of the bridge is fairly clear, but this misses the point about the actuality of the process of putting up a bridge, reducing it to merely an engineering activity. The telos of the bridge permits a positivist approach to the task of building a bridge.[6] It is less clear what the telos of an entire culture or economy could be, and without teleology it is difficult to determine the correct organisation of an economy or culture (leaving aside for the moment the question of whether we are able to more or less separate these assemblages into discrete boxes such as 'culture' or 'economy').[7] This leads to the recognition that distinct forms of economic organisation can emerge, reflecting particular institutional and cultural arrangements. These arrangements are crystallisations of historical struggles and strategies, and shape economic organisations and activities in ways that have a direct and continuing impact upon individuals, families and communities. A Canadian firm or a Chinese firm involved in the same economic activity may conduct themselves very differently in relation to issues of health and safety, care of workers, decision-making processes and expectations, organisational culture and values; so much so that experience of working in one or the other firm would be a distinct enough experience to make a difference to the shape of one's life

With the end of the Cold War, capitalism lost its ideological coherence. The ending of the Soviet system and Deng Xiaoping's reforms of the Chinese economy suggest that there was no socialist alternative to capitalism. Thus, it has become easier to see the different inflections of 'the logic of capitalism' manifested in a variety of institutional and cultural assemblages that help identify the distinct patterns of a mixed economy. The integration of production and consumption on a planetary scale ensured that the world economy was firmly organised along capitalist principles. A number of economic approaches existed that were broadly based on the free market but diverged in crucial details and thus produced distinct models in which the mix of instructions, priorities and levels of economic activity varied significantly. The Anglo-Saxon, European, Scandinavian and Japanese versions of the mixed economy reflect the priorities of different cultural formations and histories. Within this vernacularisation of capitalism, there is no reason why it should not be possible to articulate a distinct Islamicate variant of the mixed economy.

There may not be an Islamic way to build a car or a mousetrap, but there is no reason why there could not be an Islamicate way. Even if we are to conclude that human wants are potentially infinite, it does not follow that they are universal beyond a very basic level. As the example of Robinson Crusoe illustrates, a shipwrecked English plantation owner loses neither his Englishness nor the quality of being a plantation owner. Crusoe needs to engage in activities to ensure his existence on the desert island, to balance his wants with the means available to him. His quest for shelter and food, however, are all shaped by his encultured understanding of what food and shelter are, and what resources and skills are available for him to produce the goods and services he needs. Crusoe may have left English society, but its values and practices do not leave him and continue to shape him even on a desert island, for example, planting a cross with the date of his arrival there. If the story of

Robinson Crusoe shows how difficult the idea of an abstracted *homo economicus* is, the case for an Islamic economics cannot be dismissed simply. Those critics of Islamic economics who see Islamic banking as a rather clumsy attempt to escape the prohibition of *riba* miss the point: all economic activity makes sense only in relation to a complex of cultural and social relationships. There is little doubt that Islamicate practices have an impact upon economic activity. For example, it is likely that the per capita consumption of alcohol or pork is relatively low among Muslim communities. These consumption preferences not only have a local effect—for example, the establishment of halal butchers and eateries in areas with concentrated Muslim populations—but also major social effects. For instance, the argument can be made that the demand for cotton, due to restrictions on the use of silk by Muslim men, may have played a major role in stimulating the demand for cotton and producing an unprecedented level of urbanisation in Iran.[8] It does not, follow, however, that specific Islamicate practices (legal, consumer, investment) provide an essence that could account for the 'long divergence' between the economies and the societies of Europe and Muslimistan.[9] There is nothing wrong in expecting an Islamicate society to empower economic activities and institutions that reflect its priorities and values. The problem with Islamic economics is not that it does not follow the abstract universal standard of what is deemed to be the purpose of an economy, nor is it the problem of being contaminated by the logic of capitalism in its very effort to oppose it (Tripp, 2006); rather, that it is to do with the understanding of Islam upon which it seeks to ground its economic programme. The challenge for attempts to establish an unequivocal Islamic identity in the fibre of state and society is twofold: how to map out the journey from Islam to the Islamicate, and how to make that journey. Given the idealism that is the dominant strand in this genre, one could be forgiven for thinking that Islamic economics would at least be able to map out a journey from Islam to the Islamicate: that it should be able to demonstrate an isomorphic relationship between precepts found in Islam and principles established for a normative framework that can regulate the field of economic behaviour. It could be argued that the project of Islamic economics should not be seen as a 'war of manoeuvre' that immediately takes hold of society, but rather as part of a 'war of position' by which Islamists will build their utopia brick by brick, institution by institution. Islamic economics then is for Islamists a substitute for the absence of state power, for ultimately a proper Islamic economy can only come about through an Islamic state. The role of Islamic economics, then is to Islamise society as preparation and expectation of an Islamic order to come. In the next section I want to focus on the idea of an Islamic state as a means of fixing an Islamic identity.

III

It could be argued that an Islamic state has hardly been more successful than Islamic economics in bringing about an Islamic society. The question of what is Islamic about an Islamic state is homologous to projects to establish the Islamic character of economics. In his book, *Who Needs An Islamic State*, Abdelwahab el-Affendi is very aware that descriptions of ideals without effective strategies to implement them are of limited use. He purposefully attempts to avoid descriptions of Islamic order which are simply idealisations of canonical narratives—his analysis injects a degree of pragmatism into the question of the Islamic state. He does not simply repeat the canonical formulations by which the relationship between Islam and the state are most negotiated; his work is not a direct extension from classical Islamicate political thought to the current situation of the *ummah*. Rather, his description of the ideal Islamicate state is that it is based on attempts to situate the question of Islamicate polity in the current situation of the *ummah*, and thus his formulations are marked by a degree of pragmatism, which transforms the question from the realm of utopian wish-fulfilment to the domain of strategic thinking. el-Affendi's thesis makes the valuable point that classical Islamicate political thought is, for the most part, dominated by views in which questions of governance are treated as questions of moral leadership. Such thinking not only demands that only exemplary ethical figures should govern, but also that the governed should act in such a way that corresponds to the highest values associated with an Islamic code of conduct. As el-Affendi points out, such demands are more likely to be disappointed. Idealist political thought cannot provide an analysis that is not grounded in morality: success and failure become judgements on the character of individual rulers and their entourages, rather than reflections on the complexity of circumstances. This is the case even among the first four caliphs: the difference between the governance of Omar and Ali, for example, is difficult to ascribe to the lack of virtue of Ali in relation to Omar (el-Affendi, 2008). The dominance of normative rather than prudential political thinking within Islamicate circles not only persisted for a long time, but the canonisation of such political thinking also has an impact on the Orientalisation of Islamicate thought. Rather than seeing the difficulties of the early Islamicate leadership as a product of difficulties of republican-type institutions attempting to govern an imperial order, as el-Affendi (2008:165–8) insightfully suggests, it is presented as a morality tale of corruption and virtue demonstrating the violence at the heart of the venture of Islam.[10] The persistence of this mode of thinking continues to complicate the task of analysing the actualities of the circumstances that the *ummah* is currently experiencing. A normative political philosophy that becomes largely a description of an ideal institutional arrangement, which can be culled from the reading of the Qur'an, seems to function as political analysis. Such a reading often seeks to discover human rights, electoral representation, and other such elements in a sacred text, which are then used to justify the arrangement.

El-Affendi (2008) sets out to provide an analysis of the contours of an Islamicate state in a post-caliphate Muslimistan. He positions it against the traditions of such utopian constitutionalism, which remains a dominant genre of writing political thought in the *ummah*. To this end, he provides an understanding based neither on repeating the canonical formula to be found in works of classical Muslim writers such as Marwardi, nor a simplistic extrapolation from the sacred literature. Rather it is based on the direct experience of the difficulties of contemporary Muslimistan. El-Affendi eloquently suggests that for the Islamic state to be considered to be legitimate it has to fulfil five major conditions. First, an Islamicate state has to be what el-Affendi calls democratic. By this he means not only a state in which electoral mechanisms are the principal means of changing governments, but also that an Islamic state cannot be imposed. The decision to establish it must be based on the consensus of all its citizens, Muslim and non-Muslim. Second, it has to be independent and self-reliant. He adds that it has to be guided by 'firm moral convictions' and be 'noble' in its rejection of conspicuous consumerism (ibid.: 91). This would suggest that its independence is not to be located purely at the level of governmental practice, but must have both cultural and economic dimensions. Third, an Islamicate state has to be 'outward looking' and must seek to represent the collective interest of the *ummah* and promote the 'shared outlooks' of Muslims within the international institutions that regulate the conduct of the world. While el-Affendi does not argue that an Islamic state has to be a great power, it is clear that, for him, an Islamic state cannot restrict its interests narrowly to that of an ordinary nation-state. Fourth, el-Affendi envisages not a monolithic entity but rather a plural polity. His version of an Islamic state could be described as being based not on the Westphalian trinity of one government, one land, one people, but rather it would be a 'community of communities'. Fifth, it should be 'light of humankind' and embody a philosophy of giving.

Clearly, the Islamic state envisioned by el-Affendi that was independent, cosmopolitan, had a commitment to defend Muslim interests and which enjoyed the support of its total populations (including Muslims and non-Muslims) would be a political structure in which the beliefs and values that Muslims hold about Islam would be operationalised and would help to limit injustice and cruelty. The question arises, what would be Islamic about such a state? While many Muslims would find such an Islamicate state to be something that they could endorse and support, the difficulty arises that, despite his intentions, el-Affendi's version of the Islamicate state exhibits a set of normative injunctions without clear mechanisms about how these injunctions are to made effective. In this regard, el-Affendi demonstrates the difficulty of escaping idealism while trying to theorise the Islamicate state to come. Despite his prudence, el-Affendi only manages to replace the idea of virtuous ruler with a republic of virtue. It remains unclear how the normative investments that el-Affendi makes ('democracy', pluralism, universalism, cosmopolitanism and anti-consumerism) would arise from the structure of the envisioned polity itself. It may be that political theory without normative scope is impossible, or rather it is only possible to those who are locked into foundationalist epistemology and maintain value/fact distinction, even if making gestures to its impossibility. The problem that those who wish to advocate an Islamicate state face, however, makes the temptations of idealism seductive because such idealism can be used to cover a major lacuna in any conception of the Islamicate state: what exactly is an 'Islamic state'? Where do we locate the Islamic character of such an entity? The problem faced by Islamic economics and the Islamic state is not empirical. Nor is the problem hardwired into Islam per se; that is something to do with the 'essence' of Islam.

The establishment of a polity that would be considered representative of Islam by the *ummah* does not require more normative exhortations, but the means of translating the norms associated with the best understanding Muslims have of such an ideal state into the machinery of administration and governance. In other words, Islam has to be inscribed in the institutional ensemble of the organisations, practices and values of a state. This translation cannot be simply organised around a series of injunctions, for example, legislation to enforce *salat*, *hudood* punishments or the sharia. One can imagine a state that declares its commitment to Islam loud and clear, enforces *salat*, builds big mosques, but still will not be seen by the *ummah* as an Islamic state since its version of Islam remains narrow, its attitudes to other Muslims xenophobic and its accountability to its population (let alone the *ummah*) absent. For the paradox that Muslims face is that state forms that emphasise the ontic understanding of Islam are precisely those that undermine the ontological status of Islam. Thus, the challenge for any attempt to secure an Islamic state is not empirical (though those challenges are difficult enough to overcome) but also philosophical: how can a sense of Islam that emphasises its ontological characteristics be determined by a structure that emphasises its ontic aspects?

A polity that is based on an ontological understanding of Islam is perhaps the only one that could win broad approval from the *ummah* as being a truly Islamic state. The task of establishing such a state would require not only the construction of a successful hegemonic project, but also the tutoring of the *ummah* in how to read the emergent state, how to place it in a context that decolonises the Islamicate past as a way of clearing the ground for the future for Muslims. Thus, the act of state-building is epistemic as well as socioeconomic. In the following sections I want to analyse what conditions need to be fulfilled if there was to be a successful Islamist hegemonic project able to combine economy, culture and state into an integrated Islamic(ate) order.

A hegemonic project involves the interpellation, mobilisation and coordination of diverse demands into a specific programme of action based on political, cultural and intellectual leadership. A hegemonic project needs to disorganise dissent into its aims and objectives and institute practices, organisations and values that confirm its view of the world. It is possible to analyse the conditions that facilitate the success of any hegemonic project (Jessop, 1990: 209–11).[11]

Any hegemonic project is faced with an existing state form, the structure of which privileges some hegemonies over others. The state is not a neutral space equally open to all political forces and possibilities (Jessop, 1990: 209). In the case of any potential Islamist hegemonic project, it would have to confront a state form dominated by Kemalism and supported by the current international system. The dominant form of the state in Muslimistan is the *mukhabarat* state. This is the form of state that emerged following formal decolonisation of the European colonial empires and in the context of a bipolar world order. In this environment the threat was not external (because inter-state war was regulated by the two superpowers) but internal. As such, this type of state developed an elaborate apparatus to deal with potential internal threats, safe in the knowledge that the external security of the state was underwritten by the superpowers. The *mukhabarat* state used extensive intelligence services and systematic torture to prevent popular mobilisations. Such states were able to discard popular legitimacy because they relied upon support from superpowers to maintain them in power. The War on Terror has shifted the axis of threat from internal to external, as US military predominance erodes national sovereignty and the lack of a counterweight to US hegemony lowers the threshold for US intervention. States that are going to exercise their sovereignty can only do so by ensuring that they enjoy popular legitimacy and support. Regimes that rule by torture and intimidation are unlikely to be able to count on the support of their people when they become caught in the cross-hairs of the War on Terror. As Roberto Unger astutely observes: 'Faced with a mixture of unbelievable slogans and unmistakable coercion, ordinary men and women will withdraw into their families and career in search of whatever tangible advantage they can secure' (2004: 404). Consequently, any attempt to bring about a transformation in Muslimistan currently faces the challenge of defeating the cynicism that often masquerades as wisdom. The representations of other Islamist hegemonic projects (such as the Islamic revolution in Iran or the rule of the Taliban in Afghanistan) and their various claims have helped to create a degree of scepticism about the possibility of a successful Islamist hegemony devoid of violence, tyranny and incompetence. This is the landscape that structures much of the political order in Muslimistan. It clearly has an inbuilt tilt against

Islamist hegemonic projects, but this landscape is strategically selective, not structurally determining. In other words, the unevenness of the landscape that any hegemonic project faces is not immutable and appropriate strategies can overcome the disadvantages while the inappropriate ones can succumb to them (Jessop, 1990: 353).

A successful hegemonic project needs to be able to articulate the heterogeneous demands arising from various mobilisations and formations so that they transcend their local, particular and sectional interests to become a metaphor for the well-being of society in general. This involves the construction of subjectivities of significant forces and their integration into the hegemonic project, and 'the repudiation of alternative interpellations and attributions of interest' (Jessop, 1990: 209–10). In most situations, any Islamist hegemonic project is most likely to be faced with an opposition that includes the military and security apparatus, the deep state and large sections of internationally integrated liberals, ethnically marked minorities, as well as Kemalist true believers.[12] This could mean that those who oppose Islamists often begin with a base of 20 to 30 per cent of the population that is, at best, ambivalent about the Islamist project, if not fanatically hostile.[13]

A successful hegemonic project has to play a major part in balancing and 'maintaining the complex ensemble of the state apparatus' (Jessop, 1990: 210). It is surely not accidental that the Islamist groups that have been most successful in establishing a hegemony without overthrowing the Kemalist order in mass insurrection are those that have demonstrated governmental competence: for example, the Justice and Development Party (AKP) in Turkey, Hezbollah in Lebanon and Hamas in Palestine. The ability of Recep Erdoğan to run an effective mayoral government in Istanbul (1994–1998) did much to pave the success for the AKP in subsequent years. A hegemonic project that seeks to transform the status quo is assisted by being able to present fragments of the future it advocates for society (Unger, 2004: 411). If they are to be able to establish a successful hegemonic project, Islamist groups need to be able to show the way in which they would mark the movement from Islam to the Islamicate, both in the banalities of mundane governance but also in the conduct of their own organisational affairs.

A successful hegemonic project needs to be able to establish 'a policy paradigm within which conflicts over competing interests and demands can be negotiated without threatening the overall' (Jessop, 1990: 209–

10). We have seen in the cases of both Islamic economics and the Islamic state the difficulty that many Islamist projects confront when trying to translate the pieties of an Islamicate future in order to come to terms with the banalities of governance. As we saw in el-Affendi's account, the desire for an accountable, cosmopolitan, 'progressive' and independent Islamic state does not easily translate into policy terms that are the currency of a competent statecraft. Partly, this difficulty is the product of the way in which a repertoire of available policy options has been hegemonised by Kemalism. Partly, it is a product of the idealist tenor of much Islamist thinking: that is, a belief that an organisation that is committed to 'true Islam' will automatically be able to turn that society into a Utopia. Partly, it is a result of the difficulties that many Islamist groups have had in avoiding the sense in which their policies, interests and demands have a one-to-one relationship with Islam itself. While the opponents of Islamists make much of this difficulty, and do not see how it is often tempered in practical terms, there is a problem in generating a specific policy paradigm from Islam.

V

To travel the distance from Islam to the Islamicate should be the easiest journey a Believer, or perhaps the most difficult one that a society of Believers can attempt. An Islamist hegemonic project is difficult precisely because it has to navigate the movement from Islam to the Islamicate as a political enterprise. There is no extra-historical or extra-ummatic way of establishing a relationship between Islam and the Islamicate. What I mean by this is not only that there is much debate about what constitutes the appropriate translation of Islam into the horizon of the lived experiences of ordinary Muslims, but that there is no way of settling this conversation authoritatively by reference to a force outside the *ummah*. In the following chapters I am going to expand on this claim but let me state it boldly now: for all practical purposes Islam is more or less what the *ummah* understands it to be at any one time. Let me introduce a number of caveats here, which I will develop later. It is important to note that 'more or less' refers to the possibilities of understanding Islam in ways that do not carry an imprint of the ummatic agreement. This does not stop those who hold that understanding of Islam from holding it. Thus, while I see the *ummah-*

wide interpretation of Islam to be decisive, I do not see it as being total or closed. The second caveat is that by emphasising the *ummah* I am rejecting the liberal individualism that often finds expression in the declaration that 'I am a Muslim in my own way'. Such declarations are often made in the context of others claiming to determine what it means to be a Muslim—a prerogative often ascribed to the *mutawah* that disciplines Muslimness but a similar function is also performed by the Orientalists who would determine how many times a Muslim must pray to be counted as one, or if they only keep the fast but do not give *zakat* are they only 20 per cent Muslim?[14]

There is no map or pattern or method that can be used to make that journey from Islam to the Islamicate, which itself is not part of that movement. Of course, it could be argued that there is a map, if not method, and that is the one provided by the sunna or hadith and all the true Believers have to do is follow that straight path. In the next chapter I want to deal with this argument, but now I want to refer back to the claim I made at the start of this book: Islam is the name that gives Muslims a name.

Islam for Muslims functions as a quilting point: a name that unifies a discursive formation. For Islam to play this part does not mean that it is a signifier without signified for that would be mere noise (Sayyid, 2003: 34, Laclau, 2005: 102–17), rather it is a signifier that condenses the network of signifieds thus giving belonging (to a specific discursive universe) and their meaning in that totality. It is precisely because Islam functions like this for Muslims that it is impossible for it to be tied down to its signifieds through an elaborate enumeration. For such an enumeration would be both endless and contested. This is not because they are not features of Islam, which most Muslims would agree with most of the time, but that no feature of Islam could exhaust what Islam means. Only an understanding of Islam that emphasised the ontic would be reducible to a set of its key features, but because Islam is an ontological category for Muslims such a reduction is unsustainable. In a series of letters to President Khamenei, Ayatollah Khomeini declared that the Islamic Republic of Iran could abrogate any aspect of Islam to ensure its survival. Critics saw this declaration as the retreat of Islamism into raison d'état or secularism.[15] By placing Khomeini's statement in the schema dominated by the distinction between secularism and religion, what is missed is the way in which Islam came to be disclosed in

Khomeini's interventions (intellectual and governmental). For despite declaring the possibility of the abrogation of Islam, Khomeini refused to allow the use of chemical weapons by Iranian forces in retaliation for their use by Saddam Hussein's army, with perhaps considerable consequences for Iran's war effort. Khomeini's understanding of Islam was primarily in ontological rather than ontic terms. Islam could not be exhausted by its various manifestations; it was not just a religion among others. The ontological nature of Islam allows it to go beyond its historical and contextual determinations. What we see in Khomeini's letter is not simply a recalling of the category of *musalala* (used by the *ulama* for centuries) but rather its radical reworking as an iteration of the irreducible ontological nature of Islam. Can such an ontological understanding of Islam be contained in the caliphate? Is there a power great enough to hold to such a vision of Islam? In the next chapter I will turn to this question by looking at the struggle between the ontic and the ontological in the reading of the Qur'an and its relationship to the *ummah*.

10

HERMENEUTICS

I

One of the many things that Muslims are blamed for is the destruction of the ancient library at Alexandria. The story goes that Amr ibn al-'As, the Muslim general responsible for the conquest of Byzantine Egypt, was approached by a Coptic priest asking that Muslim conquerors safeguard the ancient wisdom contained in the library. Amr ibn al-'As wrote back to Caliph Omar asking him what should be done: Omar's reply is along the lines: 'If the books agree with the Qur'an, we do not need them, and if they are opposed to the Qur'an destroy them'. When they hear this story, many Muslims would see another Orientalist calumny, while those who are of Orientalist persuasion would see this as a prime example of Islamic obscurantism. What is challenging for those who want to dismiss this as an Orientalist tale, is that the story is reported by Muslims. Muslim chroniclers, writing almost five hundred years after the purported event, are the primary source for the story and why would they wish to spread a rumour that would hold Islam in a bad light? The question, I think, rests upon the place of the Qur'an among Muslims. In the previous chapter, we saw the difficulty of fixing an Islamic identity to the economy or the state. This is important to how we argue that a Muslim great power would be Islamic. If, as argued earlier, Islamic economics or the Islamic state cannot ground the Islamic nature of a Muslim great power, can the Qur'an? More specifically, can the ethical-legal content of the Qur'an be a basis for a sociopolitical order? In the rest of the chapter, I will explore this possibility.

II

Ayatollah Khomeini wrote, 'Now if I say a few words concerning certain verses of the Qur'an, I do not in any way claim to be expounding their ultimate meaning. What I say represents a possibility not a certainty; I do not say, "This and nothing else is the true meaning"' (Khomeini, 1981: 367).

The idea that reading the Qur'an is based on a possibility of interpretation rather than a certainty of meaning is an observation both commonplace and disavowed. It is commonplace as it is historically the way in which Muslims as a collectivity have actually comported themselves in relation to the Qur'an. It is disavowed because there seems to be a regular demand from most Muslim communities that the Qur'an should provide us with a certainty of meaning that can ground Muslim conduct, both individual and collective. In other words, the Qur'an not only founds the *ummah* but also acts as a foundation.

Asama Barlas (2002: 203–5) makes helpful suggestions about how this tension between the possibility of interpretation and certainty of meaning could be resolved. Barlas defends the idea that the Qur'an is polysemic, in other words, it has a capacity to generate multiple forms of reading, but she tempers this by rejecting 'interpretive relativism', that is, a belief that all readings of the Qur'an are equally valid. There seems to be an obvious tension between the claims of polysemy and the rejection of relativism: if the Qur'an is polysemic then any interpretation is possible; to insist that not all interpretations carry equal weight seems to undermine those polysemic claims. One way around such a tension is to assert that polysemy is strictly limited. Barlas elaborates such a limit by arguing that the Qur'an reflects the nature of the Divine, and therefore its meaning is limited by an understanding that it cannot transgress 'divine ontology'. This, as Barlas concedes, is a theological argument. She then goes on to offer a non-patriarchal reading of the Qur'an.

While I certainly have a great deal of sympathy with Barlas's position, I think a theological attempt to ground the polysemy of the Qur'an does not resolve the tension, but simply displaces it from the body of the Qur'an to the nature of the Divine. The theological underpinning of an 'unreading' of the Qur'an may be perfectly valid for Barlas's project, but my concern is with its wider implications regarding a theological grounding of any possible Islamicate political order. This theological displacement has a number of critical effects on the quest for an Islamicate political order, often expressed in the slogan 'the Qur'an is our constitution'.

The claim that the Qur'an is our constitution makes sense because a constitution is also a text that brings forth a political community. One could argue without too much difficulty that the Qur'an fulfils such a role and constitutes the *ummah*. One way of understanding this *ummah* is to see it as the community formed by Muslim readers of the Qur'an. There is, however, a more prosaic understanding of constitution that sees it as set of procedural rules (written or unwritten, formal or informal) by which any polity is governed. This idea of the constitution seeks in the Qur'an a codification of the rules of procedure that an Islamicate polity can use to guarantee good governance. In other words, the Qur'an should be the foundation of any Islamicate political structure; for only by building a state around the Qur'an can we ensure its Islamic character. In previous chapters we have looked at the question of what would be distinctive about an Islamicate political order. The idea that the Qur'an can provide the constitution of such a polity would appear to guarantee its Islamic identity. Such a guarantee, if at all possible however, would mean a resolution of the tension between the possibility of interpretation and the certainty of meaning. In this chapter I want to suggest some ways in which it may be possible to resolve the tension without demanding a theological foundation for an Islamicate order.

III

A Muslim is someone who believes that the Qur'an is the record of what God said to the Prophet (pbuh). It follows that for Muslims the reading of the Qur'an has a unique significance that it cannot have for non-Muslims, be they politicians or columnists or polemicists doubling up as scholars or even serious scholars. I would argue that for non-Muslims the significance of the Qur'an is secondary in that its importance is derived from the value that Muslims attach to it. While anyone can have an opinion about the Qur'an, it is the opinion of Muslims that is of primary importance, for in a sense Muslims as a collective body comprise the

Quran's main stakeholders. Others may hold opinions that could influence Muslim opinion, but they have no direct access to the Qur'an's significance. This has to be stated forcefully since there is a tendency among Western Orientalists and polemicists to claim an expertise in the field of Qur'anic studies that supersedes the understanding of inexpert or untutored Believers (al-Azami, 2003).[1] This claim of expertise, which is reinforced by Western supremacist discourse, has to be resisted: it is the Muslims' reading of the Qur'an that matters, for it is only for Muslims that the Qur'an truly matters. For Muslims, reading the Qur'an is not a mere scholastic or polemical exercise; rather it is one of the conditions of their very possibility.[2] In what follows I want to confine my remarks to the relationship between Muslims and the Qur'an.

As Muslims we revere the Qur'an as an object, allocating it pride of place in our homes, treating it with care, keeping it bound nicely if not ornamentally and using it as a 'trump' card to win arguments with our Muslim friends.[3] We seem, however, less able or willing to accord it the respect it deserves as a text. To suggest that most Muslims do not treat the text of the Qur'an with respect would seem to fly in the face of the experience of many Believers, for do we not take verses of the Qur'an and make amulets out of them, incorporate them in our prayers, refer to them in our conversations? Surely, this suggests that Muslims do respect the Qur'anic text. What I mean by respecting the text of the Qur'an, however, involves undertaking a reading critically shaped by our awareness of the nature of its textuality. Different texts imply different reading strategies. We do not read a shopping list the same way we would read a poem; we do not read a technical manual the same way we read a novel. What kind of text is the Qur'an?

The major challenge in any reading of the Qur'an goes beyond linguistic difficulties such as the divergence between the Arabic of the Prophetic era and contemporary Arabic, or the challenge of translation from Arabic into other contemporary languages. The major challenge is, as Ingrid Mattson points out, epistemological: 'how can a Muslim be certain that she has grasped the true meaning of the Qur'an' (2008: 184).[4] How should a Believer read the Qur'an with respect to the majesty of its revelation? The Qur'an has elements of biography but it is not the biography of various prophets (like Abraham or Moses), nor is it the biography of the Seal of Prophets.[5] Nor is the Qur'an simply a set of instructions, though again it contains such elements (Wadud, 1999:

32). The Qur'an is not organised throughout in narrative or chronological form: the verses are patterned in terms of length, while the surahs eschew a straightforward linearity. Reading the Qur'an means reading a non-linear text, and reading a non-linear text is not an easy task. Of course, Muslims are helped in this endeavour by the way the Qur'an asserts its role as a guide accessible to all those who wish to be guided. In other words, there is a suggestion that those who seek guidance from the Qur'an will find it, despite the complexities of its textuality, and will succeed in unveiling the meaning of its ayahs. I will return to this point a little later, but now I want to examine an amalgam of ideas that posit the Qur'an as the foundation of a political order, ideas that valorise the distinction between political structures that are 'man-made' (sic) and those that are Qur'anically ordained.

It is estimated that of some 6,238 verses in the Qur'an there are at least 228 that refer to public affairs and the regulation of social, economic and legal relations (Ramadan, 2001: 13–14). This would suggest that the Qur'an presents itself as a text that cannot be contained within the confines of the post-Enlightenment (Western) Christian definition of a distinct religious sphere (Asad, 1993: 27–30). This seems to allow Muslims to use the Qur'an to found a constitution and, of course, this is what many Muslims attempt to do.

The use of the Qur'an to underwrite a political dispensation can also be found among contemporary Muslim scholars who can be seen as working towards the development of an Islamic liberation theology (Tariq Ramadan, Farid Esack, Abdolkarim Soroush, Rachid Gannouchi). What is common to these projects of liberation theology, despite the various differences among specific writers, is the attempt to fill the content of a political position by reference to Islam. The use of the Qur'an to buttress our views is not only confined to writers with overt political concerns, it is one of the key features of Muslim life. There are a number of difficulties with this strategy that I would like to consider. First, there is the common problem of selecting the various citations. Second, there is a problem of interpretation. To be fair, this is a point that astute readers of the Qur'an are aware of. Their solution to these problems is to make an important distinction between the Qur'an as divine and immutable and its reading as historically conditioned and mundane (Ramadan, 2001: 14). Abdullah Saeed elaborates this distinction by grouping the various approaches to the reading and understanding of the Qur'an in terms of its ethical-legal content into those carried out by textualists, semi-textualists and contextualists (2006: 3). For textualists, the linguistic content of the Qur'an is sufficient to be understood. The Qur'an is autonomous and its social and historical contexts are accidental to meaning. Semi-textualists, according to Saeed, also believe in the sufficiency of literal content and also reject any concession to its context, but express their conviction in the autonomy of the Qur'anic text in a 'modern idiom' (ibid.). Contextualists, in contrast to those who believe in the irrelevance of the context of the Qur'an, believe that the situatedness of its originary enunciation, its subsequent interpretation and circulation determine its ethical-legal content. For all interpreters of the Qur'an there is a specific challenge: how to contain the polysemy of the Qur'an. For textualists and semi-textualists, language itself is sufficient to do the bulk of this work. For contextualists the problem is of greater scope, but none of these approaches can simply avoid the problem. One way of limiting polysemy is based on the intention of the author, for example, legal disputes often entail deciphering the intention of the legislators in promulgating a particular law.[6] This, as Farid Esack (1997: 73–5) points out, is very difficult to do when the author is divine and all-knowing and all-mighty. We cannot access the 'mind' of God, and attempts to transcend our fundamental limitations lead to what might be best described as 'spiritual positivism',[7] namely the attempt to use scientific discourse to compensate for our limited ability to understand the 'mind' of the Divine, thus, for example, concluding that pork and alcohol are forbidden to Muslims for health reasons. In other words, lacking access to the 'mind' of God, we resort to using a human tool (science) as a mechanism of disclosing and apprehending the import of divine will. Superficially, this seems like an attempt to make science serve God, but in fact entails the privileging of scientific discourse over the Divine. Revelation thus leads to the divinisation of science. Since it makes the logic of God equivalent to the findings of science itself, God becomes the object of scientific laws, uncovered by human minds. Such an approach confuses scientific descriptions of the universe with the reality of the universe itself. This leads to an epistemological fallacy in which scientific descriptions of creation are taken as creation itself or, otherwise stated, scientific descriptions of reality are considered to be reality itself.[8] The positivist strategy towards knowing God is deeply flawed, both in epistemological terms (there is no reason to assume scientific descriptions are more accurate in themselves than other kinds of descriptions—a flower described by a biologist is not more of a flower than one described by a poet—the descriptions serve different purposes) and in Muslim theological terms (by making the Divine secondary to science, which is a human endeavour, one closes the gap between the human and the Divine, leading to a diminishing of the Divine to the level of the human). Positivist readings of the Qur'an cannot help us know the mind of God or assist in any attempt to construct a legal framework from the Qur'an. The problem of authorial intentionality is further complicated in this case because the Qur'an insists that those who seek to know what God has ordained will do so. It constantly affirms its clarity for those who wish to experience it. At the same time, it reminds its readers to recognise the transcendent nature of the Qur'an, which cannot be contained within human cognitive horizons. Ultimately, all interpreters of the Qur'an whether they be textualists (or semi-textualists) or contextualists have to respond to the limits of Qur'anic polysemy with analogical extrapolations. Over the years, Qur'anic hermeneutics has developed a rich panoply of techniques and categories to uncover the meaning of the Qur'an so that, as much as possible, its ethical-legal content is both consistent with its spirit and relevant to the actuality of the circumstances in which Muslims find themselves.

IV

The reported conduct of the Prophet (pbuh) fleshes out some of the concepts of the Qur'an, and his 'operationalisation' of its precepts is authoritative and absolute. The record of his 'operationalisation', however, has a number of limits to it. First, there are empirical problems regarding the authenticity of the hadith and sunna; problems that cannot simply be resolved by an act of faith that extends the epistemological privilege of the Prophet (pbuh) to scholars who compiled the hadith literature. Despite their skill in scholarship, and the rigour of their methodology, it is naïve to dismiss the possibility of the persistence of an inauthentic hadith. This can only be done by degrading the exceptional status of the Prophet, since it entails an admission that Qur'anic scholars attained such levels of excellence that rendered them incapable of errors or lapses, and instead led them to partake of the ontological privilege of the Prophet (pbuh). In other words, their exceptional calibre instilled in them an almost Prophet-like understanding of the substance of the Qur'an. Such conclusions would be difficult to maintain while accepting the centrality of the Lord of Medina to Islam.

Secondly, the Prophet (pbuh) was situated in a particular historical context; thus we do not know whether the Prophet (pbuh) would consider text messaging as being a permissible way of divorcing.[9] In the absence of direct Prophetic example, Muslims have to rely on various processes of reasoning by which we can try to work out the significance of the example of the Prophet (pbuh) in different historical contexts. This expansion is an intellectual activity, subject to all the vulnerabilities of any human action. This is something that most commentary on the Qur'an accepted long ago; the difficulty, of course, arises from our construction of the process of reasoning. Is reason something that is historically constructed or is it something permanent? If one believes that reasoning is permanent then one concludes that the various techniques of interpretation developed by Qur'anic scholars are based on permanent categories, which cannot be succeeded by alternative strategies or concepts. In Western thought, reason became Reason in the Enlightenment with the abandonment of a God-centred universe. The Enlightenment spawned the cult of Reason as an attribute that was universal, changeless and manifest in the thoughts and actions of educated and socially privileged European men; while the thoughts and actions of non-Europeans, women and the dispossessed came to be viewed antithetically as unreasonable or irrational. Belief in Reason is undermined by history. One does not have to look very far or deep to see how different communities have constructed what they consider to be Reason at different times. For example, the idea that white people of European descent were biologically superior was considered reasonable (at least by white Europeans) until very recently. If one accepts that reason is a path that different communities adopt at different times to make sense of their world, then one has to accept that reason is a historical process without permanent categories or universal validity. This suggests that, while techniques formulated by classical scholars of the hadith reflected their concerns, those techniques should not be confused with the issue of interpretation itself. Other techniques reflecting the concerns of the *ummah* at present may yield different emphases and different insights.

The space between the text of the Qur'an and the reconstruction of its meaning by Muslims cannot be closed without extending the epistemological privilege of the Prophet (pbuh) to scholars such as Bukhari or to Reason itself. Such expansion has the necessary effect of reducing the status of the Prophet (pbuh) by making his unique role substitutable by other humans or by abstracted technique; this would necessarily undermine his uniqueness. I would suggest that Muslims must be wary of such a course of action. The space between reading the Qur'an and understanding the Qur'an cannot be closed. We cannot say that our interior mental state is the same as the mental state of the creator of the Qur'an. It follows that we can never be absolutely clear that our interpretations of the Qur'an are correct, except in so far as we are all part of communities who express their Muslimness in particular forms. In the absence of knowing whether our interpretations of the Qur'an are correct or not, we have to rely on communal conventions to guide us. These conventions help bridge the gap between the reading and the understanding of the Qur'an. Conventions, however, are no more successful in accessing the 'mind of God' than our interpretive techniques; conventions cannot tell us if we understand the Qur'an because we understood what God 'intended',[10] but they can tell us what understanding means now in the context of the present *ummah*. Thus, Barlas's evocation of theological rhetoric to support her reading of the Qur'an is based on a set of tacit agreements regarding the nature of God that have hegemonised the *ummah*, so much so that they can be taken as being axiomatic.[11] Thus her argument that divine self-disclosure is the key to interpreting the Qur'an is sustained by accepting that the principles of *tawhid*, and the impossibility of God committing *zulm* (cruelty), are ontological characteristics of God. Barlas uses these taken-for-granted ideas about God to help 'deconstruct' a patriarchal reading of the Qur'an. That is, she takes notions about which there is widespread agreement and extends their logic in areas where there is a great deal of disagreement. Even though Barlas claims that her 'unreading' is based ultimately on theology, I would contend her theology is itself based on shared conventions regarding Muslim beliefs. In other words, theology is grounded hegemonically, which means theology is not outside the political.

Conventions provide guidance about what is correct or incorrect, for any particular community. So we learn to pray and we learn to comport ourselves by being part of the *ummah*, which arrives at certain agreements about what constitutes a 'proper' understanding of the Qur'an, hence the centrality of the Qur'an-*ummah* nexus.[12] These conventions, however, are the result of historical compromises and struggles; in other words they are the product of political processes. What is conventional today may have once been an issue of great uncertainty and disagreement. For example, in most Muslim countries women are allowed to drive, and most Muslim countries that introduced a universal adult franchise included women—before Switzerland did (where women were given the right to vote only in 1970). The agreements about the interpretation of the Qur'an rely on the fact that human beings are historically situated creatures.

The historical and contextual nature of the interpretation of the Qur'an introduces a tension within the Qur'an-*ummah* nexus between the transcendental and the historical; the Qur'an transcends and overcomes all attempts at limiting and mastering it within a specific historical frame. There is always a possibility that future groups of Muslims may question or reject some of our current understandings of the Qur'an. The divine nature of the Qur'an points to its characterisation as a text that cannot be particularised. The historical and finite nature of the *ummah*, its humanness, limits the possibility of establishing conventions that can master historical development. In this field between the transcendental text and its historical community of readers, it is possible to isolate two different methods of trying to settle the tension. The first tendency would seek to extend the historical to claim the transcendental, in other words, arguing for the historical nature of the Qur'an itself.[13] According to this approach the Qur'an is a text of its time, it occurs in history and, as such, it can be said to simply reflect the circumstances of its revelation. This is the position most clearly identified with the contextualists. Elements of it, however, can be found in interpretations that, for example, divide the Qur'an into a transcendental Meccan portion and a historical Medinan section.

The second strategy is to expand the transcendental, to argue that revelation of the Qur'an does not simply occur in human history but consumes it. The historical is denied in the name of the transcendental and human understanding becomes transhistorical. This approach would suggest that revelation of the Qur'an and its meaning is outside history; it is not specific to any time or any place, and what the Qur'an reveals are universal systems of knowledge that are not reducible to any particular moment. This clearly is the objective of textualist (and semi-textualist) readings, except that the transcendentality of the Qur'an is contained within its language. What both these approaches have in common is an attempt to settle the tension in the Qur'an-*ummah* nexus by a process of decontestation.

Decontestation refers to words and concepts whose meaning is no longer the subject of struggle or conflict: it refers to the distribution of names and functions that are settled and generally accepted (Rancière, 1998). The decontestation of the Qur'an would make it transparent. This seems to be a good thing, since most Muslims would welcome a situation in which the meaning of the Qur'an was no longer subject to differing interpretations, but rather the source of unity. Most Muslims aiming at decontestation are guided by the best of motives and noblest of concerns. For decontestation would, in their minds, mean a unified *ummah* organised around an agreed vision of Islam that is based on unanimity regarding interpretations of the Qur'an. This would provide the *ummah* with a mechanism for conflict resolution and the preservation of unity since in case of disputes all that would be required would be a reference to the Qur'an. Since all Muslims would agree on all that the Qur'an says and means, the Qur'an would cease to be a subject of reflection or meditation but simply become a bundle of maxims that we could utilise without having to engage with the richness and profundity of the text or with the extent of its impact upon our existence. Decontestation would make the Qur'an a collection of platitudes and clichés. It would simply become the agglomeration of common sense possessed by most communities—a set of assumptions and values that people resort to rather mechanistically without probing their deeper significance. This transformation of the Qur'an into ready-made instant bon mots or slogans would mean that, while it gained in accessibility and intelligibility, it would lose its power to challenge the current set of received ideas and practices. Decontestation opens the path towards the banalisation of the Qur'an, and the denigration of Islam into a form of ancestor worship, since the capacity of the Qur'an to guide the *ummah* depends on its capacity to remain fresh, to not become a set of platitudes, but remain full of meaning, and thus significant.

The decontestation of the Qur'an implies its depoliticisation. The depoliticisation of the Qur'an presents the possibility of a depoliticised Islam. The vision of a depoliticised Islam has great appeal for many Muslims, as well as Islamophobes (Muslim and non-Muslim). The decontestation of the Qur'an also appeals to Islamophobes since it promises the depoliticisation of Islam by neutralising it. That is, Islam would be confined to specific arenas of life concentrated around 'rites of passage', but it would not interfere in the process by which Muslims conduct themselves in relation to other people. A depoliticised Qur'an would be a Qur'an that has lost its power to move its readers. A depoliticised Qur'an would be absorbed by prevailing social norms and would be, by definition, a text that is sedimented and absorbed within society. Such a Qur'an could be a source of morality, but not of ethics.

A Muslim is someone who reads the Qur'an to commune with the Divine.[14] Any attempt to use the Qur'an as a means of guaranteeing the Islamic nature of a polity is itself a sign of a loss of confidence in Muslims. For it is suggested that the Islamic character of a political order can be demonstrated only by its adherence to the Qur'an. Such a view fails to understand that identity is the outcome of a system of differences, in other words, the nature of an Islamic order will be founded on the principle of what it rejects.

The Qur'an-*ummah* nexus has to be preserved in a form in which the Qur'an is a horizon towards which the *ummah* has to move. This means that the Qur'an cannot be absorbed into the *ummah*. It cannot be the centrepiece of a purported Islamic constitutional order in which selected verses are used as pillars of support. Such an edifice threatens the integrity of the Qur'an by making some verses superior to others and thus de facto undermining the totality of the Qur'an. There is a need for a set of standards that would allow us to judge whether the legal order itself is just. This standard has to stand outside the legal framework to allow the legal framework to be subject to its guidance. The Qur'an cannot be made law for it has to remain above the law, to ensure that the law continues to be just. In other words, there is a need to be able to judge any law, to prevent the law becoming just another tool in tyranny's armoury. This way the Qur'an provides a criterion by which the law can be judged and found to be tyrannical. This, in fact, is what Muslims have always done: judging that concrete manifestations of polities that claim to be Islamic do not meet Qur'anic criteria of what it means to be Islamic. In other words, Muslims are happy to accept that Muslim governments composed of fallible humans (alas, usually men) can be judged and found wanting in relation to the vision of justice articulated by the totality of the Qur'an.

The early Islamicate state had no problem in using administrative techniques, personnel and other resources from previous political entities (principally the Persians and the Romans). It could do this in the context of a 100-year jihad that brought regions as far flung as Spain and Sind under Muslim dominion. The confrontation between the Muslim state and its enemies guaranteed the Islamic identity of the semantic order founded by the revelation of the Prophet (pbuh). The distinction between Muslims and anti-Muslims has to be a political one. It has to have meaning for life itself, and cannot simply be a distinction without substantive qualities. The Qur'an at its most powerful offers its readers a challenge: it makes them think about the manner and direction of their lives and how they can aspire towards being rightly guided. At this level the glory of the entire Qur'an comes into play; all its verses produce an effect upon the Believer that cannot be reduced simply to the linearity of its writing, the content of its stories or to the majesty of its injunctions, for beyond these moments the Qur'an provides a means of accessing the transcendental.

So Muslims read the Qur'an for guidance, as substance for meditation, but most of all they read the Qur'an to feel the imprint of the Divine. Thus, the choice to submit to Islam is a choice invested with purpose; it changes the way in which we Muslims conduct ourselves, it makes our actions resonate as part of a wider fabric, but most all it is the way in which we know how to become Muslim. One can see how deep this impression can be when looking at some of the most anti-Muslim Muslims who still cannot escape the way in which Islam marks them, even at the superficial level of their names.

Many Muslims want the Qur'an to provide a rock-like foundation; some Muslims want to see in the Qur'an the possibility of iron-like laws, that cannot be twisted or bent by unscrupulous men (alas, again mainly men). Time, however, can cause iron to rust and the hardiest rocks to turn to dust. Perhaps it is more useful to see in the Qur'an a promise. The strength of a promise comes not from its intrinsic nature but rather from the nature of the relationship between the parties. I would like to suggest that we Muslims reject the short-term and easy comfort of decontesting the relationship between the Qur'an and the *ummah* in order to allow the Qur'an to play its unique role in our lives, a role for which no legal code or institutional settlement can be a substitute. This allows the Qur'an to be a source of prayer, reflection and meditation, a criterion of good and evil, 'a demand for something better'. Atomistic readings of the Qur'an in which a particular Muslim may pluck a particular verse because it speaks to her at that moment in her life are fine for individuals, since the purpose of such selections is not to find a master metaphor that makes the rest of the Qur'an intelligible, but simply to find in a particular verse something that resonates with one's current circumstances. Such individual recitations do not have the same impact as attempts to select specific verses as a means of instituting a specific social-economic disposition. The Qur'an is too important for the *ummah* to be reduced to a banner that masks our unwillingness or incapacity to project our Muslim identity into the future. The Qur'an can give direction, solace and hope, but its institutionalisation in systems of governance cannot replace the struggle to stake out a distinct Muslim presence in the world.

V

Ali Shariati pointed out the *ummah* is not constituted by 'ties of blood or soil': its only point of unity is a common view of the world. Common to this view of the world is a vision of a constellation of communities joined by the reading of the Qur'an. Any reading of the Qur'an cannot be a purely private individual reading. Such readings are impossible, since reading is a communal practice because language itself is a social institution. To be a Muslim requires an engagement, however distant, with other Muslims (both living and dead). In other words, being Muslim is an inheritance from the *ummah*'s past and a coping with the present *ummah*. We are Muslims in relation to the *ummah* in general and, in particular, whatever part we are most aware of. It is impossible to be a Muslim alone, for being a Muslim can never be a purely private act; it has to partake of the social.[15]

Nor can Qur'anic readings be mapped onto the territorial divisions of the *ummah* (whether they take the form of dynastic states or nation-states). As the Qur'an circulates throughout the *ummah* both in terms of its spatial extension but also historically (how it was interpreted by the *ummah* in previous periods), attempts to sanction specific readings through the use of state power are always likely to be interrupted. A closed reading of the Qur'an is unsustainable. This does not mean that all interpretations have equal weight: in practical terms the Qur'an is not completely open to all readings. At any particular moment there is a hegemonic reading. Crucially, this hegemony is *ummah*-wide and alternative interpretations have to engage with infrastructures of that hegemonic reading.

Theological rhetoric is one of the means by which Muslims may attempt to hegemonise interpretations of the Qur'an. The recourse to theology cannot provide the foundation of an Islamicate social order, since theology already assumes an internal relation to a community in which its statements carry weight. In other words, theology is internal to the social. The persuasiveness of Barlas' account derives partly from the shared view of divine ontology that binds the *ummah*, for example, the Divine is against *zulm*.[16] The attempt to theologically found a polity not only risks the polity becoming a reflection of divine ontology,[17] but more importantly, it denies the political. The objection to theological foundations is not simply in terms of their presumed negative consequences, but rather that the objection is theoretical. The projects to hegemonise the interpretations of the Qur'an are internal to the *ummah*; the use of divine ontology to settle disputes and transform our understanding of the Qur'an has significance only in the context of societies that share such an understanding of the Divine. To agree that God does not practice *zulm* does not help us, for not only do we not have an apodictic mechanism for deciding what *zulm* is exactly at any given moment, but also that our understanding of the nature of the Divine is itself based on shared social practices and how they interact with more idiosyncratic readings provided by our biographies (which, of course, are also social practices). We 'learn' to be Muslims by knowing how those around us, the networks and associations that we are thrown into, comport themselves as Muslims. Being a Muslim does not (contrary to dictates of Orientalism and its internalised variants and the more rabid spoutings of Islamophobes) mean being an automaton; nor, however, does it mean being atomised sovereign individual consumers randomly selecting what it is to be Muslim. For example, someone who declares themself to be a Muslim and drinks alcohol may narrate or be narrated as a 'bad Muslim' or 'liberated Muslim'. They may feel guilty about drinking and admit what they do is wrong but lack the qualities to stop drinking. On the other hand, they may see drinking as being irrelevant to being a Muslim, and may justify it by arguing that the Qur'an only forbids arriving drunk to your prayers. They may rejoice in drinking and see it as an act of asserting their individualism and abandoning what they consider hidebound conventions. The background to all these cases is the overwhelming opinion in the *ummah* that drinking is haram, so those who are marked by their Muslimness drink in relation to that marking.

The de facto starting point for Muslim conceptions of *zulm* and the nature of the Divine is current ummatic common sense, that is, crystalised and banalised interpretations of the canonised readings. Our readings (like all readings) cannot be purely private isolated affairs, if for no other reason than that language and all signifying practices are social. Divine ontology can ground the reading of the Qur'an for Muslims, because it is the bedrock of belief, beyond which no believing woman or believing man can go; this grounding is not theological but political. That is, it is a consequence of the way in which a certain society has been instituted: the existence and morphology of the *ummah* ground Muslim understanding of the nature of the Divine.

An Islamicate political order requires the Qur'an to be a reminder—a call to ethical excellence—that should be able to deconstruct any existing arrangement, whether economic, cultural or moral; as such it cannot be identified with any ontic order. The Qur'an is the needle and its readings the threads by which the *ummah* is stitched together. These communities of readers can never do complete justice to the Qur'an, because the meaning of the Qur'an is constructed holistically and therefore all readings are going to be partial readings. The superficial and unrealisable objective in which only a uniform interpretation of the Qur'an can provide the *ummah* a sense of purpose and unity and act as foundation for its political structures has to be abandoned. What unifies the *ummah* is not a uniform interpretation of the Qur'an, but rather a common recognition of its ability to orient Muslims. We may all pray for different things, but we Muslims all pray in the direction of Mecca.[18] The possibility of different interpretations of the Qur'an is not a failure of Muslims to understand or to agree, but a recognition of the finitude of humanity. It is precisely because the Qur'an requires interpretation, that is, because of the textuality of the Qur'an, that we have the condition of the possibility of the *ummah*.

Given the space that the Qur'an occupies emotionally, sociologically and onto-theologically, perhaps it is not that hard to understand why Muslims would retell the story of Caliph Omar's decision to burn the Royal Library in Alexandria. The library in Alexandria represents the totality of empirical knowledge. In contrast, for Muslims the sublimity of the Qur'an transcends all factual statements: it is not a book that any human could write, for it is a book of absolute judgements, a book of ethics.[19] In the next chapter, I will discuss why ethics cannot give a positivity that would allow it to become the bricks and mortar of an Islamicate polity. The story of the burning of the library of Alexandria was told by Muslims, not because they endorse obscurantism or because it reveals the fanatical dogmatism of the early Muslims but rather because it highlights their understanding of the ethical nature of the Qur'an and an appreciation of the impossibility of turning ethics into mere facts. The Qur'an makes all other books unnecessary because it transcends relative judgements and points Believers towards the Absolute. In other words, the Qur'an, above all else, tells us what is the good, not what is good for a particular purpose. Ethics trumps all claims of empirical knowledge. Perhaps the burning of the library of Alexandria is a story that demonstrates that the pre-colonial Muslims believed without apologies that the companions of the Prophet (pbuh) understood the ethical nature of the Qur'an.

11

ETHICS

I

'Mohammed of Arabia ascended to the highest heaven and returned; by God, if I had reached that point I should never have returned'.[1] Mohammed Iqbal sees in this frank and moving admission the stark difference between the mystic and the prophetic (Iqbal, 1981: 124–5). A mystic has no obligation beyond a personal communion with the Divine, unlike a prophet, who has to use his personal experience of the Divine to communicate to a wider audience, as a means of bringing about a transformation of not only an individual soul but of society as whole. A messenger of God has to impart knowledge of what is good, whereas a mystic only needs to experience the good as the emanation of the Divine. In reforming society a prophet has to participate in public life, in the affairs and concerns of the many, rather than in the cultivation of the one. The prophetic appears to combine the ethical with the political. As Iqbal describes it, the Prophet (pbuh) returns: 'to insert himself into the sweep of time with a view to control the forces of history, and thereby create a fresh world of ideals' (ibid.: 124). To make a 'fresh world of ideals' is an act of foundation, and as such a political act.

The creation of a world is inherently political. To bring forth a new order of things means working in a context in which sedimented practices, habits and conventions must be shaken if not discarded. It means instituting different routines, different organisations, and different ways of thinking and behaving. Such a task has to be accomplished in a setting which comes to be dominated by those who are in favour of transformation and those who want to conserve what is already in place. Depending on the scale and intensity of reforms, an antagonistic relationship will be established in which those who support the reforms and those who oppose them become reconfigured as friends and enemies. This antagonism between friend and enemy, as has been previously mentioned, is the key defining feature of the political.

At several points throughout this volume I have argued for the primacy of the political in the analysis of social relations and the elaboration of strategic orientations. These arguments have been made *en passant* with the hope that by the end of the book the overlapping features of what constitutes the main contours of my position would become increasingly clear. Before proceeding any further, it might be useful to draw out the main themes that are associated with the primacy of the political.

It should be clear that the political does not designate a region, or a specific sphere of activity (parliament, ministries), but is a condition. The political is not only a description of what happens in governments, legislative assemblies and councils. It is not just the conversations that princes and pretenders have with their advisers. There is no specific domain of human activity that is the place of the political. The political erupts when a distinction between friends and enemies takes hold. The formation of enemies (and thus friends) occurs in relation to a conflict which divides a grouping into antagonistic blocs. The intensity of the distinction, in other words the intensity of enmity and amity, determines the depth and range of the political.

A condition of intense hostility is one in which there are no structures that are able to contain the antagonism experienced by the differing parties. The conventions, rules, routines and other regularities which pattern our life become contested. A hostility that is so intense can logically only end in an existential struggle, in the face of which there is potentially no bond, convention or rule that cannot be set aside. The difference between a game and a fight is precisely the difference between structured competition, in which it is clear what kind of behaviour is permissible, what is winning and what is losing, and open conflict, in which all conventions become eroded. The political arises where there are tears in the social fabric which cannot be stitched together. They are no longer able to ensure compliance or provide certainty. The uprooting of layers of sedimented social conventions forces an attempt to impose a re-ordering. This re-ordering must be done even when there is no longer an acceptance of the correct method of undertaking such a task. For example, in many societies conflict is domesticated by an electoral mechanism. The electoral mechanism, however, may itself become part of the conflict, and we see the spectre of elections in which the apparent losing party disputes the electoral verdict (in Iran in 2009, the US presidential elections of 2000 and in Algeria in 1994).[2]

Third, the political describes the practice of hegemony: the attempt to establish a structure and institute new social patterns and arrangements. It is the institutionalisation of social relations. In other words, the routines we live are not intrinsic or natural. They are neither hardwired into our genes nor are they universal responses to common stimuli. Practices become routinised when there is no conflict about their workings, when the behaviour that they depend upon elicits formulated and almost automatic responses. The political then is precisely the terrain prior to the establishment of rountinised practices; it is the moment in which disputes about the nature of the routines takes place.

Fourth, as can be seen from the above, the political is highly corrosive of stability or social order. It potentially risks transforming any difference into an antagonism. The re-description of social relations in terms of friends and enemies would make any society impossible. The political necessitates politics. By politics is meant not only the wheeling and dealing associated with its practitioners, but rather a set of complex arrangements (formal, informal, institutional and personal) by which the political is tamed.[3] Politics is the way in which any social order establishes processes by which the gap between signifiers and signified can be policed, marshalled and given the appearance of suture. Politics then is a constant effort to tame the antagonisms inherent to the political: it is the domestication of the political. The primacy of the political arises from the recognition of the contingency in the construction of all social relations. In a world without foundations, the political is the means by which the social is instituted (Laclau, 1990: 33–41; Sayyid and Zac, 1998).

II

The Messenger of God's mission questioned and subverted many of the patterns of social life that had governed Makah, seemingly for time immemorial. His message disrupted many of these conventions and inaugurated a new semantic order. The political nature of Islam arises not only from the dual role played by its founder—as ruler and religious guide—but also because Islam announced a new world. Solidarities and loyalties based on differences other than Muslim and non-Muslim became weakened, as the frontier between those who declared themselves to be Muslims and those who opposed them increasingly came to dominate aspects of life, disrupting and reconfiguring ties of kinship, wealth and authority. The success of the venture of Islam was such that not only did the return of the Prophet (pbuh) signal the political, but also the beginning of the politics of Islam, a politics able to contain the political impetus of Islam itself.

The relationship between Islam and politics has conventionally been divided into two camps. There are those who maintain that Islam as religion does not separate itself from politics, and those who see any attempt to associate Islam with politics as a threat to its integrity as a religion. The figure of the Lord of Medina is crucial in these debates, for those who wish to see in Islam a combination of religion and politics point to his dual role. Those who wish to oppose this view do so by countering that being ontologically privileged the Prophet (pbuh) could combine both roles, but this is not the case for contemporary Muslims, and outside Orientalist fantasies it is difficult to argue that an essence of Islam is located in its foundation and this essence governs all its various temporal and spatial permutations. Thus, if the polity ruled by the Lord of Medina was the only uncontested example of an Islamic state, it does not follow that the state is necessary for the perpetuation of Islam. Among the ranks of those who oppose the articulation of Islam and politics can be found those who see a path towards nihilism in the mobilisations and struggles in the name of Islam. It is argued that the use of Islam by politicians corrupts and taints its spirituality, and the violence perpetuated in its name by groups associated with Al-Qaeda (whether the association is institutional or figurative), with apparently little qualms for 'collateral damage' and a scattergun approach to targets which include those who describe themselves as Muslims, seems to threaten social order in many parts of Muslimistan. The declaration by Sayyid Qutb that all contemporary Muslim societies are in a state of *jailiyyia* has, it seems, opened the door for a reinscription of the friend/ enemy distinction onto the interior of the *ummah* with tragic consequences. Islam is being distorted by its association with the political, so the argument goes.

The echoes of this argument can be found in Pervez Manzoor's succinct commentary on Carl Schmitt which concludes with a firm reminder that 'Islam means the sovereignty of the Transcendent and not of the political' (Manzoor, 1999: 4). So while Manzoor is content to accept the value of much of Schmitt's critique of liberalism and 'humanitarian imperialism' he concludes that the insistence on the primacy of the political has the effect of putting politics above morality, and such a view can be dismissed as being nihilistic. According to Manzoor what a Muslim thinker is required to do is 'not the annunciation of a *political* charter that establishes Islam's compatibility with current world-order, but a *moral* vision that addresses the malaise of our common humanity' (ibid.: 5). Strangely enough, one can find the support for this position in Sayyid Qutb's discussion of the career of Ali, the fourth caliph (35–40/656–61). Qutb argues that if Ali had become caliph after Omar, the Islamic(ate) state would not have experienced the corruptions associated with the Umayyads (Qutb, 2000: 264). Uthman's election as caliph and the challenges that Ali faced when he was subsequently elected caliph demonstrate the serious difficulties inherent in being a ruler who is guided by higher considerations than mere expediency. Qutb implies that the failures of Ali's rule arose not from his alleged shortcomings but his virtues. In other words, Ali's decision to conduct himself only in ways that would be consistent with Islam prevented him from carrying out actions that could have defeated the Umayyad counter-revolution (ibid.). This belief in Islam having a moral purpose beyond the narrow (often grubby) calculations associated with politics is fairly commonplace. The familiar conception of politics and morality sees them as mutually exclusive terms. Those who engage in politics often act in ways that are condemned by morality. This is a position shared widely among Muslims. It could be seen in its most explicit form in pre-Khomeini Jafari, and Zayidi *mazhabs*, in which all political activity was considered to be corrupting. Hamid Dabashi (2013) also reaches a similar conclusion arguing for a rejection of the binarism that he associates with the Islamist (and to be fair the neo-conservative) desire to order the world in terms of exclusive oppositions—Islam and the West, secularism and the religious—in favour of Islamicate ecumenical cosmopolitanism. Breaking the binary is also the central theme of the various counter-jihad/counter-radicalisation programmes initiated and facilitated by many Western plutocracies as part of the War on Terror.[4] The quest to reject the distinction between friend and enemy, however, simply leads to another iteration of those who are our friends (those who reject the binary of friend and enemy) and those who are our enemies (those who accept the friend/enemy antagonism). The problem of conflict lies not in its existence but rather in how we comport ourselves with reference to it. The opposition between morality and politics is one of the constant refrains trotted out by those who want to tell the difference between moderate and radical Muslims, between Muslims and Double Muslims. It is an argument that states that Islam has to be understood as morality and that seeks to rule any articulation of Islam and the political as out of order.

I think it is useful to reinforce the distinction between morality and ethics that is often blurred. By morality I refer to an embedded, institutionalised code of behaviour about what is good and proper, and what is not. All societies are moral in that they have rules of conduct which determine proper behaviour. All morality, however, always has the possibility of failure in that the ideas of what is good and proper become detached from the actual behaviour that is supposed to embody these qualities. Or what is considered to be moral works against other ideas of what might be better. Ethics on the other hand describes the constant possibility of a better union between what is and what ought to be.[5] The ethical involves a sustained reflection and intervention in the field of the moral, a constant questioning and demanding that current mores of a community correspond ever closer to the spirit of the 'law' rather than just its letter. The ethical evokes a horizon where the correspondence between the practices of what is good and proper and the articulation of the desire of what is good and proper is tighter. The ethical can invalidate any existing moral conduct by showing that the practice of morality in a specific context produces what can be only understood as immoral outcomes. So, for example, it could be argued that to punish theft in situations in which many individuals find themselves unable to support themselves or their families would be unethical even if theft is considered to be morally improper conduct. The ethical always has the potential to trump the moral. The Prophet's (pbuh) ethical message questioned and eventually displaced the morality of Arabian society of the time. The breaking of idols could be construed as an act of immorality (from the point of view of many anti-Muslims in Makah) but also a supremely ethical act.

To attempt to exclude the political from Islam means to also exclude Islam from its manifestation in a set of social relations. If Islam is not manifested in social relations, it simply disappears, except as an archive, since only an idealist conception of Islam could guarantee its existence without any social context. Such a form of idealism would not be sustainable. Thus to argue for an Islam external to the political is to argue for the emptying of its ethical potential and its eventual dissolution. The ethical impulse in Islam makes any ummatic morality provisional and potentially able to be subverted and rectified in the name of an Islam 'to come'.[6] Not an Islam which has not been realised yet, but rather an Islam that is not possible to realise: an Islam which is not grounded in any essential form but rather as a horizon which orients and structures Muslim aspirations.

The moralisation of the political is not the subordination to ethics but rather a betrayal of the ethical potential of Islam. For example, fatwas issued by various individuals on whether martyrdom operations or suicide bombings are permitted 'in' Islam are largely ineffective since they are based on a morality which those who engage in such operations reject in favour of an ethical impulse. This logic can be seen at play in the much publicised fatwa by Muhammad Tahir-ul Qadri. Qadri presents a meticulous and detailed example of traditional Islamicate scholarship in setting out his refutation of the use of suicide bombing (or martyrdom operations).[7] The *Fatwa on Terrorism and Suicide Bombings* sets out to demonstrate, through the use of Quranic verses and prophetic traditions, that not only does Islam prohibit terrorism but terrorism is a rejection of faith (*kufr*) (Qadri, 2011: 5). Qadri, however, does not only provide answers to questions like can Muslims use violence to promote their values (ibid.: 7) or can terrorism be justified (ibid.: 12), but uses the classic question and response format of the fatwa genre to conclude that Muslims should not rebel against governments unless those governments are preventing the actual practice of Islam:

Islam holds the peace and tranquillity of society in general, and of Muslim state in particular, so dear that it is does not allow people to raise the banner of revolt in the name of confronting injustice, oppression and other vices committed by the ruling elite. The banner of rebellion against a Muslim state cannot be raised unless the rulers commit explicit, declared and unequivocal disbelief and use force to prevent the performance of religious rituals like prayers (Qadri, 2011: 10).[8]

The moral code of Islam—its injunction to promote peace and coexistence—is used as a bulwark against the ethical impulse to correct injustice and end oppression. According to this view, no Muslims could (or even should) protest against, say, the Saudi regime because despite the unjust and oppressive nature of that regime it permits prayer. What is most troubling about Qadri's conclusion is not its specific content—that it can be said to be justifying tyranny—but rather its understanding of Islam as primarily ontic.

III

The *Fatwa on Terrorism and Suicide Bombings* is based on the assumption that Islam is a set of rules and algorithms which determine which types of actions comply with these rules and which violate them; algorithms which authorised religious scholars decipher and determine. Therefore it is possible to say what exactly is within Islam and what is not. It is a commonplace observation that most Muslims would accept that there are certain kinds of behaviours which are forbidden to Muslims, for example, eating pig meat of any kind. The prohibition on eating pork would appear to be an example of a rule that scholars have determined from the text of the Qur'an and the context of the Prophet's (pbuh) sunna. The meaning of Islam can be reduced to a set of regulations which govern the actions of all Believers. In fact, such a view of Islam is to be found not only among those who criticise it but also among those who are its most adherent supporters: Islam is simply a matrix of rules. The legalism that Qadri puts in the service of a vision of 'a moderate Islam' is not something exclusive to those who recognise in his canonical citations a formation that is addressed as 'Sunni'. Similar practices are to be found among all major branches of the venture of Islam. The scholasticism of this methodology is based on a metonymic displacement of Islam itself to classical Islamic scholarship.

Dabashi (2013: 133–34) provides an example of an impassioned denouncement of such a metonymic move. He rails against the presumptions of the *ulama* to determine what is or is not Islamic, who is or is not a Muslim, what are or are not penal offences. In his rejection of the legalistic-scholastic methodology, Dabashi attacks the claims of authority of Islamic scholars.[9] In perhaps an unfortunate phrase, he asserts the privilege of the natality of his Shia belonging, to make the point that religious scholars cannot determine his Muslimness. In less erudite hands, this rejection of religious scholarship's claims of authority leads to the notion of being a Muslim as an exercise of individual choice: being a Muslim in my own way. A critique of the methodological scholastic legalism that succumbs to a methodological individualism does not take us very far. It is difficult to make the case that we should reject the scholarly expertise of the *ulama*, without also dispensing the product of that expert knowledge. It is not clear why claims for authority by religious scholars are more problematic than the claims for authority demanded by scholars from Universities of Columbia or Leeds or Cape Town.[10] Scholarship, craft, study, and judicious and sustained engagement have value. The autodidact *alim* is as (if not more) pernicious as any organised, audited group of religious scholars. I would argue that a rejection of scholastic legalism does not imply a retreat into the wilful Cartesian subject determining his or her understanding of Islam as sovereign and complete.

The *ulama* are legitimate actors in the venture of Islam. The problem is not that Qadri and others in scholastic-legalistic framing are exceeding their proper authority, but rather, the method they are following is going beyond what it can bear. This can be seen in the claim that Qadri shares with those who he vehemently opposes like the Taliban and Al-Qaeda: Islam is a complete way of life. If Islam is a form of life, than it follows that it cannot be reduced to a matrix of rules, as following rules involves the practice of how those rules are obeyed and followed. One cannot trace in a linear fashion the movement from the statement of a rule to its implementation. This is why when well-meaning Muslims are called upon to account for an action committed by individuals in the name of Islam, the recourse to the argument that this action is not found in the Qur'an, while having some rhetorical purchase, is inadequate, since it is possible for any action to be made consistent with a rule. An example of this is provided by Qadri himself. The chain of citations that he uses to bind Muslims against what he calls so unproblematically 'terrorism' is full of interpretive shifts that belie his insistence on transparent reading of canonical texts as means of determining an Islamic position. For example, Qadri concludes that rebellion against a Muslim government is prohibited (ibid.: 10). A hundred pages later, however, he provides a

Prophetic example, the meaning of which is that one should only obey what is right (ibid.: 118). Those who wish to rebel will mobilise citations like those given on page 118 and those who oppose rebellion will refer to citations on page 10.[11]

In the approximately 500 pages of the *Fatwa on Terrorism and Suicide Bombings*, there is no serious attempt to conceptualise or define what terrorism is. This allows Qadri to introduce parenthetically the semantic equivalence between the phrase 'creating mischief in the land' and terrorism (ibid.: 97). This is not to accuse Qadri of shoddy scholarship, or to even suggest that such a 'translation' is invalid, but to point out that neither terrorism nor 'mischief in the land' have a transcontextual apodictic meaning. The application of rules cannot be grounded upon rules for applying rules, because in all such rules there will be an interpretative element. The meaning of following a rule is not given by the rule itself but rather by the culture, which says this is what it means to follow this rule.[12] It is not the *ulama* that determines what Islam is, or who a Muslim is; that is the province of the *ummah* as a totality at any given time.

It is for this reason that arguments for being a Muslim in one's own way collapse. As I have argued in the previous chapter, there is no way to be a Muslim except through a relationship with the *ummah*: past, present and future; even if that relationship is based on denial of the *ummah*. Being a Muslim cannot be exclusively a matter of private indulgence or whim, for being a Muslim means being in a relationship with other Muslims through which we learn and unlearn what being Muslim means or should mean. One can only be a Muslim in one's own way, as other Muslims are Muslims in their own way. The social nature of this 'one's own way' cannot be easily set aside. There is no monadic Muslimness. Being a Muslim means to partake in social practices which are constitutive of being part of a community. This is not peculiar to Muslims but rather the consequences of the impossibility of following rules except against the backdrop of a cultural setting which makes rule following possible.

Qadri's fatwa is a move in a language game which Muslims play: the canonical chain of citations, the admonishments that Islam does not permit this or that. The condemnation on moral grounds of those who cause 'mischief in the land' can always be trumped by an ethical call to correct the mores that afflict society. No chain of citations, no fatwas can foreclose such calls. The political needs to be embraced because it cannot be escaped. The proliferation of armed struggles throughout the *ummah* reflect not religious illiteracy or moral depravity but the absence of legitimate politics that can orient Muslims towards a better future. To reject the political in favour of the legal or the transcendent is to condemn Muslims to the fate of a people without history. At several points in this volume I have hinted that the articulation of the political and Islam is not necessarily a bad thing, rather it is the best hope for the future of the *ummah*. The political, however, needs to be domesticated by politics. The domestication of the political can take many different forms, reflecting various histories, commitments and entanglements. Islamic(ate) governance can be a form of the domestication of the political. The problem for those who advocate a form of Islamic(ate) governance is that the claim that such an entity would be ethical is both necessary and impossible. It is necessary because the appeal of Islamic(ate) governance as an instrument of rectifying injustice and bringing about a harmonious state of affairs is what provides it with traction among Muslims. It is impossible because an ethical state is unsustainable since ethics cannot be made concrete, and as soon as they become concrete and codified it becomes morality. Wael Hallaq (2013) would argue that construction of a moral community is the central task of what he describes as Islamic governance.[13] A moral state cannot be ethical as morality is provisional and open to a call for justice, which is permanent. The caliphate cannot be an Islamic(ate) state, which is a state that is bound by the demands of an ethics of Islam. If the caliphate is not ethical, then what is the point of it and why should Muslims struggle against tremendous odds for a chimera that will not deliver them justice and prosperity? The caliphate cannot deliver the ethical but it can fuel Muslim agency and empower the possibility of achieving an ethical horizon.

The caliphate is a polity which represents a global Muslim subjectivity. The caliphate is not merely an historical institution but rather an overdetermined ensemble around which questions of the governance of the *ummah* and the relationship between Muslim biographies and Islamicate histories are played out. The caliphate is a concentration of meanings about how the venture of Islam fits into the world. The ability of Muslims as a 'collective will' to make their own history, to project themselves into the future, to elaborate and enrich their sense of who they are and who they wish to be rests upon the possibility of the caliphate. In other words, without a great power to anchor the Muslim presence in the world system, the myriad problems that confront the *ummah* are going to be difficult to resolve. Of course, the challenge of a great power that is Islamicate is how to guarantee its Islamic character into the future. We have seen a number of projects that have sought to deliver a guarantee of an Islamic character through the establishment of Islamicate economics, the Islamicate state, or an Islamic constitution, and I have suggested that none of these can promise an Islamic great power. This question also overshadowed the second: how can Muslims create a great power that they can call their own? Dreams of ideal Islamic constitutions and wishes for an aggrandisement of Muslim power abound. The lack of Muslim unity is commonly bemoaned. Gatherings of Muslim politicians frequently pass resolutions calling for greater Muslim unity. As we discussed in Chapter 8, the historical tried and tested route for achieving great power has been blocked by contemporary arrangements of the international system. Muslims who wish for a great power of their own would need to pioneer an alternative route or the world system would need to be radically restructured. To some extent the difficulty of securing the Islamic(ate) character of a polity has tended to undermine thinking of the way in which to secure a great power for Muslims.

Any strategy has to have a clear sense of the interest it is trying to further. There can be no interest without there being a subject. Devising strategies on how to get an Islamicate great power is a futile exercise if there is no subject for whose interest one can make calculations and schemes. Getting an Islamicate great power means having women and men who are willing and able to work towards that end, because they identify their interests with a sense of who they are and who they want to be. It seems paradoxical that an Islamicate great power assumes a Muslim subjectivity as the condition of its possibility but it is precisely that subjectivity that it is supposed to protect and project into the future. To devise a strategy requires the cultivation of a subject. It is commonly assumed that there is already a ready-made Muslim subject around which it is possible to build a strategic project. Throughout this book I have shown that I am deeply sceptical of this assumption. Muslim subjectivity, in its 1,400-year post-Revelation history, has not been constant, it has not meant the same thing or had the same significance. Therefore the cultivation of a Muslim agency is the essential task of any project that aims to move towards an Islamicate great power. The strategy for establishing an Islamicate great power needs to be based on cultivation of ummatic Muslim subjectivity. The heterogeneity of a Muslim subject position cannot be a barrier to an Islamicate great power. As I have argued in previous chapters, there is no reason to assume that the heterogeneity of Muslims is qualitatively different from that found in China or India. It is possible, to argue that what unites India is its 'Hinduism'—there is no linguistic, ethnic or cultural homogeneity which makes it possible. It remains unclear why Islam would be insufficient to bind an Islamicate great power.[14]

Sohail Daulatzai describes a promising vector of Muslim agency and suggests:

the Muslim International is not geographically located. Instead it is composed of not only multiple and overlapping diasporas that have resulted from slavery, colonialism, and migration, but also by communities and collectives that have been shaped by uneven and disparate relationships to nation-states, capitalism, and imperial power, a zone of struggle and solidarity in which new kinds of politics emerge. The Muslim International … shapes and is shaped by the convergent histories and narratives that are central to the shared struggles of these overlapping diasporas. For those diverse histories and narratives are what influence the various modes of resistance and forms of mobilization that have continued to challenge power in enduring ways (Daulatzai, 2012: xxiii–xxiv).

The translation of the facticity of the *ummah* into the 'Muslim International' requires its mobilisation and transformation into a political agent. What Daulatzai seems to be pointing to is an innovation of a post-national Muslim politics, in which the Westphalian state does not constrain the expression of an Islamicate identity, and this expression is articulated with various decolonial discourses, in such a way that the Muslim International becomes the surface of inscription for decolonial demands. What is important to note, however, is that the cultivation of Muslim agency cannot be confined to a pietistic component. It requires intellectual and cultural expression that inserts the Muslim subject into the world. Muslim agency requires a counter-narrative that decolonises the global hegemony of the Plato-to-NATO story that makes flesh the colonial hierarchy of the West. What the non-West decolonial counter-narrative would lead to is the relativisation of the centrality of the Western enterprise as a template for the future of the world. In conditions in which an Islamicate great power seems impossible to achieve, the formation of a collective will on a global scale (the Muslim International) helps to bring about a strengthening of the capacity of Muslim subjects to imagine themselves as Muslims into the future. This imagining of an alternative future is an important first step towards planning for a better world. The counter-narrative that is decolonial and global would allow Muslims to fit their biographies with consistency and hope into a history. To prevent the Muslim International being simply a crystallisation of Muslim agency as permanent opposition it will be necessary to see it as moving towards the caliphate.

The answer to the Muslim question is the caliphate. (Of course, as I have tried to show throughout the pages of this volume, there can be no actual answer to the Muslim question since that is not a proper question, so to say that the caliphate is the answer to something that is not a question is a deconstructive gesture which targets not only the difficulty of transforming the quest for Muslim agency into a question but also the nature of the caliphate itself.) To recall the caliphate is not just to strive to bring it back, but to remember it and the historical sequence it projected and protected. The caliphate then is an actor on the world stage. It is the possibility of a redemptive conclusion to the diasporic condition of the *ummah*. The point of gaining power is not to simply keep on challenging those in power, but to build a new world, and this world cannot come about except through an exercise of power. It cannot be maintained except through the exercise of power. Groups that are unable to accept the impossibility of a world without power are condemned to permanent opposition. This does not mean that all exercises of power are equivalent but rather that the struggle is over different configurations of power, and not the utopian dreams of its elimination. Power can be tamed, but not abandoned. The caliphate would mean a reconfiguration of power not its elimination through a state of permanent opposition.

The caliphate does not have to be ethical; it has to be capable of building a world in which Muslims are not a scandalous presence. Its identification as an Islamicate entity arises not from the particular way in which it promotes or practises Islamically ordained behaviour, but rather, it can be a surface of inscription in which different projects and different paths to achieve a better fit between what is actual and what is ideal can be the subject of meaningful experiments. Its Islamic identity arises from its insertion into a historical sequence that connects with the past and forges a new future, in which it is antithetical to the prevailing world order. The caliphate offers a domestication of the political on an ummatic scale through the institution of the politics of Islam. A politics that is not theologically confined and conceived, but rather a politics in which Islam's presence in the world is made manifest.

IV

A manifesto for achieving the caliphate would have to innovate the strategies by which previous iterations of a great power have been brought into the world. The most common strategy for such an enterprise is based around the capture of a state apparatus by a dedicated vanguard of Islamists who then use the power of the state to bring about transformations of society in line with Islam, the benign effects of this transformation reverberate across the *ummah* and similar movements and transformations come to pass. Such narratives do not take into account the antagonistic nature of the entire enterprise: changing society in substantial ways means confronting those who are entrenched in the current order and identify with it. Any transformation that is worth accomplishing must mean a redistribution of resources and privileges, which mean that it does not follow that state capture by an Islamist vanguard or mass party will not generate resistance among various Kemalist forces, resistance that could be mobilised by external actors to hinder and thwart the Islamist projects of transformation.[15] So any attempt to have an Islamicate great power has to be less a restoration and more an innovation. What has to be innovated is not only the strategy for achieving the caliphate but a philosophy that can capture what the caliphate is. This is innovation not merely at the level of its institutional configuration (as a mechanism and criteria for selecting leadership) but at the level of what the meaning of the caliphate is.

The demand that the caliphate be an ethical state to justify its Islamic character is impossible to achieve. The caliphate that may come is not and cannot be an Islamic state. The dream of a caliphate at its most emancipatory is a dream about Islam as the articulation of the ethical and the political. To actualise the dream means translating the articulation of the ethical and the political into an institutional ensemble that can house the politics of Islam. The caliphate is not then an Islamic state in which its very structures and subjectivities can be reduced to a privileged interpretation and codification of a specific morality. This has even been the case historically, in which states which were considered to be primary expressions of Muslim sovereignty were characterised by Muslim scholars as being those that implemented the sharia. The sharia was always supplemented by other customary practices, it was not reducible to its literal kernel, as repeatedly demonstrated by analysis of court rulings in sovereign Islamicate polities.[16] Rather, the caliphate becomes the vehicle of social justice, prosperity and freedom under the sign of Islam. Its Islamic character arises from its narration as part of a historical sequence, its opposition to other historical possibilities and the rejection of the anti-Muslim. There is no algorithm for determining any of these processes. There is only a politics; the caliphate is the space for the politics of Islam.

In the absence of a central organisation able to coordinate the activities and responses for the achievement of the caliphate, the task of going towards the horizon of the caliphate has a number of paths. There is the path that emphasises armed resistance. Insurgency has been most successful when it has formed a phase of national liberation wars. It can be argued that national liberation wars have been one of the most successful forms of armed struggle. Through national liberation wars in many places the colonial order has been defeated. The successes of national liberation wars lead many groups who wish to change the order to try and imitate this form of armed struggle. Successful national liberation wars were often characterised by armed forces based in rural areas, gaining control of territory sufficient for the insurgents to exercise functions of government. This is the condition of dual power, where parallel institutions to the official state are established, creating an alternative society, which can act as a blueprint for the time when the insurgents gain power, as well as challenging the monopoly of the official state. The expansion of this liberated territory then culminates in the encirclement of cities (where the power of the colonial state is concentrated) and the final overthrow of the colonial regime.[17] The attempt to apply the national liberation strategies in many parts of Latin America, but also in the United States and Europe, however, has not been successful. This is largely because, in the conditions of highly urbanised societies, where the infrastructural reach of the state was far more intense and sustained, it proved almost impossible to create spaces of dual power, in which alternative models of socioeconomic organisation could be implemented.

The shrinking of the rural population through the process of urbanisation, the expansion of surveillance technology and the capacity of the state to penetrate its periphery, has made it difficult to secure a base area necessary for the establishment and exercise of dual power.[18] There is, however, another difficulty, namely that the friend/enemy distinction, which was sharply drawn and regularly enacted in the colonial order, where the colour line marked the colonial and the colonised, becomes blurred and confused in countries after formal decolonisation. In Muslimistan, national liberation wars, as a way of bringing about an Islamic(ate) state or the caliphate, have disintegrated into endemic violence without clear direction. The promiscuity with which targets are selected suggests that violence has a function that is divorced from a clear strategy. Without an effective overarching strategy, acts of violence begin to have their own rationality and purpose as acts of piety rather than actions in service of tangible ends. Confronted with the sustained violence of the American War on Terror, without the insulation of a state structure able to resist or limit the efficacy of American arms, armed resistance fragments into endemic violence which weakens rather than strengthens the expression of Muslim agency. The demagogisation of the lesser jihad reflects the inability of current Muslimstani states to conceptualise, let alone coordinate, resistance to the continued marginalisation and sublaternisation of the *ummah*. Non-state actors took up the task of achieving a political transformation through armed conflict with the American global order. In many regions this passing of the duty of jihad from governments to groups has gone further where individuals have begun to describe their acts of violence in terms of jihad. This movement from jihad as the province of the caliphate, to being a province of sub-caliphate governments, to being presumed an obligation of vanguard armed groups, to a 'lone wolf' operation indicates a progressive de-politicisation of the jihad and its separation from a strategy of liberation.[19] As a consequence, the lesser jihad is no longer a means but becomes an end in itself. The devolution of jihad from state to individual risks transforming the political into an expression of piety. This is not to argue for the abandoning of the principle of armed struggle, but rather highlighting that armed struggle has to be matched with clear and effective strategy, the impulse of which is emancipatory rather than authoritarian. The attempt to mobilise Muslims as political agents cannot be exclusively or mainly based on coercion or the fear of coercion.

Another path to the caliphate is one which emphasises cultural resistance over simply armed resistance. The caliphate could be achieved by a radical cultural transformation. Projects of cultural resistance have for the most part focused on preserving ways of life and most Islamist groups continue to read cultural struggle from the register of a morality. In this approach cultural resistance takes mainly a prohibitive form, its response to the perceived decadence of societies that Muslims find themselves in. Issues of inequalities, well-being and injustice, are all presented as signifiers of a moral corruption, which the correct application of Islam will resolve. The cultural policy of too many Islamist organisations becomes locked into being repressive rather than creative: continually forbidding rather than presenting alluring alternatives to the present state of affairs. The construction of a critical culture cannot be seen as a second order task, which focuses on shoring up a very narrowly conceived understanding of social behaviour and practices.

Recalling the caliphate requires not so much a cultivation of spiritual purity, or armed struggles to overthrow the existing order, but more importantly an elaboration of cultural production that encompasses the full gamut of what constitutes human life. If Islam is a way of life then its artistic and cultural productions must reflect that totality. In the realm of popular culture, Islamicate cultural production has gained some global influence primarily in the fields of music (particularly hip-hop and qawali).[20] Recalling the caliphate means a cultural struggle that is directed towards a horizon which is mundane, as well as spiritual. Since 1945, American global hegemony has been multi-dimensional. It has not rested simply on having the largest economy or one of the strongest military forces.[21] It has benefited from the way its cultural productions (cinema and popular music) have helped articulate and make its values and interests globally influential. A focus on the cultural production rather than prohibition would enrich and broaden what it means to be Muslim. It would also help construct an alternative to the prevailing global 'common-sense'.[22] An example of this can be seen in the way in which the story of Palestine is most likely to be narrated and policed through a Zionist prism throughout American society—in contrast, the same story among most members of the *ummah* is likely to be told through anti-Zionism. Muslims thousands of miles from Palestine are able to see in the plight of the Palestinian people something that they have empathy for. The spread of the anti-Zionist narrative has become one of the threads that connect the *ummah*. There is no reason why the struggles of Muslims in Kashmir, Burma and Chechnya could not become another common thread connecting and binding an ummatic culture. Harnessing cultural output to the production of the Islamicate rather than the policing of the Islamic would support the conditions for the articulation of a global Muslim counterpublic.[23]

Counterpublics are supplemental to hegemonic conceptions of public space, authority and debate. A counterpublic is constituted in conflict with a dominant public and its cultural horizon is marked by the awareness of its subordinated status (Warner, 2002: 423–5). Islamic(ate) counterpublics exist throughout the *ummah*, but for the most part they remained confined within the Westphalian cage of isomorphism between government, territory and culture. A global Islamicate counterpublic would operate at the transnational level, in opposition to the public of the 'international community' announced by Western powers.

A global Islamicate counterpublic is more likely to be established given the current arrangement of forces than a base area which acts as the crucible of the caliphate. To the extent that Islamicate counterpublics already exist, the task of articulating a global Islamicate counterpublic is not as challenging as building something from scratch. This is not of course to assume that attempts by Muslims to forge such a counterpublic will only be met by the cut-and-thrust of debate at the hands of their opponents. The War on Terror has ripped the liberal-democratic imaginary in which Western power saw itself (and was seen by those with short memories) as being a benign force which would not permit its values of freedom of speech and human rights to be abandoned. The compulsory force-feeding of one-third of Guantanamo inmates, drone strikes, and the disclosure of the mass surveillance and complicity of major American companies in the exercise of empire, have made it difficult to sustain the illusion that Western power is a force for good, and that liberalism is incompatible with systematic and sustained cruelty, or that reasoned argument and debate will be sufficient to resolve conflicts.[24]

Attempts by Kemalist governments to regulate and discipline the Islamicate counterpublic by the use of all the coercive machinery available to a state should give anyone pause for thought—the production of cultural outputs that point towards the caliphate would not have overcome coercive and disciplinary counter-measures. The advantage of a global Islamicate counterpublic animated by moving towards the direction of the caliphate is, however, two-fold. First, such a march towards the horizon of the caliphate does not require central coordination for its efficacy. It emerges as biographies connect with a sense of a historical stream.[25] Cultural production both in its everyday banal sense as well as in terms of a specific domain (art, music, literature) arises from multiple points of contact and connection, so given the scale of the *ummah* and its historical depth, the resources to present an alternative vision of the world is potentially difficult to police. Second, the sense of political direction given by recalling the caliphate helps to limit the risk of being swept-up by the immediate and overtaken by events and thrown off course by small disappointments and large deceptions. Recalling the caliphate is a means of standing for something as a way of avoiding falling for anything.

The most successful national liberation wars were those that were able to combine a controlled armed struggle with a cultural transformation. That is, campaigns in which the coercive and persuasive were locked together; in other words, national liberation wars as forms of hegemonic struggles. The caliphate could only come about through a hegemonic struggle. The challenge the *ummah* faces is how such hegemony can be established without a coordinating organisation, without a nascent Islamicate sovereign great power. Recalling the caliphate is the name for a hegemonic project that seeks to decolonise the *ummah*.

It could be argued that statism inherent in the notion of the caliphate limits its liberational potential. The Muslim International and an Islamicate global counterpublic would become redundant if an Islamicate great power was to be realised. An Islamicate global counterpublic would, however, cease to be if there was an Islamicate great power. Would not the caliphate's statecentric approach to mastering of the political diminish the capacity of Islam to be a corrective to the abuse of power? Would not the emergence of an existing caliphate subvert the sublaternity of the counterpublic and reduce its ethical potential?

Recalling the caliphate cannot be a plea for a restoration. It is also a recollection, a remembering of something less than perfect. An entity that both inspires and disappoints. An entity that was flawed and in need of reform, and at the same time an entity that promised to secure a Muslim presence and project Muslims into the future. Recalling the caliphate promises the possibility of a rejection of eurocentrism without a collapse into authenticity. The caliphate is not the Islamic state ruled by the Lord of Medina. The caliphate does not end in the second *fitna*, it does not end with the Mongol sack of Baghdad and it does not end with the proliferation of caliphs throughout Muslimistan.[26] The idea of the caliphate transcends the limits of the institution, as it anchors the political presence of Islam in the world.

Recalling the caliphate then is not simply the recovery of a narrative of glory and power but also recovery of its ignoble corruptions. The flaws and difficulties of an entity are as necessary as its strengths and benefits, because they give directions to a future which is not utopian but is worth working towards precisely because it is not utopian. The caliphate is not an ethical institution, rather it is an institution in which there is recognition of its ethical deficit. The common historiographical convention that divides the caliphate between the first four rightly guided caliphs and the rest is another admission of the ethical deficit of this institution. The caliphate is in a state of suspension between the ideal ethical state represented by the Medina polity and the various Kemalist states in which the historical sequence that began with the revelations to the Messenger of God is ruptured. The strategy for recalling the caliphate cannot have the character of a blueprint, but rather of poetic possibilities, which inspires and reorients Muslims to the practical task of protecting the *ummah* and projecting it into the future.

It is possible to sketch out various steps by which the caliphate could re-emerge: for example, the Turkish parliament transferring the office of caliph to the Organization of Islamic Cooperation (OIC); or by treaty in which the various major countries within the OIC which are accountable, transparent and independent form a viable confederation. One can then imagine all sorts of reforms of the institutions that would transform the OIC into a caliphal institution: weighted voting according to population, establishment of coordinating offices for social development, defence, financial, healthcare, promotion of the Islamicate—the problem is how to bring about an environment in which such decisions are made by those able to effect them.

In this process of making a space in the world for the *ummah*, the caliphate can open up the range of options available for the organisation of a global order in which the fundamental diversity of the planet is underwritten by multipolarity rather than disciplined by faux universalism. Muslims have been the most visible targets of the War on Terror; they have been conscripted into an emerging political consciousness, by the never-ending war. They trade stories comedic ('flying while been Muslim'), horrific (the visceral sadism in the force-feeding of the hunger strikers in Guantanamo) and heroic (daily grind of living under occupations in Palestine, Kashmir, Chechnya and Burma). The conversations of the *ummah* are now irredeemably coloured by the War on Terror as Kemalists and Islamists adjust to the banality of its execution. In these glimmerings of stories that break the cracks of hegemonic discourse, the possibility of alternatives exist. For the invisible casualties of the War on Terror include not only the dead and disappeared, but also the hollowing out of freedoms loudly proclaimed by the West and now quietly disavowed in order to prevent terrorism. The cosmopolitan dream of a well-regulated world in which a legal framework would promote and protect human rights has been cruelly exposed.[27] The search for alternatives to the current order, the attempt to articulate a vision of the world in which justice and prosperity prevail, seems to come unstuck not only in the face of American unipolarity but also in terms of trying to generate universal values from the European heritage which does not bracket the coloniality of that heritage. Recalling the caliphate can contribute to opening the possibilities of construction of an alternative world order. The caliphate's coming would be based on the rejection of the nation-state with its uneasy mixture of universalism and particularity. At the same time it would be a rejection of cosmopolitanism with its desire to replace the international order of multiple states with a world government based on internalisation and perpetuation of a liberal social imaginary.[28] The caliphate makes sense as one of the pillars of a fundamentally multiple world, where pluralism and multiculturalism are inscribed in the architecture of the world order. It strengthens the possibility of the post-Western world and post-*mazhabi* Islam.

Recalling the caliphate recognises that it is an exercise in world-making and that its poetic nature arises from the way in which it characterises the world and attempts to realise that world through its performance.[29] Recalling the caliphate means understanding that the challenges that confront Muslims collectively are neither religious nor cultural but political, and their resolution can only be found in a politics in the name of Islam. This politics has no necessary content other than that struggled over in the historical sequence inaugurated by the return of the Prophet Muhammad (pbuh). Islam is neither a religion of peace nor a religion of war—rather Islam is a language that Muslims use to tell stories about themselves. Recalling the caliphate, then, is a decolonial declaration, it is a reminder that Islam is Islam, and for Muslims that is all it needs to be.

To the Giver of intelligence and wisdom, eternal praise in abundance.

NOTES

1. NAMES

1. Perhaps postcolonial theory is just an extended footnote to this quote by Ibn Khaldun and this volume simply another extension of this footnote.
2. One could object and say that a name is simply a label that is attached to an object. A change of label does not change the object itself. Such an objection can only be made in a universe in which the distinction between linguistic phenomena is sharply divided from material phenomena or from reality itself. But reality is itself a human invention: that is, we experience the universe through the facticity of humanness, and between humans and the world is language, which we cannot simply jump over.
3. The phrase 'people without history' as Eric Wolf explains was used by Marx and Engels to describe East European nationalism that they considered not to be a harbinger of modernity. Wolf's book *Europe and the People Without History* used the phrase ironically as a means of arguing that cultures studied by anthropology were not pristine worlds lost in time but rather a result of the processes of European global expansion. See Wolf (1982) for more details.
4. Smith (1995: 22–4) lists having a name as one of the five key features that define an *ethnie*.
5. For example, after the fall of Nineveh in 614 BCE, the Assyrians began to disappear from memory. It is unlikely that Assyrians as biological entities ceased to exist, but they vanished as an ethno-political entity. See Simo Pampola's (1999) arguments for the continuity of Assyrian identity beyond the collapse of the Assyrian Empire.
6. Throughout this book when two dates appear, the first refers to the Hijri calendar and the second to the Common Era.

7. Schulze (2000: 24–5) points out that in 1900 there was only an Islamicate public space in the Ottoman Empire, Iran, Afghanistan and the Arabian peninsula—the rest of 'Muslimistan' was under European hegemony.

8. The concept of the vernacular intellectual has been developed by Grant Farred (2003).

9. Given the demographics of Nazi concentration camps, its inmates would have overwhelmingly been of Jewish heritage, Roma, homosexuals and, of course, communists.

10. A number of prison memoirs have emerged as well as information gleaned from confidential official sources detailing the treatment of those deemed to be 'enemy combatants'. See Moazzam Begg's (2006) story of his plight in the American global gulag. See also Rejali's (2007: 503–18) analysis of the use of torture in the War on Terror. Darius Rejali's meticulous and exhaustive account of modern torture demonstrates that the use of torture in the War on Terror is not an aberration but rather Western democracies (France, United States, Britain) have been pioneers in the development of torture techniques.

11. I would like to acknowledge Dr Hesse, connoisseur of the stand-up art for reminding me of this skit.

12. See Mamdani (2005) for an elaboration of this dialectic between 'good' and 'bad' Muslims.

13. This grounding, as I will argue in more detail in subsequent chapters, is ultimately political.

14. I owe this reading of Heidegger primarily to Iain Thomson (2005). A number of arguments are advanced to reject the possibility that any context could be organised around a single logic. Most of these criticisms are arguing for the complexity of any context and attempting to point to the various countervailing tendencies within that context. Such criticism sees complexity in empirical terms; in other words, it seems that a society of a million people would be less complex than a society of a hundred million. Moreover, it fails to recognise that a context is itself not an empirical object but rather a product of a particular intervention. The framing of the context requires a logical order. All contexts are based on relationality; therefore, their organisation as contexts will always involve patterns of exclusions and inclusions. This system of inclusions and exclusions will be organised around a set of principles, and that set of principles would constitute the logic of the context.

15. Stephen Howe (2011) believes that: 'A mythical Islam has apparently acquired a kind of immunity from the demands of contextualisation, of attention to internal diversity and change and to structural determination, which are posed to historical and social studies of almost all other ideolog-

ical formations. In a period when "imagined communities", "invented traditions" and the "social construction of knowledge" are the commonplaces and even clichés of contemporary intellectual work, Islam became widely exempt from these elementary stipulations'. As we will see in the next chapter such deliberations are a staple of Eurocentric writing on matters Islamicate.

16. One of the common refrains in writing on Muslims is to see Muslimness as a façade for ethnicities. This evidence is in accounts both popular and academic which continue to describe Muslim imperial formations in terms of their assumed ethnic markers (Arab or Turkish empires). It is evidenced in contemporary studies which see ethnicity at play in Muslim mobilisations in Western plutocracies. See for example, Sami Zubaida and the ever so provocative Stephen Howe's interventions on the subject.

17. See Sayyid (2003: 36–9) for a critique of the notion of local 'litte Islams'.

18. That is the language game played around ideas of Western exceptionality and centrality.

19. See Sayyid (2003: 31–46) for a detailed discussion of the differences between 'weak' and 'strong' Orientalism.

20. Grosfoguel concedes the cumbersome nature of this formulation but maintains that its heuristic value outweighs its inelegance of expression (personal communication).

21. See Fazlur Rahman's gentle scepticism about the possibility of a priori rules for the production of Islamic thought (1984: 11).

22. Of course, all three positions contain within them a host of heterogeneous outlooks and proclivities, and my use of these strands of critical thinking is pragmatic rather than devotional.

23. The dirty war (*guerra sucia*) referred initially to the campaign of eradication of left-wing guerrillas and their assumed supporters by the Argentine military junta (1974–1983). It then came to be a more generalised form of counter-insurgency operations based around the education of Latin American military and police officers at the School of the Americas in waging armed conflicts against domestic subversive threats. The War on Terror can be seen as an expansion of the logic of the dirty war on a global scale directed at Islamists and their assumed supporters.

2. LIBERALISM

1. See Donald Pease's (1999) insightful analysis of Khatami's attempt at dialogue.

2. By 'Muslimistan' I mean the countries of the world in which Islam is dominant—for all intents and purposes it approximates the membership of the

Organization of Islamic Cooperation, with a few possible tweaks, for example the exclusion of Mozambique and inclusion of Bosnia Herzogovina, see Sayyid (2010). Compare the idea of Muslimistan with Marshall Hodgson's notion of Islamdom (1977: 58).

3. See Mouffe's (2005: 10–11) discussion of liberalism and its inability to conceptualise the political as both the realm of antagonism and collective formation.

4. Iranian president Mohammad Khatami, interview by Christiane Amanpour, CNN, 7 January 1998, http://edition.cnn.com/WORLD/9801/07/iran/interview.html, last accessed 17 Apr. 2012. In what follows I am indebted to Donald Pease's (1999) article on the use of Tocqueville by Khatami.

5. Ibid.

6. The argument being advanced here does not depend on the degree to which the *New Republic* can be considered as representing American journalism, rather, what is instructive about the *New Republic* is how it illustrates the logic of the discourse of Westernese in relation to Khatami's attempt to build a dialogue of civilisations.

7. This resonates with classic Oriental fantasy in which the white man (sic) can pass himself off as the 'Other', but the 'Other' cannot imitate the Western. So much so that people born and brought up in European metropolises continue to be marked as irredeemably 'Other' and questions about 'where they come from' continue to be asked at any social function.

8. See Pease's (1999) discussion of Tocqueville within contemporary American political culture.

9. Amanpour (1998).

10. There is almost certainly a false belief that use of 'Old Nick' to refer to the Devil was based on Machiavelli's first name Nicolo.

3. SECULARISM

1. I discuss the difficulties of atomistic readings of the Qur'an in Chapter 10.

2. A small group of critics of the Israeli Zionist project do so in purely Judaic terms, denying the possibility of the establishment of a state of Israel in the absence of the messiah.

3. This is not to deny that in recent years secularism, in the United States at least, was primarily discussed in terms of arguments about the separation of church and state in the context of the cultural and political advances made by the *Nasrani* Right. It would be fair to say, however, that with the advent of the War on Terror as the grammar of global governance, the discussion on secularism as a problem for the world is increasingly inflected through Islamicate examples and instances.

4. This, of course, applies only to the dominant version of modernity and its relationship with Western identity. See Martin Jacques (2012) on a distinct East Asian modernity.

5. Of course, this does not mean that there are no Muslims who refute the claims of secularism. In fact, in the wake of the global dirty war, many organisations have emerged in Western plutocracies who advocate secular or moderate Islam (Progressive Muslims, Muslims for Secular Democracy). It is the case, however, that there are many more Muslims who are critical of secularism as it is deployed as a means of disciplining Muslimness.

6. Donner remarks on the viciousness of the First and Second Civil Wars among the early Muslim community, and their narrow range of elite participants so that the wars could often appear as intense and uncompromising family feuds (2012: 189).

7. Common to all three types of regime would be the de facto identification between the universal and the Western.

8. There are, of course, other reasons, including the difficulty of actually knowing what a particular divine decision is.

9. Pandey shows how in the immediate aftermath of Partition there remained a great deal of uncertainty about the extent to which the 'Muslim minority' in India was Indian (1999: 610–61).

10. The homology with racism and Western plutocracies is worth noting: racism continues to be presented as being an exceptional state of affairs rather than something that continuously shapes the modern Western order (Hesse, 2004a).

11. As stated earlier in fn. 3, the US may have been an exception to this, since prior to 9/11, the debate around secularism took the form of contestations around church and state relations, or most furiously around the struggle between pro-choice and pro-life groupings.

12. I argue this point in more detail in Chapter 7.

13. See Chapter 7.

14. The coup that removed Mohammed Morsi from power in Egypt was justified in terms of the necessity to keep religion out of politics, or specifically, to keep Muslims (in the form of the Muslim Brotherhood) out of power. See Beach (2013).

15. I discuss the idea of democracy as the means of disclosing the Western kernel beneath all other cultural accretions in Chapter 5.

4. RELATIVISM

1. Perhaps the loss of the caliphate has made too many Muslims fearful. Perhaps the sight of so much Muslim blood being shed in so many different places makes them worry about the future of Islam itself.

2. Notwithstanding the Muslim involvement in anti-Iraq war movements in Western plutocracies.

3. See Birt's (2007) discussion of Islam-West *kulturkampf* in contemporary Britain.

4. See Chetan Bhatt (1997) and Sami Zubaida (2007) for examples of work which sees the multiculturalist policies of the British state as supporting Muslim essentialism. In addition to academic writing, there is also the work of provocateur commentators who make the same point such as Martin Bright, Melanie Philips, Daniel Pipes and Nik Cohen.

5. In contrast, one can see the attempt John Keane makes to demonstrate the 'ecumenical' nature of his vision of global civil society by including Muslims as active partners in this venture, rather than as just silent spectators or supplicants. Keane makes an effort to narrate his vision by drawing on non-Western sources, including Islamicate figures.

6. For a description of high life that any European colonial hand would recognise see Chandrasekaran (2007).

7. See for example the statements of principles of the Project for the New American Century, http://www.newamericancentury.org/statementofprinciples.html, last accessed 28 Feb. 2013.

8. See Liz Fekete's analysis of the counter-jihad movement (2012).

9. Rumy Hasan's *Multiculturalism: Some Inconvenient Truths* (2010) is an excellent example of this genre, in which the author's opposition to Muslims is joined with a belief that multiculturalism undermines Enlightenment values.

10. For a discussion of logical incoherence of publically self-proclaimed ex-Muslims see Birt (2007).

11. For example, David Cameron, prime minister of Britain has spoken of a 'cultural apartheid' by which Muslims apparently self-segregate. See Brian Klug's (2011) discussion of Cameron's Munich speech.

12. See, for example, the Ousley report which accused Muslims of enforcing segregation by sending their children to local schools where 90 per cent of the pupils were from Muslim backgrounds. Oddly, but consistent with this genre, the existence of all-white schools was not seen as being segregationist nor was the argument made that its Anglo-British parents pulling their children out of local schools that made them segregationists. See Finney and Simpson's critique of the prevalence of such segregation in Britain (2009).

13. This, of course, would also apply to any other political project, be it Islam or China or the United States.

14. One thing that Edward Said's work has made clear is that academic neutrality or consistency has not always been present in the study of the Orient.

See, for example, Brendan O'Leary's comments on the way in which Bernier's conceptualisation of Oriental despotism contradicted his own descriptions of Indian society (1989: 57) or Springborg (1992) on Weber.

15. It is interesting to note that during the Cold War, in Europe at least, it was the Soviet Union and its satellites that were accused of repressing freedom of expression, and it was the Western broadcasting organisations that were routinely and rather unsubtly censored by electronic jamming. It is important, however, not to suggest that there was no political censorship in Western plutocracies, but just that, given liberal governmentality, it was often privatised.

16. See Slater's (1994) discussion of Baudrillard, pp. 94–6.

17. See for example, Niall Ferguson (2004).

18. In semantics, lexemes that are unmarked tend to be less restricted in the range of contexts in which they can be used than marked lexemes. For example, tiger refers not only to male of the species but also the species in general whereas tigress (which is marked by addition of a suffix) refers only to a female tiger (Lyons, 1968: 305–11).

5. DEMOCRACY

1. As Sarantakes (2005: 83) points out this view was clearly held by the creators of *Star Trek*, who saw different political systems not in terms of their socioeconomic efficiency but that a democratic society would value life and a non-democratic society would not and be based on fear and terror.

2. Interestingly, we discover that the mirror universe counterparts of the *Enterprise* who had been transported to 'our' *Enterprise* had been immediately recognised and detained. This is explained by the capacity for rational beings to appear as savage, a capacity that savages lack—they cannot get away with pretending to be civilised. Readers will immediately recognise another Orientalist trope. See Said (1985).

3. 'Mirror Mirror,' *Star Trek: The Original Series*, Season 2, Episode 33, originally broadcast on 6 Oct. 1967.

5. See comments by supreme leader of the Islamic Revolution Ayatollah Seyed Ali Khamenei who once again underscored that Islamic revolution (rather than the American invasion of Iraq) was the inspiration for the 'Arab Spring', http://english.farsnews.com/newstext.php?nn=9107126223.

6. For example, Held (1995) acknowledges that Athenian democracy is a fundamental source of inspiration for Western political thought. Similar views can be found from any cursory glance at the corpus of Western political thinking.

7. Both Held (1995) and Hornblower (1993) concede that democratic elements may have Phoenician and Mesopotamian antecedent.

8. Simon Hornblower (1993) suggests that democracy begins with Sparta and the institution of a constitution that called regular meetings of a popular assembly.

9. As elegantly explored by Patricia Springborg (1992).

10. The recognition of Orientalism within Classical studies has led to a number of recent works that have begun to devalorise the Ancient Greek experience and, in particular, its relationship with the Persian Orient.

11. It was not unusual to have juries of 6,000 from the total citizenry (those who held full political rights) of around 30,000 during the fifth century BCE. For details of the level of mobilisation see Ober (1996).

12. See for example, the Achaemenid History Workshops project of reappraising and reconceptualising the Greek historical record, so that it is seen more as part of Greek cultural conventions, rather than as a transparent reading of the world of the ancient Greeks, especially Kuhrt and Sancisi-Weerdenburg (1988). The hazards associated with such a revision of one of the West's foundational narratives can be seen in the debate generated by the publication of Martin Bernal's *Black Athena* (2001). Alas, too often the social sciences continue to rely on versions of ancient history, which someone like Weber would be familiar with, and refuse to acknowledge the transformations that have occurred in the discipline and which put into question many of the easy assumptions about the West and non-West.

13. See Fuss (1989) for a fuller examination of the nature of essentialism.

14. Populism can be seen as a category that emerges to explain a divergence between Democracy and Western identity that cannot be resolved by an expansion of the boundaries of the West (see S. Sayyid, 2003).

15. Žižek sees in democracy the master-signifier of the capitalist world order, rather than a Western-dominated world order (2002: 273). In this regard, there seems to be an overlap between Samir Amin's understanding of Eurocentrism as capitalism and Žižek.

16. The relationship between Islamism and the West is rather complex. For a set of arguments that see Islamism as anti-Western—in a cultural sense, not necessarily in a geopolitical sense—see Sayyid (2003).

17. This, of course, is the ambition of John Keane's (2009) magnus opus *The Life and Death of Democracy*. What follows is based on Keane's attempts to displace Eurocentrism from the narrative of democracy.

18. See Barkcin (2000) for an insightful analysis of the relationship between post-Cold War Western realpolitik and the export of Democracy.

19. Given the affinity between the neo-conservatives of the Bush administration and Reaganism it is worth reflecting on the Reaganite project of promoting democracy in Latin America during the 1980s. Carothers points out that there is a very strong tendency within the United States to see its

political institutional arrangements as the essence of Democracy itself, rather than merely one possible institutional configuration among many others (1993: 249).

20. Žižek sees in the democratic consensus the exclusion of any possibility of imagining alternative social, economic and political arrangements (2002: 167).

6. FUTUROLOGY

1. The Mahdi is an eschatological figure that features in various popular Islamicate beliefs. The Mahdi is considered to be a figure who will establish a redemptive rule over the world prior to the Day of Judgment. Among some groups the Mahdi is identified with the return of the twelfth Imam who among the Jaffari *mazhab* is considered to have gone into occultation in 259/873, while others identify the Mahdi with the return of Isa (Jesus).

2. *Dune*, Dir. John Harrison, Tandem Communications, 2000, TV Series.

3. In what follows, I confine my remarks to the world constructed in Frank Herbert's first *Dune* trilogy and the mini-series *Dune* (2002)—this means I have nothing or little to say in this piece about David Lynch's film version of *Dune* (1985), except that it is interesting to note that there are only two or so incidental references to the Mahdi in the entire film. Nor do I comment on subsequent *Dune* novels by Frank Herbert.

4. This is not to discount science fiction outside Western modernity, for exampleTurkey.

5. This description is inspired by Heidegger's, *The Question Concerning Technology*, esp. pp. 13–19. Also see Kass (1993), esp. pp. 2–8, where Kass defines technology as a means of rational and instrumental calculation by which the world is ordered so that it achieves the highest levels of efficiency and control with the least expenditure of effort.

6. See Gray's (2004) comments on p. 42.

7. See Khalid Bahyedeldin, 'Islamic themes in Frank Herbert's Dune', 12 September 2004, http://baheyeldin.com/literature/arabic-and-islamic-themes-in-frank-herberts-dune.html. The site is useful for showing the influence of Arabic vocabulary, in particular in the construction of the *Dune* universe.

8. Frank Herbert in Dune Genesis http://www.Dunenovels.com/news/genesis.html.

9. I would not want to suggest that Herbert deployed exclusively Islamicate themes, clearly there are references to other world cultures and histories—many of the rituals of the Fremen are extrapolated from the Apaches, for example. However, the Islamicate influences clearly predominate in the world of *Dune*.

10. See Jane Park's study of what she describes as the 'oriental style' in Hollywood's representation of the future. In particular, her reading of *The Matrix* (Park, 2010).

11. One could argue, for example, that Herbert's handling of intrigue in *Dune* is rather unsatisfactory, for the initial impetus for the action of *Dune* is the decision by the Emperor Shaddam IV to hand over the most valuable resource (the planet Arrakis) to a potential challenger, Duke Leto. Even though this handover is a trap, the bait being used seems too valuable and an unnecessary risk. Intrigue in the *Dune* universe often comes across as melodramatic rather than Machiavellian.

12. See Springborg's (1992) reflections on the relationship between Orientalism and the development of political theory as another front in the antagonism between West and the non-West.

13. It was increasingly influenced by the Persian lexicon, initially through the medium of post-Achemenid Hellenistic monarchies and subsequently by the increased direct interactions with the renewed Persian Empire under the Sassanid Dynasty from the third century CE onwards.

14. Of course, there is little doubt that the later Muslim rulers began to absorb Persianate and Roman lexicons of power.

15. See al-Azmeh (2001: 63) for a pedantic rejection of the ex nihilo character of the first Islamic polity. Unfortunately, such a reading is too literal and fails to acknowledge that, strictly speaking, the category of 'ex nihilo' is only possible if one accepts the notion of an absolute origin. That is, a moment beyond which one cannot go to explain a causal relationship. In human history we are confronted not with absolute origins but contingent beginnings, that is, causal relationships can always be found to recede on the horizon. As such, 'ex nihilo' can mean no more than the provisional statement of relative newness rather than the appearance of something out of nothing.

16. The 'revolutionary' nature of the formation of the Islamic state had already meant that the reliance on pre-Islamic Arabian political categories was not adequate for the task of ruling an empire much larger than any previous imperial order.

17. This is the Roman army following reforms generally associated with Diocletian's reign. See Fergus Millar (1993: 191–3) for evolution of the rank of dux within the Roman army.

18. For an analysis of some of these binary oppositions see the work of Ali Shariati (1979) who articulates the messianic impulse with the revolutionary potential of mobilisation under the sign of Islam.

19. 'The Omega Glory' was released during the second season of the original Star Trek series in 1967, as the Vietnam War moved towards its climax.

Star Trek: The Original Series, Dir. Vincent McEveety, Desilu Productions, First broadcast 1 March 1968.

7. DIASPORA

1. Castells places Islamist movements within the genre of religious fundamentalism and suggests that religious fundamentalism has been present 'throughout human history'. While we should not take this hyperbole too literally, it is clear that Castells's definition of fundamentalism has been taken without reservation from the 'Fundamentalism' project, which sees fundamentalism as a species of dogmatism that has been a constant in human history. Following this observation, Castells argues that 'Islamic identity is constructed on the basis of a "double deconstruction"'' (2001: 15) in which subjects must deconstruct themselves as national citizens or ethnic groups and '(W)omen must submit to their guardian men'. Castells refers to surah IV (v.34) as a way of justifying this claim. Of course, it is equally possible to pluck other verses from the Qur'an to demonstrate that the Qur'an is one of the few sacred texts that makes continual and frequent references to 'believing men and women', 'believing woman and man', and so on.

2. Castells also seems to conflate Ali and Hussein, by giving the date of Ali's assassination as the date of Hussein's martyrdom.

3. For example, the dispute surrounding the publication by Danish newspaper *Jyllands-Posten* (30 September 2005) of twelve cartoons depicting the Prophet (pbuh) was transformed once the Muslim community in Denmark was able to mobilise the rest of the *ummah* on its behalf.

4. See Ouis (2001) discussion of the significance of a McDonalds in Mecca.

5. For example, it can be argued that the part of the intensity of debate generated by the publication of *Black Athena* was the way it questioned the originary moment of the Plato to NATO sequence.

6. As Hirst and Thompson (1996) argue, the scale of population movement in the wake of the dismantling of the European empires (including the Soviet Union) does not compare in scale with the movement in the nineteenth century, when millions of Europeans settled in the Americas, and parts of Africa, Asia and Oceania.

8. CALIPHATE

1. Even if there was to be a conflict about distinct administrative arrangements, those administrative structures would be overdetermined so that they symbolise something more than mere bureaucratic procedures. Even one of the most liberal of revolutions, that which founded the United States of America,

was not a struggle at its core about the quality of distinct administrative arrangements.

2. Of course, the more theologically inclined could argue that redemption for Muslims is only possible if Muslims simply return to the way of the Prophet (pbuh) and His pristine message. Such a liberal understanding of redemption would negate the political, since individual salvation cannot be the basis of collective action, thus it cannot be a source of politics. This is similar to the criticism that Roy (1994) makes regarding what he describes (rather problematically) as 'neofundamentalism'.

3. Sabet (2008: 97–124) makes a powerful case for the conceptual richness of Khomeini's theorisation of the *velayat-e faqih*.

4. This list is in defence of freedom of speech, gender equality, opposition to sharia law and opposition to the establishment of the caliphate. It is interesting to note the self-referential quality of these points: the opposition to Muslim autonomy is not based on a rejection of Muslim demands. These demands demonstrate the self-referential quality of the discourse against Muslim autonomy, a single narrative that sees the Islamist enemy as the enemy it would like to face, rather than the enemy it does face.

5. For it was the decision by Mustafa Kemal to effectively abolish the caliphate by transferring it to the Grand National Assembly that helped to lay down the conditions of the possibility of Islamism. See Sayyid (2003: 57–63).

6. Like many major institutions, the caliphate has different significance at different points in Muslim history. For example, the title Guardian of Holy Cities began to assume far greater importance than the title of Caliph following the Mongol sacking of Baghdad (Bulliet, 1994: 172–75). It is also the case, that much of European writing on the caliphate was conditioned by the contestation over the role of the Ottoman order and its ability often circumscribed but still powerful enough to provide some sort of check to European colonial encroachments (Khan, 2007). Given the proximity of Ottoman domains to the centre of European power, and the duration and intensity of its various conflicts with European forces, and considering the fate of other Asian polities (such as the Mughal Empire), the capacity of the Ottomans to sustain themselves is a remarkable achievement which no amount of compromises, miscalculations and capitulations can erase. Despite all the caveats and disappointments of Ottoman rule, they continued to represent a continuity of an independent Muslim presence in the world. The *ummah* increasingly recognised this achievement as one Muslim state after another fell under European colonial control, so that by 1900 the Muslim populations of the British, Dutch, Russian and French empires dwarfed that of the Ottomans. Even then, half of all the population of free Muslims, that is Muslims not living under European colonialism, were under the rule of the Ottomans (Schulze, 2002: 25).

7. Of course, most conventional Muslim reflections on the caliphate would consider being male a necessary rather than a contingent qualification of being a caliph. There is, however, no reason to assume that the caliphate could not be a collective office or occupied by a woman. The office of the caliphate would not be immune to hegemonic constructions and contestations.

8. There is a debate as to when to date the 'decline' of the Ottomans. There are a number of possibilities: the failure to take Vienna in 1689, the treaty of Karlowitz in 1699 where the Ottoman Empire accepted the right of Russian patronage of their Christian Orthodox subjects, or 1798 and the Napoleonic invasion of Egypt, or the de facto secession of Egypt in the 1840s or the imposition of financial administration in 1870. I tend to favour the sequence of wars beginning with the First Balkan War and culminating with the First World War as the point when the Ottoman capacity to be a great power was shattered. Even in 1914 the boundaries of the Ottoman state included the following countries: Turkey, Iraq, Syria, Lebanon, Palestine, Yemen, Jordan and parts of Saudi Arabia including Hejez. Such a state would probably be the second or third most populous Muslim country in the world and certainly have the largest GDP. It is very likely that it would be in the first rank of Islamicate countries and possibly on par with other regional giants. Little wonder that Imam Khomeini acknowledged the Ottoman state's value, despite being monarchical and many of its rulers being corrupt, as a guarantor of Muslim independence. See Khomeini (1981: 49).

9. The term 'great power' was first used in relation to the five key participants in the Congress of Vienna.

10. In the interregnum between the Cold War and the War on Terror there was a widespread belief that military capacities were no longer sufficient to guarantee great power status. The belief that the age of warfare was over can be seen in the experiments by the US military to develop non-lethal weapons, as well as the idea that a reduction in military forces was possible and would signal the new age of liberalism and democracy. This was to be the 'end of history'. The events of the Gulf War and subsequent colonial-style occupation of Iraq and Afghanistan seemed to re-emphasise the utility of military capacity in maintaining great power status. See Waltz (1979) for a discussion of the significance of military power in anarchical systems. See also Hirst (2001) for an analysis of the relationship between coercion and persuasion as the source of the capabilities of a great power.

11. For counter-intuitive consequences of such an eventuality see Mouffe (2005: 76–83, 115–18).

12. Obviously if there is a high degree of homogeneity among the great powers around core values and norms this would limit the capacity of rival groupings in weak states to appeal to contending great powers, and there-

fore their freedom of movement, as was the case when great powers formed a white club. See Furedi (1998).

13. Tariq Ali's various outpourings give constant if rather repetitive expression to the idea that Muslim subjectivity is too fragile for what he would consider a 'progressive' politics. More specifically, the division of Pakistan in 1971 is a staple of South Asian historiography where the independence of Bangladesh in 1971 is already inscribed in the formation of Pakistan in 1947. See Ali (1983, 2005).

14. For example, in many ways the French did not become French until the 1880s.

15. Zubaida's (2007) review of Tariq Modood's book on multiculturalism (2007) displays the usual inability to comprehend Muslim identity.

16. It is also an open question whether without Indian military intervention East Pakistan would have seceded.

17. Ian Lustick (1997) rejects these arguments in his investigation of why the Middle East does not have a great power, but what he says has a wider application. Factors 1–4 are based on his discussion. Though his analysis is limited to the failure of Arab nationalism to produce a Middle Eastern great power, his conclusions are relevant to account for the difficulties of an Islamicate great power emerging in the post-Ottoman universe.

18. Data provided by the Organization of Islamic Cooperation presents a pitiful level of trade between its members.

19. Part of the problem is the way in which Westernese preserves for itself the enterprise of politics. Therefore, Western statesmen tend to be narrated as magisterial and prudential figures in comparison with non-Western statesmen. Only a handful of non-Western practitioners are accorded the status of acting prudentially (Mahatma Ghandi and Nelson Mandela), and again their personal conduct is seen as quasi-saintly and thus above politics. The contrast between the dominant discourses surrounding Mao or Khomeini with Ghandi and Mandela is telling, as is the degree to which each of these figures presided over major cultural and socioeconomic transformations.

20. There is an extensive literature about the metrics of a great power. For my purposes, the use of GNP is indicative of orders of magnitude rather than strictly predictive. Any list of Muslimistani states based on scale would include most of these ten countries. So, for example, the list of the ten most populous Muslimistani countries would substitute Morocco for Malaysia; the list of the ten largest militaries would add Syria and Morocco and leave out Nigeria and Malaysia. Of course, any such list is very crude and makes no allowance for geopolitical positioning (contrast Nigeria's paramount position in at least West Africa with Pakistan's impressive metrics being undermined by its location in regions containing India, China, Russia and,

via the occupation of Afghanistan, the European Union and the United States. See Map of the Muslim World (forthcoming).

21. According to the *Pew Global Attitudes Project* report (Pew Research Centre, 2006), Muslims surveyed both in Muslimistani countries (Pakistan, Jordan, Turkey, Indonesia, Nigeria and Egypt) and in Western plutocracies (UK, Spain, Germany and France) assert the primacy of their Muslim identity over their national affiliation. Among Muslims in Nigeria, 71 per cent identified with being Muslim as being primary compared to only 51 per cent of Nigerian Christians. Only in Indonesia primacy of Muslimness did not reach a majority. This is clearly in contrast to commentators who deny the primacy of Muslim identities.

22. For example, the international political movement Hizb ut-Tahrir which has branches throughout the *ummah* organised a meeting on 13 August 2007 attended by 80,000 to 100,000 people in Indonesia in support of the idea of a caliphate. See BBC News 13 Aug. 2007, news.bbc.co.uk/2/hi/asia-pacific/6942688, last accessed 5 Mar. 2013.

23. See for example, Chantal Mouffe's argument that terrorism is a consequence of a unipolar world (2005: 76–82).

9. ORDER

1. Debate about Iraq's post-Saddam flags can be found at http://news.bbc.co.uk/2/hi/middle_east/3660663.stm. See also Al Jazeera http://english.aljazeera.net/English/archive/archive?ArchiveId=3328. See also Cockburn and Usborne (2004).

2. The measures included very public coverage of Saddam Hussein at prayer, the attempt to establish his family lineage as belonging to Sayyids, that is, those who claim or whose ancestors have claimed they are directly descended from the Prophet (pbuh); and more bizarrely the copy of the Qur'an written using the blood Saddam Hussein donated over a two-year period as ink.

3. See Charles Tripp's powerful analysis of the way in which Muslim intellectuals have responded to the capitalist transformations of Islamicate societies (2006).

4. The two notable exceptions are Malaysia and Turkey, which seem to have produced high growth rates for over a decade under governments which are certainly 'Islam friendly'. One also needs to discount the oil-fuelled economies of the Arabian Peninsula whose economic development has almost exclusively been a function of the export of oil.

5. Kuran's criticism is severely hindered by the way in which his work falls within the genre of Eurocentric accounts of 'the European Miracle'. A forceful critique of this genre can be found in Blaut (2000).

6. See Bent Flyvbjerg's (1998) detailed study of the machinations that led to the Aalborg project, a three-year plan to integrate environmental and social factors in dealing with private motor vehicle use and the provision of a bus terminal. Flyvbjerg's study takes place in a medium-sized Danish town. Francis Fukuyama (2011) sees Denmark also as the criterion of what an actually existing Utopia might be like: an effective state, a transparent and just system of law, and accountable government.

7. Economy and culture are discursively constructed fields of activities and networks; they are not the uncovering of pre-given entities. The construction of such discursive fields has changed over time.

8. This is argued by Richard Bulliet (2009), who provides a persuasive account of the prevalence and persistence of the middle Persian language following the Muslim conquests. Middle Persian became the second language of the Islamicate commonwealth, not because of its intrinsic qualities or the qualities of the speakers but because of the transformations that Bulliet describes in the urbanisation and de-urbanisation of Iran.

9. Kuran makes the argument that Islamicate financial and legal practices blocked the economic development of the Middle East thus making these societies vulnerable to European colonial enterprise. The teleology of Kuran's account downplays the mutability of social practices. In the Islamicate context this is provided by the division policed by the *ulama* and others, between the immutable core of belief and the contextual needs of the common good. There is no reason to assume a priori that Muslims could not adapt their practices if it became necessary to do so. This line of argument is akin to the one which Giancarlo Casale points out that continually chides the Ottomans for not setting out to discover America, forgetting that Columbus did not go in search of America but India and the Ottomans had an idea where it was and how to get there (2010: 11).

10. A comparison between the early Islamicate state and its transition to empire and the Roman republic's transition to empire shows how assassinations, civil wars and usurpations were common as both political entities attempted to manage the crises produced by the acquisition of empire. What is remarkable, of course, is that despite these challenges, the degree to which Islamicate and Roman polities managed to expand and sustain that expansion over many centuries, unlike Sparta or Athens. See Morris (2009).

11. My discussion of a successful hegemonic project is based on my reading of Bob Jessop's work. In particular, his strategic relational approach has a number of insights that can be harnessed beyond a concern with the contours of a modern capitalist state in its Western form. Jessop argues, however, that the state only properly emerges with the development of state discourses. This would seem to suggest a sharp distinction between state-like

formations, which were characteristic of the pre-modern, and the modern state. Recent studies on non-modern states suggests that this distinction is perhaps another iteration of Orientalism, and that the boundaries between many non-modern states of the past and modern states may, on occasion, be overdrawn.

12. See for example, the coalition formed and coordinated by the Egyptian deep state which helped empower the military coup that overthrew Mohammed Morsi, the first democratically elected president of Egypt. See Talal Asad's (2013) observations on the coup.

13. This figure is purely illustrative and is based on approximations of the level of support as indicated in controlled electoral contests in various parts of Muslimistan.

14. A recent example of this is provided by Oliver Roy's observations on what could be described as parvenu Muslims—though he does not use the phrase, but the tone suggests it (2004).

15. Surely, it will not surprise anyone to learn that among his Western critics were Oliver Roy and Giles Kepel.

10. HERMENEUTICS

1. Al-Azami would seem to suggest that only 'views of practising Muslims' should count (2003: 341). Of course, such a neo-Khajarite perspective leaves open the question of how much practice one needs to be a Muslim.

2. The relationship between Muslims, Islamicate heritage and non-Muslim experts is discussed in Asad (2003: 224–5).

3. See Mattson (2008) for an elegant description of the centrality of the Qur'an in Muslim life.

4. It is possible to detect within Mattson's account of the Qur'an a subtle unreading of patriarchy: by focusing on female characters and believers, she manages to portray a relationship between the Qur'an and its readers who are not axiomatically male.

5. The Qur'an is not like the New Testament, which can be described without too much difficulty as a biography of Jesus told by four different writers. Recent biblical scholarship has suggested there may have been over thirty such biographies or gospels during the first century in Roman Palestine.

6. Cf Barlas's (2002) comments regarding the nature of the Divine as a means of unreading patriarchy in the Qur'an.

7. I was introduced to this felicitous expression by Mohammed Siddique Seddon.

8. For example, the description of a hydrogen atom only having one electron is seen as one confirmation of *tawhid* by some commentators. Of course,

this example made more sense when science did not consider there to be anything smaller than electrons—in a world of quarks and strange attractors it becomes more difficult to sustain 'one electron, one God'.

9. See for example, the ruling made by a Malaysian court in 2001 permitting divorce by SMS (Podger, 2001).

10. Of course, any kind of anthropomorphic expression that calls upon God to act has to be understood as a metaphor, since it is difficult to think how the supreme being, knowing all, can be described in human terms like 'acting' and 'intending'. Perhaps the all-powerful, all-knowing infinite can only be.

11. It should be clear that by 'rhetoric' I do not mean anything pejorative or trivial, but rather I follow Stanley Fish's (1989: 347) definition in which rhetoric is another word for anti-foundationalism.

12. But different schools within Islamicate history may privilege certain sections of the *ummah* (e.g. the *ulema*). I would suggest that what is decisive is the *ijma* of the *ummah* rather than the *ulema*, even if the *ijma* of the *ulema* may often be the crucial step in securing the *ijma* of the *ummah*. It is not necessary, however, that the *ulema* are always in the vanguard of forming a consensus. Too often in Islamicate history they have been echoes of certain sectional interests rather than the voices and leaders of all social sectors.

13. Esack (1997: 53) suggests that the Qur'an is primarily addressed to the people of Hejaz at the time of the Prophet (pbuh).

14. I am grateful for AbdoolKarim Vakil's formulation and discussion of this point.

15. The argument against the private Muslim is similar to the argument Wittgenstein makes about the incoherence of private language: if it is private, it is not a language, and if it is a language it cannot be private. This is slightly different from the more conventional way in which religious practices are inserted in post-Enlightenment schema regarding the private and public spheres of any society.

16. One can see a similar strategy in the work of Muslims who try to argue that the Qur'an admonishes homosexual violence but not homosexuality itself. The overwhelming weight of current opinion among Muslims would currently reject such an interpretation, and may continue to do so, or such an interpretation may become hegemonic. See Kugle (2003).

17. This danger is further enhanced if one considers how the expansion of the infrastructural capacity of the state allows it to regulate the most intimate aspects of human life (Mann, 1986).

18. I am not aware of any significant demand among Muslims that praying in the direction of Mecca is oppressive or authoritarian, or something that needs to be 'reformed'.

210

19. In his lecture on ethics Wittgenstein (1993) makes a distinction between judgements of relative value (for example this is a good pen) that can be turned into factual statements and judgements of absolute value that cannot be reduced to factual propositions. This leads Wittgenstein to suggest that if there was a book of ethics it would 'with an explosion destroy all other books in the world'.

11. ETHICS

1. Abdul Quddus of Gangoh cited in Iqbal (1981: 124).
2. In Algeria in 1994, the military stepped in to prevent the Islamist FIS from gaining an electoral victory and thus initiating the Algerian civil war. Another example provided by the US presidential elections in 2000 in which the election came to be decided by results of a state governed by the brother of the Republican candidate and legality of the electoral process determined by nine American supreme court judges along partisan lines. Or the process by which what came to be called the Green Movement in Iran refused to accept the legitimacy of the re-election of President Ahmadinejad in 2009. In all these cases, the electoral process becomes part of the conflict to varying degrees.
3. See Mouffe (2005: 8–34) for a discussion of the difference between politics and the political. Overlapping distinctions between politics and the political can also be found in the works of Carl Schmitt, Ernesto Laclau and Jacques Ranciere. Also Frederick Bailey (2001) who makes a similar distinction on the basis of a 'social anthropological' analysis of power.
4. See for example, the UK government's 'Prevent Strategy'.
5. The source of 'the ought' is not necessarily anything innate in human nature, but is rather the condition of what arises from inter-textuality.
6. Compare this with Derrida's formulation of 'democracy to come'. Derrida's post-metaphysical conception of democracy does not point to an unrealised ideal but an unrealisable objective (1994: 73–83).
7. Qadri is not purely a traditional scholar; part of his training and was gained (including a doctorate) from a Westernised educational system: the University of Punjab.
8. Ironically, three years after publication of this fatwa, Muhammad Tahir-ul-Qadri organised a popular mobilisation in Pakistan (the long march) in which he tried to use extra-parliamentary measures to force the government of Pakistan to resign. His call for such measures was based on the well-known corruption of the members of the government.
9. Dabashi mainly directs his criticism at Mohsen Kadivar, who is considered to be a 'progressive' and supporter of the Green Movement in Iran, but it is

precisely because Kadivar is not a hidebound religious scholar that Dabashi's criticism has an exemplary quality and can be seen as a critique of the juridicalistic domestication of Islam, see Dabashi (2013: 110–66) for more details.

10. For example, academics can be found making interventions in all kinds of fields of human endeavour: from members of the medical profession who seek to regulate the health of the population, to economists who advise governments on how to achieve particular outcomes, to anthropologists who advise the American military on the most efficient ways to wage the War on Terror.

11. For examples of similar discussions among groups of Muslims see Hirschkind (2006).

12. This conclusion draws upon Wittgenstein's discussion of the following rules. See Wittgenstein (1958), see also Kripke's (1982) elaboration of this insight and Winch (1990).

13. Hallaq (2013) sees the state as a modern construct and therefore does not believe that there was a pre-modern Islamic state, hence his use of the term 'Islamic governance'. He shares this view of the modernity of the state with Bob Jessop. I prefer to see the modern state as a particular iteration of the spatialisation of power, and thus I am persuaded that the state begins with the Sumerians. See Mann (1986) for a history of the state.

14. By Hinduism I do not mean a set of precise beliefs and ritual practices— that constitute it as a religion—but rather an entire contentious ensemble formed by cross-cutting webs of meanings and interactions and comportments, formal and informal, elite and subaltern, orthodox and heterodox through which a sense of Hinduism is expressed.

15. See Asad's (2013) commentary on the anti-Muslim Brotherhood coup in Egypt.

16. See for example, the work of Mathee (2011) on court records found in Timbuktu. Mathee used a collection of fatwas to understand the social context from which they emerge, and in doing so demonstrates how flexible the implementation of the sharia was and how its interpretations were debated. The tension between the literal and metaphorical in the very practice of sharia belies any notion that a living polity could simply implement the sharia, ready-made off the shelf. Even those Muslim sisters and brothers who are staunch in their conviction that the sharia is absolute and immutable would have to allow interpretation at a point at which they need to apply a specific rule to a specific case: they have to interpret whether the case is appropriate for the application of that rule. For example, is a case of sexual violence best dealt with by the rule about the prohibition of adultery? See also Pierce (2003).

17. This description is primarily based on the Maoist conception of national liberation struggles. It could be argued that part of the failure of insurgency strategies in these contexts was intellectual: marked by the abandonment of the concept of protracted war articulated by Mao to a model based on Che Guevara's foco theory of insurgency. See Mao (1963).

18. Perhaps, one of the differences between the intractability of the insurgency in Afghanistan and Iraq is that Afghanistan has retained many of the features that facilitate a 'classical' national liberation war. The rural/urban balance and the existence of large number of landscapes impenetrable to sustained state intervention, meant that especially during the summer months the remit of the Karzai regime was often reduced to Kabul and its environs.

19. For example, in 2011 Roshonara Choudhry, a top university student, was found guilty of stabbing a British MP who supported the war in Iraq. Choudhry was born in east London and is of Bangladeshi heritage. Choudhry explained her attack as being motivated by the desire to defend all Muslims. There is little evidence that Choudhry's action was planned with her escape in mind, nor was it clear what purpose would the stabbing of one MP have on a strategic or tactical outcome. See http://www.guardian.co.uk/uk/2010/nov/03/roshonara-choudhry-jailed-life-attack

20. For analysis of the relationship between hip hop and Islam, see Alim (2006).

21. Martin Jacques in his study of the rise of China lists a dozen attributes of American global hegemony including: world's largest economy; one of the highest GDPs per capita; one of the most technological, innovative economies; majority of best-rated universities in the world; English as global lingua franca; Hollywood domination of world cinema; New York City as predominant city in the world; value added from products that are branded as American; and US military expenditure is four times more than nearest rival. See Jacques (2012: 497).

22. Gramsci makes a distinction between 'common-sense' which is the embedded 'spontaneous philosophy' of the masses, consisting of superstitions, folklore, inherited assumptions and contradictory beliefs and good-sense (1971: 421). This common-sense has to be made ideologically coherent and turned into what Gramsci describes as good-sense: a new set of popular beliefs and values critical of the prevailing hegemonic order (1971: 323–6).

23. See Charles Hirschkind (2006) for a discussion of the concept of the Islamic counterpublic.

24. See the video made by the human rights organisation Reprieve in which the rapper Yasiin Bey agreed to undergo the force-feeding procedure deployed against the hundred hunger strikers in Guantanamo. http://www.

guardian.co.uk/world/video/2013/jul/08/mos-def-force-fed-guantanamo-bay-video, last accessed 20 July 2013.

25. This sense of historical stream does not have to be metaphysical, it can be rhetorical. Of course, given my intellectual proclivities I would say it is rhetorical.

26. Richard Bulliet (1994: 172–5) makes a very persuasive argument about how in the absence of an effective caliph following the Mongol capture of Baghdad, the Hajj become the centre of (Sunni) Islam. This shift was signalled by the way in which the office of caliph was eclipsed by the title of Guardian of the Holy Cities (currently used by the head of the Saudi regime). The shift from the caliphate to the Hajj can be seen as a move from the political to a private piety. As it should be clear, by the caliphate I refer to something much more than an institutional ensemble monopolised by a particular dynasty.

27. For example, the difficulties Edward Snowden had in trying to secure asylum.

28. See Mouffe (2005: 90–118), for a critique of the cosmopolitian world order.

29. Warner (2002: 422) describes the process of 'poetic world-making' in similar terms but in relation to the formation of publics.

BIBLIOGRAPHY

el-Affendi, A., *Who Needs an Islamic State?*, London: Malayasia Think Tank, 2008.

——— *Who Needs an Islamic State?*, London: Grey Seal Books, 1991.

Agamben, G., *Homo Sacer: Sovereign Power and Bare Life*, Stanford, CA: Stanford University Press, 1998.

Ahmed, S. 'Chicken Tikka Masala', In Ali, N., Karla, V., and Sayyid, S., (eds) *A Postcolonial People*, London: Hurst, 2006.

Aktay, Y., 'Who Needs a Moderate Islam?' www.muslimistan.net, posted 27 April 2007, http://muslimistan.net/?p=68, last accessed 6 Nov. 2013.

Ali, A.H., *Infidel: My Life*, New York: Free Press, 2007.

——— *The Nehrus and the Gandhis: An Indian Dynasty*, London: Picador, 2005.

——— *Can Pakistan Survive?*, Harmondsworth: Penguin, 1983.

Al Jazeera http://english.aljazeera.net/English/archive/archive?ArchiveId=3328

Alim, H. S., 'Re-inventing Islam with unique modern tones: Muslim hip hop artists as verbal Mujahidin', *Souls: A Critical Journal of Black Politics, Culture, and Society*, 8, 4 (2006), pp. 45–58.

al-Azmeh, A., 'Postmodern Obscurantism and "the Muslim Question"', *Journal for the Study of Religons and Ideologies*, 2/5 (2003), pp. 21–47.

Amin, S., *Eurocentrism*, trans. Russell Moore, London: Zed Press, 1989.

an-Nabahani, T. and Hizb ut-Tahrir, *The Islamic State*, London: Khalifah Publications, n.d.

Anthias, F., and N. Yuval-Davis, *Racialized Boundaries: Race, Nation, Gender, Colour and Class and the Anti-Racist Struggle*, London: Routledge, 1992.

Arendt, H., *The Origins of Totalitarianism*, New York: Meridian Books, 1958.

Armstrong, J., *Nations before Nationalism*, Chapel Hill: University of North Carolina Press, 1983.

Asad, T., 'Neither heroes or villians: a conversation with Talal Asad on Egypt after Morsi', *Jadaliyya*, 23 July 2013, http://www.jadaliyya.com/pages/index/13129/neither-heroes-nor-villains_a-conversation-with-ta, last accessed 25 July 2013.

———— *On Suicide Bombings*, New York: Columbia University Press, 2007.

———— *Formations of the Secular: Christianity, Islam and Modernity*, Palo Alto, CA: Stanford University Press, 2003.

———— *Genealogies of Religion: Discipline and Reasons of Power in Christianity and Islam*, Baltimore, MD: Johns Hopkins University Press, 1993.

Aydin, C., *The Politics of Anti-Westernism in Asia: Visions of World Order in Pan-Islamic and Pan-Asian Thought*, New York: Columbia University Press, 2007.

al-Azami, M.M., *The History of the Qur'anic Text: from Revelation to Compilation: A Comparative Study with Old and New Testaments*, Leicester, UK: Islamic Academy, 2003.

al-Azmeh, A., 'Postmodern Obscurantism and "the Muslim Question"', *Journal for the Study of Religons and Ideologies*, 2/5 (2003), pp. 21–47.

———— *Muslim Kingship*, London: IB Tauris, 2001.

———— *Islams and Modernities*, London: Verso, 1993.

Bahyedeldin, K., 'Islamic themes in Frank Herbert's Dune', *The Baheyeldin Dynasty*, 12 September 2004, http://baheyeldin.com/literature/arabic-and-islamic-themes-in-frank-herberts-dune.html

Bailey, F. G., *Treasons, Stratagems, and Spoils. How Leaders Make Practical Use of Beliefs and Values*, Boulder, CO: Westview Press, 2001.

Barber, B., *Jihad vs. McWorld: Terrorism's Challenge to Democracy: How Globalism and Tribalism are Reshaping the World*, New York: Ballantine Books, 1996.

Barkcin, S., 'Exporting Democracy to the Muslim World', unpublished paper, University of Ankara, Ankara, Turkey, 2000.

Barlas. A., 'Believing Women' in *Islam: Unreading Patriarchal Interpretations of the Qur'an*, Austin: University of Texas Press, 2002.

Bauman, Z., *Modernity and the Holocaust*, Cambridge: Polity Press, 1989.

BBC News, 'Woman jailed for life for attack on MP Stephen Timms', 3 November 2010, http://www.bbc.co.uk/news/uk-england-london-11682732, last accessed 1 July 2012.

———— 'Iraq unveils new "inclusive" flag', 27 April 2004, http://news.bbc.co.uk/2/hi/middle_east/3660663.stm

Beach, Alastair, 'Egypt's liberals seek to ban political Islamists from power' The Independent, 21 July 2013, http://www.independent.co.uk/news/world/africa/egypts-liberals-seek-to-ban-political-islamists-from-power-8724765.html, last accessed 6 Nov. 2013.

Begg, M., *Enemy Combatant*, London: Pocket Books, 2006.

Bernardi, D.L., *Star Trek and History: Race-ing Towards a White Future*, New Brunswick, NJ: Rutgers University Press, 1998.

BIBLIOGRAPHY

Bernal, M., *Black Athena Writes Back*, Chappel Hill, NC: Duke Univeristy Press, 2001.

Bhatt, C., *Liberation and Purity: Race, new religious movements and ethics of postmodernity*, London: UCL Press, 1997.

Bhattacharyya, G., *Dangerous Brown Men: Exploiting Sex, Violence and Feminism in the 'War on Terror'*, London: Zed Press, 2008.

Bilgrami, A., 'Secularism and relativism', *Boundary*, 2/31 (2), (2004), pp. 173–96.

Birt, Y., 'Ex-Muslims Excluding Muslims', *Yahya Birt*, 27 June 2007, http://www.yahyabirt.co.uk/?p=78, last accessed 8 Nov. 2013.

Blaut, J.M., *Eight Eurocentric Historians*, New York: Guilford Press, 2000.

Bobbio, N., *Democracy and Dictatorship: the Nature and Limits of State Power*, trans. Peter Kennedy, Cambridge: Polity Press, 1989.

Borges, J.L., *Collected Fictions*, trans. Andrew Hurley, New York: Penguin Books, 1999.

Brass, P.R., *The Production of Hindu-Muslim Violence in Contemporary India*, Seattle, WA: University of Washington Press, 2003.

Broadbridge, A.F., *Kingship and Ideology in the Islamic and Mongol Words*, Cambridge: Cambridge University Press, 2008.

Brown, J., *Nehru: Profiles in Power*, London: Longman, 2000.

Buck-Morss, S., *Thinking Past Terror: Islamism and Critical Theory on the Left*, London: Verso, 2003.

Bull, H., *The Anarchical Society: A Study of Order in World Politics*, London: Macmillian, 1982.

Bulliet, R., *Islam: The View From the Edge*, New York, Columbia University Press, 1994.

Bulliet, R., *Cotton, Climate, and Camels in Early Islamic Iran: A Moment in World History*, New York, Columbia University Press, 2009.

Buzan, B. and R. Little, *International Systems in World History*, Oxford: Oxford University Press, 2000.

Carothers, T., *In the Name of Democracy: US Policy Towards Latin America in the Reagan Years*, Berkeley, CA: University of California Press, 1993.

Casale, G., *The Ottoman Age of Exploration*, Oxford: Oxford University Press, 2010.

Castells, M., *The Power of Identity*, Oxford: Blackwell, 1997.

Chandrasekaran, R., *Imperial Life Inside the Emerald City: Inside Bahghad's Green Zone*, London: Bloomsbury, 2007.

CNN Interactive, 'Transcript of interview with Iranian President Mohammad Khatami', 7 January 1998, http://edition.cnn.com/WORLD/9801/07/iran/interview.html, last accessed 17 Apr. 2012.

Cockburn, P. and D. Usborne, 'Burning with anger: Iraqis infuriated by new flag that was designed in London', *The Independent* (UK), 28 April 2004.

BIBLIOGRAPHY

Cohen, R. and R. Westbrook, *Amarna Diplomacy: the Beginning of International Relations*, Baltimore: Johns Hopkins University Press, 2000.

Crossley, P. K., *A Translucent Mirror: History and Identity in Qing Imperial Ideology*, Berkeley: University of California Press, 2002.

Dabashi, H., *Being A Muslim in the World*, United States: Palgrave Macmillan, 2013.

Daulatzai, S., *Black Star, Crescent Moon: The Muslim International and Black Freedom Beyond America*, Minneapolis: University of Minnesota Press, 2012.

Davies, N., *Europe, East and West*, London: Jonathan Cape, 2006.

——— *The Isles: A History*, Oxford: Papermac, 2000.

Derrida, J., *Spectres of Marx: The State of Debt, the Work of Mourning and the New International*, London: Routledge, 1994.

Devji, F., *Landscapes of the Jihad: Militancy, Morality and Modernity*, London: Hurst, 2005.

Diawara, M., 'Reading Africa through Foucault', *October*, 55, (1990), p. 87.

Dodd, V and A. Topping, 'Roshonara Choudhry jailed for life over MP attack', T*he Guardian* (UK), 3 November 2010. http://www.guardian.co.uk/uk/2010/nov/03/roshonara-choudhry-jailed-life-attack

Donner, F.M., *Muhammad and the Believers*, Cambrige: Harvard University Press, 2012.

Du Bois, W.E.B., *The Souls of Black Folk*, London: Penguin Books, 1989 [1996].

Dune, John Harrison dir. (Tandem Communications) 2000 [TV series].

Esack, F., *Qur'an: A User's Guide*, Oxford: Oneworld Publications, 2005 [2007].

——— *Qur'an Liberation and Pluralism*, Oxford: Oneworld Publications, 1997.

Fallaci, O., *The Force of Reason*, Rome: Rizzoli International Publications, 2006.

Fars News, 'Supreme Leader reiterates Islamic identity of regional uprisings', 11 December 2012, http://english.farsnews.com/newstext.php?nn=9107126223, last accessed 11 Dec. 2012.

Farred, G., *What's My Name?*, Minneapolis: University of Minnesota Press, 2003.

Fekete, L., 'The Muslim conspiracy theory and the Oslo massacre', *Race & Class*, 53/3 (2012), pp. 30–47.

Ferguson, N., *Empire: How Britain Made the Modern World*, Harmondsworth: Penguin, 2004.

Findley, C., *The Turks in World History*, Oxford: Oxford University Press, 2005.

Finley, M., *Politics in the Ancient World*, Cambridge: Cambridge University Press, 1991.

Finney, N., and L Simpson., *Sleepwalking to Segregation?: Challenging Myths About Race and Migration*, Bristol: Policy Press, 2009.

BIBLIOGRAPHY

Fish, S., *Doing What Comes Naturally: Change, Rhetoric and the Practice of Theory in Literary and Legal Studies*, Durham, NC: Duke University Press, 1989.

Flyvbjerg, B.T., *Rationality and Power: Democracy in Practice*, Cambridge: Cambridge University Press, 1998.

Foucault, M., *Power/Knowledge: Selected Interviews and Other Writings 1972–1977*, C. Gordon (ed.), Brighton, The Harvester Press, 1980.

Fowden, G., *From Empire to Commonwealth: Consequences of Monotheism in Late Antiquity*, Newhaven, NJ: University of Princeton Press, 1994.

French, D., *The British Way in Warfare 1688–2000*, London: Unwin, 1990.

Fukuyama, F., *The Origins of Political Order: From Prehuman times to the French Revolution*, London: Profile Books, 2011.

Furedi, F., *The Silent War: Imperialism and the Changing Perception of Race*, London: Pluto Press, 1998.

Fuss, D., *Essentially Speaking: Feminism, Nature and Difference*, London: Routledge, 1990.

———— *Essentially Speaking: Feminism, Nature and Difference*, New York: Routledge, 1989.

Gilpin, R., *War and Change in World Politics*, New York: Columbia University Press, 1981.

Gilroy, P., *The Black Atlantic: Modernity and Double Consciousness*, London: Verso, 1993.

Goldberg, D. T., 'Racial Europeanization', Ethnic and Racial Studies, 29/2 (2006), pp. 331–364.

Goldberg, D.T., *The Racial State*, Oxford: Blackwell, 2002.

Gove, M., *Celsius 7/7: How the West's Policy of Appeasement Has Provoked Yet More Fundamentalist Terror—And What Has to Be Done Now*, London: Weidenfeld & Nicolson, 2006.

Gramsci, A., *Selections from Prison Notebooks*, Q. Hoare and G.N Smith (eds), London: Lawrence and Wishart, 1971.

Gray, J., *Al-Qaeda and What it Means to be Modern*, London: Faber and Faber, 2004.

Grosfoguel, R., 'World-Systems Analysis in the Context of Transmodernity, Border Thinking, and Global Coloniality', *Review*, 19: 2 (2006), pp. 167–187.

Hall, S., 'The West and the rest: discourse and power', in Halland, S. and B. Gieben (eds), *Formations of Modernity*, Cambridge: Polity Press, 1992.

Hallaq, W., *The Impossible State: Islam, Politics, and Modernity's Moral Predicament*, New York: Columbia University Press, 2013.

Heidegger, M., 'The question concerning technology', in *The Question Concerning Technology and Other Essays*, trans. William Lovitt, New York: Harper and Row, 1977, pp. 3–35.

BIBLIOGRAPHY

Held, D., *Democracy and the Global Order*, Cambridge: Cambridge University Press, 1995.

———— A. McGrew, D. Goldblatt and J. Peeraton (eds), *Global Transformations: Politics, Economic and Culture*, Cambridge: Polity Press, 1999.

Herbert, F., 'Dune genesis', The Official Dune Website, 1980, http://www.frankherbert.org/news/genesis.html

Hesse, B., 'Im/plausible deniability: racism's conceptual bind', *Social Identities*, 10/1 (2004a), pp. 9–29.

———— 'Discourse on institutional racism: the genealogy of a concept', in Law, I., D. Phillips and L. Turney (eds), *Institutional Racism in Higher Education*, London: Trentham Books, 2004b, pp. 131–48.

———— 'Introduction: un/settled multiculturalisms', in Hesse, B., (ed.), *Un/settled Multiculturalisms: Diasporas, Entanglements, Transruptions*, London: Zed Books, 2000.

———— 'Reviewing the Western spectacle: reflexive globalization through the black diaspora', in Brah, A., et al. (eds), *Globalization, Migration, Environment*, London: Macmillan, 1999, pp. 122–43.

Hesse, B. and S. Sayyid, 'Narrating the postcolonial political and immigrant imaginary', in Ali, N., V.S Kalra and S. Sayyid (eds), *A Postcolonial People: South Asians in Britain*, London: Hurst, 2006, pp. 13–31.

Hirschkind, C., *The Ethical Soundscape: Cassette Sermons and Islamic Counterpublics*, New York: Columbia University Press, 2006.

Hirst, P., *War and Power in the 21st Century: The State, Military Power and the International System*, Cambridge: Polity Press, 2001.

———— and Thompson, G., *Globalization in question: the international economy and the possibilities of governance*, Cambridge: Polity Press, 1996.

Hodgson, M., *The Venture of Islam*, vol. 1, Chicago: University of Chicago Press, 1977.

Holsti, K. J., 'Governance with government: polyarchy in nineteenth-century European international politics', in Rosenau, J. and E. Czempiel (eds), *Governance Without Government: Order in Change in World Politics*, Cambridge: Cambridge University Press, 1992, pp. 30–57.

Hornblower, S., 'The creation and development of democratic institutions in Ancient Greece', in Dunn, J. (ed.), *Democracy: The Unfinished Journey 508 BC to 1993*, Oxford: Oxford University Press, 1993, p. 2.

Howe, S., 'Aftershock: 9/11 ten years on', *Rationalist Association*, 7 September 2011, http://rationalist.org.uk/2646/aftershock-911-ten-years-on, last accessed 6 Nov. 2013.

Huntington, S., *The Clash of Civilizations*, New York: Simon and Shuster, 1998.

Iqbal, M., *The Reconstruction of Religious Thought in Islam*, Pakistan: Iqbal Academy, 1981.

BIBLIOGRAPHY

Jacques, M., *When China Rules the World*, London: Penguin Books, 2012.

Jalal, A., *Democracy and Authoritarianism in South Asia: a Comparative and Historical Perspective*, Cambridge: Cambridge University Press, 1995.

Jessop, B., *State Theory: Putting Capitalist States in Their Place*, Cambridge: Cambridge University Press, 1990.

Karsh, E., *Islamic Imperialism*, New Haven: Yale University Press, 2006.

Kass, L.R., 'Introduction: the problem of technology', in Melzer, A.M., J. Weinberger and M. R. Zinman (eds), *Technology in the Western Political Tradition*, Ithaca, NY: Cornell University Press, 1993.

Keane, J., *The Life and Death of Democracy*, London: Simon and Schuster, UK, 2009.

—— *Global Civil Society?* Cambridge: Cambridge University Press, 2003.

Kepel, G., *The War for Muslim Minds: Islam and the West*, Cambridge, MA: The Belkap Press, 2006.

Khaldun, I., *The Muqaddimah: an Introduction to History*, trans. Franz Rosenthal, ed. and abridged Dawood, N. J., London: Routledge, 1978 [1967].

Khan, S.O., 'The "Caliphate Question": British views and policy toward Pan-Islamic politics and the end of the Ottoman Caliphate', *American Journal of Islamic Social Sciences*, 24/4 (2007), pp. 1–25.

Khan, M.A, *An Introduction to Islamic Economics*, Islamabad: International Institute of Islamic Thought, and Institute of Policy Studies, 1994.

—— *Islamic Economics: Annotated Sources in English and Urdu*, Leicester: Islamic Foundation, 1983.

Khomeini, R., *Islam and Revolution*, trans. Hamid Algar. Berkeley: Mizan Press, 1981.

King, R., *Orientalism and Religion: Post Colonial Theory, India and the Mystic East*, London: Routledge, 1999.

Klug, B., 'An almost unbearable insecurity: Cameron's Munich speech', MnM Working Paper No. 6., 2011, http://w3.unisa.edu.au/muslim-understanding/documents/klug-almost-unbearable.pdf, last accessed 30 Mar. 2012.

Kripke, S., *Wittgenstein on Rules and Private Language: An Elementary Exposition*, Cambridge, Mass.: Harvard University Press, 1982.

Kugle, S., 'Sexuality and sexual ethics in the agenda of progressive Muslim', in Safi, O. (ed.), *Voices of Progressive Muslims: Toward an Authentic Engagement with Modernity*, Oxford: Oneworld Press, 2003, pp. 190–234.

Kuhrt, A., and Susan Sherwin-White, *From Samarkhand to Sardis: A New Approach to the Seleucid Empire*, Berkeley and Los Angeles: University of California Press, 1993.

—— and H. Sancisi-Weerdenburg (eds), *Method and Theory: Proceedings of London 1985 Achaemenid History Workshop*, Lieden, Netherlands: Nederlands Instituut voor het Nabije Oosten, 1988.

221

BIBLIOGRAPHY

Kuran, T., *The Long Divergence: How Islamic Law Held Back the Middle East*, Princeton, NY: Princeton University Press, 2011.

—— *Islam and Mammon: the Economic Predicaments of Islamism*, Princeton, NY: Princeton University Press, 2004.

Laclau, E., *On Populist Reason*, London: Verso, 2005.

—— *New Reflections on the Revolution of Our Time*, London: Verso, 1990.

Lawrence, B. (ed.), *Messages to the World: The Statements of Osama Bin Laden*, London: Verso, 2005.

Lieven, D., *Empire: the Russian Empire and its Rivals*, New Haven: Yale University Press, 2001.

Lustick, I., *Trapped in the War on Terror*, Philadelphia: University of Pennsylvania, 2006.

—— 'The absence of Middle Eastern great powers: political "Backwardness" in historical perspective', *International Organization*, 51/4 (1996), pp. 653–83.

Lyons, J., *Introduction to Theoretical Linguistics*, Cambridge: Cambridge University Press, 1968.

Maalouf, A., *Balthasar's Odyssey*, trans. Barbara Bray, London: Vintage, 2002.

Mahmood, S., 'Secularism, hermeneutics, and empire: the politics of Islamic reformation', *Public Culture*, 18/2 (2006), pp. 323–47.

—— 'Questioning liberalism, too', *Boston Review*, April/May 2003, http://www.bostonreview.net/BR28.2/mahmood.html

Mamdani, M., *Good Muslim, Bad Muslim: America, the Cold War, and the Roots of Terror*, New York: Three Leaves Press, 2005.

Manji, I., *The Trouble With Islam Today; A Muslim's Call for Reform in Her Faith*, Canada: Random House, 2003.

Mann, M., *The Sources of Social Power*, vol. 1, Cambridge: Cambridge University Press, 1986.

Mao, Z., *Selected Military Writings of Mao Tse-Tung*, Beijing: Foreign Language Press, 1963.

Manzoor, P., 'The sovereignty of the political: Carl Schmitt and the nemesis of liberalism', *The Muslim World Book Review*, 20/1 (Autumn 1999), pp. 3–14.

Massad, J., 'The "Arab Spring" and other American seasons', *Al Jazeera*, 2011, http://www.aljazeera.com/indepth/opinion/2012/08/201282972539153865.html

Mathee, Mohamed S., 'Women's agency in Muslim marriage: fatwās from Timbuktu', *Journal for Islamic Studies*, 31 (2011), pp.75–95.

Mattson, I., *The Story of the Qur'an: its History and Place in Muslim Life*, Oxford: Blackwell Publishing, 2008.

Mazrui, A. A., 'Pretender to universalism: western culture in a globalizing age', *Journal of Muslim Minority Affairs*, 21/1 (2001), pp. 11–24.

BIBLIOGRAPHY

McNeil, W., *The Pursuit of Power: Technology, Armed Force and Society Since AD 1000*, Chicago: University of Chicago Press, 1982.

Mignolo, W., 'Epistemic Disobedience, Independent Thought and De-Colonial Freedom' *Theory, Culture & Society*, 26/7–8, (2009), pp. 1–23.

——— *The Idea of Latin America*, London: Blackwell, 2005.

Millar, F., *The Roman Near East, 31 B.C.–A.D. 337*, Harvard, MA: Harvard University Press, 1993.

'Mirror Mirror', Star Trek: The Original Series, Season 2, Episode 33, Marc Daniels dir. (Paramount Television, 1967) [TV series].

Morris, I., 'The Greater Athenian State', in Morris, Ian and Walter Scheidel (eds), *The Dynamics of Ancient Empires: State Power from Assyria to Byzantium*, New York: Oxford University Press, 2009.

Mouffe, C., *On the Political*, London: Routledge, 2005.

Nasr, S.V.R., *Islamic Leviathan: Islam and the Making of State Power*, Oxford: Oxford University Press, 2001.

National Intelligence Council, *Mapping the Global Future*, Pittsburgh, PA: Government Printing Office, 2004.

Nienhaus, V., 'Fundamentals of an Islamic Economic Order Compared to the Social Market Economy—A Systematic Overview', *KAS International Reports*, 11 (2010), pp. 75–96.

——— 'Islamic economics: policy between pragmatism and utopia', *Economics*, 25 (1982), pp. 80–98.

Ober, J., *The Athenian Revolution*, Princeton, NJ: Princeton University Press, 1996.

O'Leary, B., *The Asiatic Mode of Production*, London: Basil Blackwell, 1989.

Ouis, P., 'McDonald's or Mecca? An Existential Choice for Muslims in a Globalized World?', *Encounters*, 7/2 (2001), pp. 16–188.

Ouseley, H., 'Community pride not prejudice—making diversity work in Bradford, The Ouseley Report', Bradford: The Bradford District Race Review Panel, 2001.

Pagden, A. (ed.), *The Idea of Europe: Antiquity from European Union*, Cambridge: Cambridge University Press, 2002.

Pampola, S., 'Assyrians after Assyria' *Nineveh Online*, 1999, www.nineveh.com/ Assyrians%20after%20Assyria.html, last accessed 8 Nov. 2013.

Pandey, G., 'Can a Muslim be an Indian?', *Comparative Studies in Society and History*, 41/4 (1999), pp. 608–29.

Pankhurst, R., 'The Caliphate and the changing strategy of the public statements of al-Qaeda's leaders', *Political Theology*, 11/4 (2010), pp. 530–552.

Park, J.C.H., *Yellow Future: Oriental Style in Hollywood Cinema*, Minneapolis: University of Minnesota Press, 2010.

Pease, D., 'Khatami's attempt at dialogue', *Boundary*, 26/3: (1999), pp. 87–114.

BIBLIOGRAPHY

Pecora, V.P., *Secularization and Cultural Criticism: Religion, Nation and Modernity*, Chicago: University of Chicago Press, 2006.

Pew Research Center, 'America's image slips, but allies share U.S. concerns over Iran, Hamas', *Pew Global Attitudes Project Report*, 13 June 2006, http://www.pewglobal.org/2006/06/13/americas-image-slips-but-allies-share-us-concerns-over-iran-hamas/

Pidd, H., 2008. 'Bishop under fire for attack on Muslim 'no-go areas', *The Guardian*, 7 January 2008, http:// http://www.theguardian.com/uk/2008/jan/07/religion.politics, last accessed on 17 Oct. 2009.

Pierce, L., *Morality Tales: Law and Gender in the Ottoman Court of Aintab*, Berkeley: University of California Press, 2003.

Pitts, J., *A Turn to Empire: the Rise of Imperial Liberalism in Britain and France*, Princeton, NJ: Princeton University Press, 2005.

——— 'Empire and democracy: Tocqueville and the Algeria question', *Journal of Political Philosophy*, 8/3 (2000), pp. 295–318.

Podger, C., 'Anger over mobile divorce ruling', *BBC News*, 11 July 2001, http://news.bbc.co.uk/2/hi/asia-pacific/1433790.stm

Porter, B., *War and the Rise of the State: the Military Foundations of Modern Politics*, New York: The Free Press, 1994.

Qadri, M., *Fatwa on Terrorism and Suicide Bombings*, London: Minhaj-ul-Quran International, 2011.

Qutb, S., *Social Justice in Islam*, trans. from Arabic by John Hardie, Oneonta, NY: Islamic Publications International, 2000.

——— *Milestones*, trans. Mohammed Moinuddin Siddiqui, Kuwait: International Islamic Federation of Student Organizations, 1989.

Rahman, F., *Islam and Modernity: Transformation of An Intellectual Tradition*, Chicago: University of Chicago Press, 1984.

Ramadan, T., *Islam, the West and the Challenges of Modernity*, Leicester: Islamic Foundation. 2001.

Rancière, J., *Disagreement: Politics and Philosophy*, Minneapolis, MN: University of Minnesota Press, 1998.

Rejali, D., *Torture and Democracy*, Princeton, NJ: Princeton University Press, 2007.

Richter, M., 'Tocqueville on Algeria', *The Review of Politics*, 25/3 (1963), pp. 362–98.

Rorty, R., *Irony, Contingency and Solidarity*, Cambridge: Cambridge University Press, 1989.

Roy, O., *Globalised Islam: The Search for a New Ummah*, London: C. Hurst and Co, 2004.

——— *The Failure of Political Islam*, London: I.B Tauris, 1994.

Rupert, M., *Ideologies of Globalization: Contending 2000, Visions of a New World Order*, London: Routledge, 2000.

BIBLIOGRAPHY

Sabet, A., *Islam and the Political: Theory, Governance and International Relations*, London: Pluto Press, 2008.

Sadiki, L., *The Search for Arab Democracy*, London: Hurst, 2004.

Saeed, A., *Interpreting the Qur'an: Towards a Contemporary Approach*, London: Routledge. 2006.

Said, E., *Orientalism*, London: Routledge, 1978 [1985].

Sarantakes, N.E., 'Cold War pop culture and the image of U.S foreign policy: the perspective of the original Star Trek Series', *Journal of Cold War Studies*, 7/4 (Fall 2005,) pp. 74–103.

Sardar, Z., 'Introduction', in Sardar, Z. and Sean Cubitt (eds), *Aliens R Us: the Other in Science Fiction Cinema*, London: Pluto Press, 2002.

———— *Postmodernism and The Other: The New Imperialism of Western Culture*, London: Pluto Press, 1998.

Sassen, S., *The Global City*, 2nd rev. ed., New York: Princeton University Press, 2001.

Sayyid, S., 'Empire, Islam and the postcolonial', in Huggian, G. (ed.), *Oxford Handbook of Postcolonial Studies*, Oxford: Oxford University Press, 2013.

———— 'Thinking Through Islamophobia', in Sayyid, S. and Vakil, A., (eds) *Thinking Through Islamophobia: A Global Prespective*, London: Hurst, 2010.

———— and Zac, L., 'Political analysis in a world without foundations', in Scarbrough, E. and Eric Tanebaum (eds), *Research Strategies in the Social Sciences: A Guide to New Approaches*, Oxford: Oxford University Press, 1998, pp. 249–67.

———— *A Fundamental Fear: Eurocentrism and the Emergence of Islamism*, London: Zed Books, 1997 [2003].

Schmitt, C., *Political Theology: Four Chapters on the Concept of Sovereignty*, Chicago: University of Chicago Press, 2005.

———— *The Concept of the Political*, Chicago: University of Chicago Press, 1996.

———— 'The age of neutralizations and depoliticization', trans. Konzett, M. and J.P. McCormick, *Telos*, 96 (summer 1993), pp. 130–42.

Schmitt, C., *The Nomos of the Earth: In the International Law of the Jus Publicum Eurpaeum*, New York: Telos Press, 1950 [2003].

Schulze, R., *A Modern History of the Islamic World*, New York: New York University Press, 2002.

———— *A Modern History of the Islamic World*, New York: I.B. Tauris, 2000.

Scruton, R., *The West and the Rest: Globalization and the Terrorist Threat*, Continuum International Publishing Group: London, 2003.

Shariati, A., *On the Sociology of Islam*, Berkeley, CA: Mizan Press, 1979.

Shaw, M., *Theory of the Global State: Globality as an Unfinished Revolution*, Cambridge: Cambridge University Press, 2000.

BIBLIOGRAPHY

Showalter, D., *The Wars of German Unification*, London: Arnold, 2004.

Slater, D., 'Exploring Other Zones of the Postmodern: Problems of Ethnocentrism and Difference across the North-South Divide', in A. Rattansi & S. Westwood (eds) *Racism, Modernity and Identity: On the Western Front*, Cambridge: Polity Press, 1994.

Sloterdijk, P., *Critique of Cynical Reason*, London: Verso, 1998.

Smith, A., *The Ethnic Origin of Nations*, Oxford: Basil Blackwell, 1995.

——— *National Identity*, Harmondsworth: Penguin, 1991.

Soroush, A., *Reason, Freedom, and Democracy in Islam: Essential Writings of Abdolkarim Soroush*, trans. and ed. by Sadri, M. and A. Sadri, Oxford: Oxford University Press, 2002.

Spivak, G., *In Other Worlds: Essays in Cultural Politics*, New York and London, 1987.

Springborg, P., *Western Republicanism and the Oriental Prince*, Cambridge: Polity Press, 1992.

Stark, R. and R. Finke, *Acts of Faith: Explaining the Human Side of Religion*, Berkely: University of California Press, 2000.

Staten, H., *Wittgenstein and Derrida*, Lincoln, NE: University of Nebraska Press, 1984.

Stevens, C.B., *Russia's Wars of Emergence 1460–1730*, Harlow: Longman, 2007.

Taylor, C., *Multiculturalism and 'The Politics of Recognition'*, Princeton: Princeton University Press, 1993.

Thomson, I., *Heidegger on Ontotheology: Technology and the Politics of Education*, New York: Cambridge University Press, 2005.

Tibi, B., 'The totalitarianism of Jihidist Islamism and its challenge to Europe and to Islam', *Totalitarian Movements and Political Religions*, 8/1 (2007), pp. 35–54.

Tripp, C., *Islam and the Moral Economy: the Challenge of Capitalism*, Cambridge: Cambridge University Press, 2006.

Turner, B., 'From Orientalism to global sociology', *Sociology*, 23/3 (1989), pp. 629–38.

Tyner, J.A. and R.J Kruse, II, 'The geopolitics of Malcolm X', *Antipode*, 36/1 (2004), pp. 24–42.

Tyrer, D. and Sayyid, S., 'Governing Ghosts: Race, incorporeality and difference in post-political times', Current Sociology, 60/3, (2012), pp. 353–367.

Tyrrell, W.B., 'Star Trek as myth and mythmaker', *Journal of Popular Culture*, 10/4 (1977), pp. 711–9.

Unger, R., *False Necessity: Anti-necessitarian Social Theory in the Service of Radical Democracy*, London: Verso, 2004.

Valensi, L., *The Birth of the Despot: Venice and the Sublime Porte*, Ithaca, NY: Cornell University Press, 1993.

BIBLIOGRAPHY

Venn, C., *The Postcolonial Challenge: Towards Alternative Worlds*, London: Sage, 2006.

—— *Occidentalism: Modernity and Subjectivity*, London: Sage, 2000.

Vzw, C., 'Introduccion', in *Suturas y Fragmentos: Cuerpos y Territororios en la Cienca Ficcion*, Barcelona: Fundacio Antoni Tapes, 2004.

Young, R., *White Mythologies: Writing History and the West*, London: Routledge, 1990.

Wadud, A., *Qur'an and Women*, Oxford: Oxford University Press, 1999.

Wallerstein, I., *Geopolitics and Geoculture: Essays on the Changing World-System*, Cambridge: Cambridge University Press, 1991.

Waltz, K., *Theory of International Politics*, New York: McGraw-Hill, 1979.

Warner, M., 'Publics and counterpublics', *Quarterly Journal of Speech*, 86/4 (2002), pp. 413–25.

Winch, P., *The Idea of a Social Science and Its Relation to Philosophy*, Great Britain: Routledge, 1990.

Wittgenstein, L., 'A Lecture on ethics', in Wittgenstein, L., *Philosophical Occasions*, Klage, J.C and A. Nordmann (eds), Indianapolis, IN: Hackett Publishing Company Inc,. 1993, pp. 36–7.

—— *Philosophical Investigations*, trans. Gertrude Anscombe, Great Britain: Basil Blackwell, 1958.

Wolf, E., *Europe and the People Without History*, Berkeley, CA: University of California Press, 1982.

Worland, R., 'From the new frontier to the final frontier: Star Trek from Kennedy to Gorbachev', *Film and History*, 24, 1/2 (1994), pp. 19–35.

X, Malcolm, *Malcolm X Speaks: Selected Speeches and Statements*, Breitman, G. (ed.), New York: Grove Weidenfeld, 1965.

Žižek S., *The Puppet and the Dwarf: The Perverse Core of Christianity*, Cambridge, Massachusetts: MIT Press, 2003.

—— in Lenin, V., *Revolution At the Gates: a Selection of Writings from February to October 1917*, ed. with Introduction and Afterword by Žižek, S., London: Verso, 2002.

—— *Did Somebody Say Totalitarianism?*, London: Verso, 2001.

—— *The Fragile Absolute*, London: Verso, 2000.

—— 'A leftist plea for "Eurocentrism"', *Critical Inquiry*, 24, 2 (1998), pp. 988–1009.

Zubaida, S., 'The Many Faces of Multiculturalism', *openDemocracy*, 5 June 2007, http://www.opendemocracy.net/faith-europe_islam/many_faces_4677. jsp, last accessed 11 Oct. 2011.

INDEX

INDEX

INDEX

Iran-Iraq War (1980–8): use of chemical weapons during, 150

Iraq: 74, 127, 129; government of, 81; military of, 150; Operation Iraqi Freedom (2003–11), 53, 80–1

Islam: 1–3, 7, 11–12, 15, 20–2, 34–5, 45, 47, 52–3, 70, 75, 77, 79, 89, 93, 117, 125, 134–5, 148, 161–2, 177, 179, 186, 190–1; collective identity of, 72; concept of the Divine, 35, 41; 'Five Pillars' of, 6; fundamentalist, 24; liberation theology of, 155; political, 172–3, 175, 183–4; Ramadan, 6; secularist interpretation of, 32; *salat*, 145; *zakat*, 138, 149

Islam, Yusuf (Cat Stevens): 71

Islamic economies: 139, 141–2, 144; absence of *riba*, 137–8; banking system of, 137–8; criticisms of, 139; development of, 135–8; imposition of *zakat*, 138

Islamism: 10, 19, 32, 50–2, 57–8, 61, 64, 77, 103, 117, 139, 146–9, 173, 183, 186; concept of, 9, 23–4, 48–9; conflict with Westernese, 60; critiques of, 54–6; essentialism, 58, 60; identity of, 49–50; ideology of, 58, 142; opposition to, 51, 75, 77–8; totalitarian image of, 48–9

Islamophobia: 54, 161–2, 165

Israel: 109

Italy: Milan, 122; Venice, 122

jailiyyia: 172

Jainism: 40

Jalal, Ayesha: 39–40

Japan: 124; Tokyo, 101

Jesus Christ: 23; divinity of, 36

jihad: 110–11; depoliticisation of, 185; violent, 185

Judaism: 23, 32, 41; collective identity of, 105

Justice and Development Party (AKP): ideology of, 147

Kashmir: 39; Indian presence in, 40; Muslim population of, 40, 124, 187, 190; Pakistani presence in, 40

Kemal, Mustafa: 3

Kemalism: 64, 77, 128, 134–5, 183, 187–9; model of nation building, 126, 146, 148; supporters of, 147

Khamenei, Ali Hosseini: 149, 199

Khan, Hulegu: Sacking of Baghdad (1258), 120, 189

Khatami, Ayatollah Mohammad: political rhetoric of, 20–5, 27–8; President of Iran, 17

Ibn Khaldun: 1

Khomeini, Ayatollah Ruhollah: 149–50, 152, 173; political rhetoric of, 28; theory of *velayat-e faqih*, 76–7, 118

Kuran, Timur: criticisms of Islamic economies, 139, 207, 208

bin Laden, Osama: family of, 119

Lagash: 122

Lebanon: 147; Cedar Revolution (2005), 83

liberalism: 26

Libya: Civil War (2011), 64–5, 83

madrasas: curriculum of, 104

Mahdi: 77, 133; use of concept in media, 85–6, 88, 90–3, 95–7

INDEX

INDEX